I found this book to be very helpful. Besides helping an infant achieve early potty training, the method in this book helps parents learn to read their baby's body language better.

Dr. William Sears, *Pediatrician, originator of the term "attachment parenting" and author of* The Baby Book

Infant Potty Training is a very interesting approach, and I do agree that it fits well with AP. . . . I do applaud your approach.

Dr. William Sears, Jr, *Pediatrician*

This book is pivotal. I read *Infant Potty Training* with great interest and then raised my own two children accordingly. I have recommended this approach to many mothers who have had success and are satisfied with the results. Unfortunately, and unfairly, the information is practically unknown to most pediatricians and parents today, but this book will surely help effect change in our society.

Dr. Simone Rugolotto, *Pediatrician and Neonatologist*

This book is a welcome addition to the child-rearing literature, expanding the range of possibilities for the modern mother and family. It is a practical, user-friendly guide to "nurturant potty training" and provides a global perspective on this important developmental milestone.

Dr. Marten deVries, *Professor of Social Psychiatry,
Sec Gen World Federation for Mental Health*

In just two generations, the knowledge that infants and babies can be potty trained has been lost to the point that few Americans realize it is possible, much less desirable. In *Infant Potty Training*, Laurie Boucke teaches American parents how to apply the gentle, loving earth-friendly techniques the rest of the world uses to nurture happier, healthier babies.

Dr. Linda Sonna, *Psychologist*

A MUST read for everyone. After reading it, you just can't go back to regular diapering. I find the whole subject fascinating, especially the cross-cultural comparisons.

Basmat Even-Zohar, *Professor of History*

Laurie Boucke

Infant Potty Training

**a gentle and primeval method
adapted to modern living**

WHITE
BOUCKE
PUBLISHING
OAKHURST, CALIFORNIA

First published May 2000 (1-888580-10-0)
Second Edition April 2002 (1-888580-24-0)
Third Edition January 2008 (1-888580-30-5)
Reprinted May 2009, July 2010, January 2012,
January 2014 (with minor edits), January 2017.

ISBN-10: 1-888580-30-5
ISBN-13: 978-1-888580-30-3

Library of Congress Cataloging-in-Publication Data

Boucke, Laurie.

Infant potty training : a gentle and primeval method adapted to modern living / Laurie Boucke. -- 3rd ed.
  p. cm.
Summary: "A resource on infant toilet training including guidelines, medical and anthropological reports, testimonials, history, philosophy, cross-cultural research, and photos from around the world. This practice is also called elimination communication"--Provided by publisher.
Includes bibliographical references and index.
ISBN 978-1-888580-30-3 (trade paper)
1. Toilet training. I. Title.
HQ770.5.B68 2008
649'.62--dc22   2007043535

WHITE BOUCKE PRODUCTIONS
PO BOX 1463, OAKHURST, CA 93644, USA
www.white-boucke.com

PERMISSIONS

CONTENTS

PART 3
TESTIMONIALS – AROUND THE WORLD

PART 4
CROSS-CULTURAL STUDIES

PREFACE

Potty training from birth or the early months of life? *Infant Potty Training* is based on an elimination training technique used in much of Asia and Africa. It has been adapted to the Western urban lifestyle in various ways, including the use of a potty or toilet, part-time pottying and part-time diapering.

Observant visitors to the countrysides of Asia or Africa will invariably witness mothers holding their infants in a relaxed and loving manner as their babies "go" on cue. Whereas Westerners consider potty training to be both a "big deal" and an ordeal, it is as enjoyable and natural as caring for baby's other needs for millions who start in the early months of life.

Part 1 of this book provides detailed information on how infant pottying works. Chapters 1–7 explain the basics and provide many tips and photos. For parents in a hurry to get started, this is all you need to read for now—the rest of the book can be read at your leisure for additional information, support and inspiration. In Parts 2 and 3, detailed testimonials by a number of mothers provide firsthand accounts. The testimonials were gathered from a cross-section of families representing different backgrounds, cultures, races, nationalities, lifestyles, income levels and education levels, demonstrating that this practice is not limited to any particular society or group. Part 4 examines nurturant child-raising practices in other societies, then presents a selection of cross-cultural writings on infant elimination training as used in many parts of the world.

Terminology

The word "go" is frequently used to mean "eliminate." The words "potty" and "toilet" are sometimes used as verbs in the generic sense of "pottying or toileting baby" and when used this way do not necessarily refer to any specific receptacles for elimination.

In the expression "infant potty training," the word "training" is used in the positive sense of a loving exchange between mother and baby. It refers to a reciprocal learning experience, a form of mother-baby training and synergy that should *never* be misconstrued in the negative sense of pressure, rigidity or coercion.

The abbreviations "IPT" (infant potty training) and "EC" (elimination communication) are synonymous and refer to the assisted infant toilet learning approach that is the subject of this book. The term "EC" is also used as a verb ("I EC'ed my baby") and noun ("We are EC'ers"). The term "elimination communication" can also refer to baby body language, vocalizations, sign language and other forms of communication that relate to a child's elimination.

The literal meaning of the terms "diaperless" and "diaper-free" is "not wearing diapers." A diaperless baby can wear training pants or underwear and still be considered a diaper-free baby.

Invented terms that fit the subject matter are also used. For example, a "pottytunity" refers to a "potty opportunity" (opportunity to use the potty or toilet). "Peequency" refers to "pee frequency."

About the Book

My first book on this topic was *Trickle Treat: Diaperless Infant Toilet Training Method*, 85 pages and published in 1991 (now out of print but still in many libraries). That book was written as a result of my own experiences and was also inspired by the fact that no other books existed on the topic.

Since that time, much new information has come to light, the practice has become increasingly popular and the attitude of Western medicine has started to change. There is now disagreement with the widely held premises about maturational readiness for toilet learning and the age at which babies can start to gain some sphincter control.

This third edition of *Infant Potty Training* is the result of recent research, cooperation and input by pediatricians and psychologists, and the sharing of information by thousands of experienced mothers. As with the earlier editions, it is a comprehensive guide for addressing parents' questions. An abridged version *Infant Potty Basics: With or Without Diapers . . . the Natural Way* was published in 2003 with frugal families, "time-challenged" readers and gifting in mind and is now availale as an eBook. Then in 2006, with the philosophy that "seeing is believing," we released a 2-hour DVD entitled *Potty Whispering*.

Parents must bear in mind that each baby is unique and will develop at her own personal pace. Anyone who desires to use infant pottying with a healthy baby in a stable home environment, who practices it correctly and exercises loving patience and diligence on a regular basis should be able to experience the many joys that ensue.

Laurie Boucke
Lafayette, Colorado
January 2014

INTRODUCTION
BY PROF. MARTEN W. DEVRIES, MD

Potty training is an important developmental milestone in all societies and therefore of universal interest to mothers and families. Cultures worldwide have given their signature to bowel and bladder training methods and back their approaches with specific ideas of what a baby is, can and should do.

Those who have studied and observed child-rearing practices across different cultural settings have been struck by the diversity of ideas, expectations and practices that guide parents and families in the day-to-day interactions with their babies and children. One observation by the influential anthropologist Caudill, who compared Japanese and American infant development and child-rearing practices during the 1950s and 1960s, has always loomed as a compelling wisdom. He was struck by the fact that the responses he observed in infants to child-care practices were in line with broad expectations for behavior in both cultures. For example, in the United States the expectation that the individual should be physically and verbally assertive, and in Japan, that the individual should be physically and verbally restrained, was observable in infant behavior as well as in child rearing. During my fieldwork in East Africa in the mid-1970s, I was similarly struck with how cultural values interacted with the constitutional characteristics of the baby.

From the cross-cultural perspective, two points emerge that are of interest regarding this volume. One is that the culture and the family project their ideas as to what an infant can actually do, often with very good evolutionary and social reasons, and thereby shape the infant's behavior. The other is that infants are capable of an immense repertoire of behavior at birth and during the first year, a fact borne out over 40 years of ethnographic and experimental study. These two aspects, that the infant is receptive to learning and can carry out an immense range of behavior, as well as being open to shaping by family and culture, provide the rationale for this book.

Ms. Boucke provides a practical update and guide to potty training, using observations of infants and maternal comments. In so doing she follows in the footsteps of earlier anthropological field studies dating to Geber. These cross-cultural studies have illuminated the diverse perspectives and the range of possibilities available to Western mothers. In photos, testimonials and descriptive material, Ms. Boucke brings this information to the Western reader in practical down-home language. The lesson from Ms. Boucke and traditional societies is that infant potty training is far more than just a chore or messy necessity, it is an important way for the family and baby to get to know one another. Boucke refutes the Western views that early training is coercive or potentially dangerous in terms of personality formation, using a world sample to show that potty training can indeed be a nurturant experience and help create a competent infant. Her selection of photos and comments make it clear that potty training can be anything but harsh.

Today, given the advance of diaper technology, it is not necessary for families to employ the time-tested method of infant toilet training. But this is a valid and effective alternative, as Ms. Boucke makes clear with examples from Asia, Africa and the USA. *Infant Potty Training* provides the opportunity for mothers to be with their infants in new, creative and loving ways. I find that the author's practical advice and clear descriptions constitute a nurturant contribution to families, pediatricians and child-rearing literature in general.

Marten W. deVries
Maastricht, Netherlands
February 2000

THE CONCEPT
&
THE METHOD

chapter 1
a wonderful discovery

When my third son was born, I dreaded the thought of another bout of conventional toilet training which would entail additional years of diapers, and began seeking a better solution. I learned the basis for an alternative approach through a mother visiting us from India. I was skeptical when she told me that "back home" in her culture mothers start toilet learning in infancy and that there is rarely a need to use "the cloths" on babies.

I challenged her to get my son to go on cue for her, which she gladly and effortlessly did. I was spellbound watching her communicate with my tiny 3-month-old son, who somehow instinctively knew what she wanted him to do. I can only describe the exchange and instant understanding between them—a stranger and an infant—as a wonderful discovery.

I used the technique she demonstrated, slightly modifying and adapting it to a Western lifestyle, and found it to be far superior to conventional diaper-to-potty-training. A detailed account of my personal experience is found in Part 2 of this book.

Who Can Use IPT?

Parents, parents-to-be, grandparents, nannies and anyone else interested in lovingly and patiently working with a child towards accomplishing potty learning in a gentle, gradual and fun way. It is best used by:

- a parent who spends at least the first 1–2 years caring for baby
- a working parent with one or more trustworthy and reliable helpers such as a family member, nanny or friend
- a parent who can use part-time pottying on a fairly regular basis such at least one potty visit most mornings and evenings

What Does It Take?

Time, diligence, patience and practice, with at least a few pottytunities (opportunities to use the potty or toilet) a day. It is important to note that this is *not* an all-or-nothing endeavor and that it is essential to maintain a healthy balance in all that you do for your child and family.

How Long Does It Take?

IPT is a gradual developmental process that carries on for many months, similar to learning to walk or talk. As with other major skills, it takes lots of practice and loving parental patience. For Western families who start before the end of the first window (around 6 months old), the average age of completion is around 2 years, although completion age can vary a lot (18 months to 27–28 months or even older). No matter what age a child finishes, babies have fairly good control of elimination for many months before completion.

IPT parents recognize, appreciate and enjoy different stages of development along the way. Depending on circumstances (age started; learning curve; health; development; environment; caregiver attitude; and expectations) and one's definition of the term "potty trained" (ability to release on cue; ability to retain and wait to go; ability to dress and undress; total potty independence, including nighttime), it generally takes from 6 months to 2 years.

How Do I Know When My Baby Needs to Go?

You can know when baby needs to go by one or more of the following:
- baby's timing (by the clock)
- baby's signals and cues (including body language and sounds)
- baby's elimination patterns
- your intuition and instinct

How Many Trips to the Toilet a Day Does It Take?

This is up to you. Each family proceeds at its own pace. Always bear in mind that it is unrealistic to expect to be on time for every elimination. This will only happen when baby has completed potty training. It is fine if you get your infant to go on cue just once or twice a day at first, then build from there as time and circumstances permit. Do not be too hard on yourself by expecting too much.

Does My Baby Have to Be Naked?

This is not a requirement. Many parents keep a diaper or training pants on their baby in between potty visits, while others prefer a bare baby bum at home. In short, it is a matter of preference and a lifestyle choice.

Is It Safe?

Of course, as long as parents have the right mindset. Parents must exercise patience and gentleness; observe and respond to baby's signals on time whenever reasonably possible; and provide proper, comfortable and loving support while holding their infants. This is a positive and nonpunitive practice. Punishment, anger and control are *not* a part of IPT. See "Avoid the No-Nos" in Chapter 7 for more about the no-nos.

What Are the Main Benefits?

The three big winners are babies, parents and the environment. In detail, IPT:

- Enhances bonding through closeness and communication.
- Responds to infants' natural elimination communication and timing.
- Taps into first window of learning for toilet learning.
- Keeps babies in touch with their own bodies.
- Reduces diaper use and negative associations (diaper rash, contact with waste and chemicals, bulk between the legs, etc.).
- Helps environment by conserving/saving trees, water, petroleum and landfill space.
- Allows babies to achieve good control early in life.
- Lets children complete potty training at a relatively young age.
- Reduces risk of urinary tract infections (UTIs).
- Combats enuresis (bedwetting).
- Reduces or eliminates embarrassing "accidents" for preschoolers.
- Yields big savings on diapers and laundry costs.

Does It Really Work?

Yes, but not without practice and effort. Success does not just happen on its own. It takes at least one committed adult and several months of perseverance to finish. In most situations, there are rewards for both baby and care-giver right from the very first days or weeks, such as acknowledgment and encouragement of baby's communication and abilities.

Does It Work with a Toddler and a Baby or Twins?

Yes, part-time IPT works well in both situations. Although your time will be limited, there is strength in numbers. For example, two or more children tend to encourage, inspire and motivate each other. For more on working with siblings and multiples, see Chapter 8, "Part-Time Pottying."

Can I Still Start If My Baby Is 6 Months or Older?

Yes, infant pottying can work just fine with late-starters. Many parents have started at 9 months, even 18 months or older, and have done okay by making some simple and logical modifications. For some, it can be tricky starting with a child who has been "trained" to go in a diaper, who wears disposables and does not associate the feeling of wetness with elimination or who is mobile (creeping, crawling or walking). It mainly depends on your convictions. For more on starting with an older baby, see Chapter 9, "Late-Starters."

Can I Do It Part Time or with Daycare?

Many families do. If you are fairly consistent, it is not confusing for your child. Strive to potty your baby on a fairly regular basis during optimal and obvious times when you are at home, such as first thing in the morning, after a feeding or before bed, including weekends and holidays. Elicit the help of other family members including siblings. For daycare, search for one that is open to IPT or that is willing to potty your baby every so often, perhaps along with the toddlers. At the very least, they should be willing to change your baby often. For more on part-time IPT, see Chapter 8, "Part-Time Pottying."

Will People Think I'm Crazy?

There are people who object to every lifestyle imaginable, so don't let this deter you. Since the 1950s, the Western world has been indoctrinated to fear and reject any form of early toilet learning, with no proven medical basis. Now that many parents have had good results with IPT, the old dogma has lost its monopoly. Pediatricians and other medical professionals are supportive and open to learning more about IPT. More and more families recognize the fact that there is a lot of money, rather than truth and sound research, behind some big product endorsements (diapers and bestselling books come to mind) and are less frightened by the myths about infant elimination training.

chapter 2
philosophy

Babies are smarter and more capable than we think. Infants are helpless in so many ways that it is hard for us to imagine such tiny beings could be aware of elimination or have some control over it.

Healthy infants are indeed aware of when they "go" and communicate this awareness, but if we don't respond, they stop communicating and eventually lose touch with the elimination functions. Most of us condition and thereby train babies to use diapers as a toilet. Later they must unlearn this training. This can be a confusing and traumatic experience for many.

If you do not believe that an infant is aware of elimination, remove his diaper and pay attention as he goes. From his facial expressions, body movements and vocalizations, you will perceive that he is aware of the muscular sensations. You can help keep him in touch and encourage muscular development. Like any other muscle, the more a baby consciously experiences and begins to exercise his sphincter muscles, the more control he can gain. At first it may just be awareness of the sensation, but he will inevitably experiment with contracting and relaxing the muscles. The earlier you acknowledge and encourage this, the earlier he can gain some control.

Infant potty learning, like many things in life, begins with association and can be approached in a rational and scientific manner as well as an intuitive and instinctive one—or a combination of both—depending on what works best for you and your baby. The rational approach involves timing and observation of elimination patterns and baby body language. The more instinctual approach involves intuition and tuning in to your baby in more subtle ways. Both are covered in detail in this book, based on this premise: *IPT is teamwork. It is not something you are doing to your baby, and it is not something your baby can do without you.*

Studies demonstrate that newborns are able to make associations, learn and remember. In 1928, Anderson Aldrich taught an infant association with the sound of a bell after just 12 rings of the bell. A 1966 study by Siqueland and Lipsitt illustrated the quick learning ability of newborns and the power of positive conditioning in reinforcing learned behaviors. Just one day after birth, babies learned to turn their heads to one side 83 percent of the time in response to an offering of sugar water. Next the newborns were taught to turn their heads to the left at the sound of a bell or to the right at the sound of a buzzer. The task was then complicated by switching bell and buzzer, with reinforcement provided only for turning the opposite way. It took the infants only 30 minutes to accomplish this.[1]

Pediatrician T. Berry Brazelton and Bertrand Cramer, MD, state that "None of these laboratory studies can be as effective in reinforcing an infant's memory as are the times when parent and infant are involved in spontaneous, reciprocal interaction, each giving and receiving rewarding cues from the other."[2] Although neither of these doctors are advocates of infant elimination training, the principle of positive reinforcement between mother and infant exists in the spontaneous and reciprocal interaction between mother and baby during infant toilet learning. And the baby-mother dyad fits this mold better than any other toilet training approach used by Westerners in the past century:

- parent-directed—based on parent leading, 1900–1960s
- child-directed—based on child leading, from 1962
- baby-mother-directed—based on reciprocal interaction between baby and mother

Brazelton argues that parents must wait until their kids initiate toilet training at around the age of 2 years.[3] An infant is a very social being. Instead of ignoring his elimination instincts and innate propensity for learning by waiting years for him to "get it" on his own, a mother can instead be an active participant in a shared symbiosis. In this way, she acknowledges and encourages his capacity for early learning. A cooperative and caring partnership shapes the heart of infant potty training.

Another way to look at an infant's natural ability to respond to elimination communication is to compare it to a Montessori "sensitive period" in that the optimum learning time for many things is in infancy when the brain is open and receptive. "A sensitive period refers to a special sensibility which a creature acquires in its infantile state, while it is still in a process of evolution."[4] Healthy infants in a stable, relaxed and loving environment can learn pottying effortlessly over the months, just as children can learn foreign languages with no effort and no accent at a young age, something that later becomes an arduous process. "There is for each developmental phase a particular and specially suited period. These are times when a child is ready to make a developmental step. If it misses the timing of this learning step, the child will make up for it much later and with a lot of struggle."[5]

Most Westerners begin teaching toilet habits when it is difficult and awkward for both child and parent. It is hard for the child because:

- His instinctive awareness of elimination has been suppressed for months or years.
- He has been encouraged and allowed to use diapers as a toilet.
- He was not encouraged to use his "toilet muscles" in infancy.
- He was not encouraged to communicate the need to go in infancy.
- He is mobile and typically does not like to spend the necessary time sitting on the potty.

It is difficult for the parent because a toddler:

- is typically not interested in potty training
- eats solid foods and makes bigger, smellier messes in his pants
- is more likely to challenge and "test" his parents
- is mobile and usually does not like to spend the necessary time sitting on the potty

Babies in non-Western societies typically complete toilet learning far earlier than Western babies. In some respects, Western mothers using infant pottying may face an uphill battle. The very concept strikes many as ridiculous, impracticable or impossible, so a mother opting for this method does not have the societal support and examples that teach, inspire and sustain mothers in traditional societies. Most women abroad have experienced infant elimination training themselves. It is and has long been the norm for them, so that women and children have a life experience of loving support from both their families and communities. Due to many generations of unwavering acceptance and positive acculturation in their societies, no one finds it unusual or strange. No doctors or psychologists frighten families with stories of psychological damage. In these cultures, babies generally don't wear diapers and are not subjected to anger, impatience, punishment or worries about keeping carpeting or fancy clothing clean and dry. They do not have to undergo diaper untraining and are free to run and play as toddlers, without interruption by boring and confining diaper changes and potty sessions.

Diapers, especially disposable ones, are a convenient but temporary solution. We attempt to "plug up" our child's disposal system with diapers in the same way as we temporarily stop the flow from a leaking pipe. If allowed to wear wet diapers on a regular basis, a child grows accustomed to feeling wet and loses his natural aversion to this sensation. This will make toilet teaching a more difficult task, no matter when you begin. If you use super-absorbent disposable diapers that always make baby feel dry by absorbing the urine into a gel, he will not learn to associate urination with wetness. When he finally begins toilet learning in earnest, whether at age 15 months or 4 years, it is likely to be difficult for him to make the cause-and-effect connection between peeing and feeling wet. Many such children are frightened to "go" anywhere but in a diaper, while others experience fear when first introduced to a toilet.

Whenever possible, use cloth diapers without a waterproof cover in order to immediately feel any dampness and remove the wet diaper. Let baby spend diaper-free time in training pants or bare-bottomed at intervals throughout the day. He will be more comfortable without a constant bulk between his legs. This will make it easier for him to maneuver, which in turn may speed up his learning of some motor skills. For example, if there is no diaper bulk to contend with, imagine how much easier it is for an infant trying to turn over for the very first time.

Training from infancy is time consuming, but dealing with elimination, cleanliness and toilet training take time no matter when you begin. If you plan to let your child self-train at the age of 2, 3 or 4 years (or even older—no one knows if or when a child will self-train), you will spend a lot of time changing diapers and dealing with laundry until that time comes. If you remain at home with your infant, you will be with him many hours a day anyway, so why not use some of the time to potty instead of delaying the task? Or if you work outside your home, potty your baby a few times in the morning and/or evening. Take the time to learn and respond to his signals instead of bundling him up and ignoring his communications.

As they grow older, most babies dislike being held down and changed throughout the day but still love being held in-arms and receiving the attention they get at potty time. By responding to their natural timing and signals, you reinforce their instinctive awareness of and communication about elimination. Both of you will benefit from the time you devote to this. Your baby is ready if you are.

chapter 3

the in-arms phase

The in-arms phase is the most unique part of infant pottying for Westerners. Since an infant cannot sit, she should be cradled securely and comfortably in your arms over a receptacle or other toilet place for this phase.

The optimum time to begin is anytime from birth through approximately 6 months. This is the first window of opportunity. If you begin after 6 months, you will need to work on unlearning and relearning elimination associations and to make some easy and logical modifications to the guidelines given in this chapter and the next. (See Chapter 9 "Late-Starters" for starting with older babies.) In short, there is no definite cutoff point, but typically, the earlier you start the better as long as starting with such a young baby isn't too tiring or stressful.

Infant pottying is more intense and demanding at the start, gradually becomes easier and less time consuming over the months and is often completed sooner than conventional Western toilet training. For many, the overall time spent dealing with diapers and elimination is also less with IPT. Despite these possibilities, I do not recommend IPT for those whose main goal is to speed toilet learning.

The six steps of the in-arms phase are:

1. Choose Your Basic Signal
2. Learn Elimination Timing and Patterns
3. Select Locations and Receptacles
4. Find the Best Positions
5. Learn about Signals and Cues
6. Understand and Commit

STEP 1: Choose Your Basic Signal

The first step involves selecting a signal to use to cue baby to go for you. Your signal can be any sound you choose. The most common signal for voiding is "potty whispering"—a sound such as "sssss" or "pssss" that imitates the sound of running water or urination. For defecation, you can use a grunting or straining sound such as "hmmmm," or just use "sssss" for both forms of elimination. Some parents prefer baby talk such as "pee pee" while others like to use a sentence with recognizable voice intonation, "Do you have to pee?" Some mothers rely on the position to be the "cue de grace" and do not use any audible signal. Use whatever feels most natural and comfortable to you. Infants can learn to associate their elimination with your cues in just a few days if you start early enough.

STEP 2: Learn Elimination Timing and Patterns

Step 2 is the observation phase and involves familiarization with baby's natural timing and elimination patterns. You can gain a general feeling for her elimination timing during one or a few sessions of about 30–60 minutes, whatever feels right for you.

Select a warm, comfortable, well-lighted place for observing the child. Lay some protective material on the carpet or mattress. Suggestions include a layer of waterproof material covered with a sheet and either a few towels or a cloth diaper. If the fountain effect proves to be a problem with a baby boy during this exercise, you can put a diaper, flannel blanket or soft towel over his groin area. Bear in mind that if you cover him, you may have to pay closer attention to ascertain exactly when he pees.

If helpful, you can keep notes or a potty log to record your baby's body language, vocalizations, timing, patterns, likely times to go or not go, or any other observations you make in relation to feedings, naps and elimination. A sample potty log page is provided overleaf.

When baby goes before, during or after a feeding, make the "sssss" sound and jot down the time. Making the "sssss" sound helps her learn to associate your basic signal with elimination. If she makes a sound or you notice a physical body signal just before she eliminates, use this to help you anticipate future elimination. Remove the wet cloth and replace it with a clean, dry one. Repeat the process for as many times as she goes after the feeding. The object of the exercise is to eventually use your notes to determine the frequency of your baby's need to go and any patterns in relation to feeding and sleeping.

| FEEDING TIME | EVENT | | NOTES |
	PEE	POO	

OBSERVATION DATE: _____   NAME: _____

Potty Log

If you're observing a newborn and still recovering from delivery, or if you don't want to leave your baby (partially) unclothed for observation, another way to study elimination timing is to place a diaper on your chest, lay her on the diaper, wait for her to go, give your basic signal when she goes and jot down the time of elimination. Replace the wet or soiled cloth with a clean, dry one, and repeat this process as many times as necessary. You can also study your newborn while holding her in-arms—some find it easiest with baby just wrapped in a cloth diaper or prefold and a blanket. Keep her warm, secure and comfortable at all times. She may go often (every 5–10 minutes) in the first weeks since her bladder is so small; her poops might be explosive and hard to predict for a while. She might cry before, during or after going for some days or weeks. Her timing and patterns may change dramatically over the first few weeks or months. While you are recovering from the birth, give yourself a realistic goal of catching just one or a few eliminations per day. Many find that the wake-up pees are the easiest to catch.

You can also study timing and patterns while using a sling or wrap. Baby-wearing is one of the best ways to become familiar and stay in tune with your baby's elimination timing and patterns since you know straightaway when she goes. It is especially beneficial in cold climates or rooms without sufficient heating. Some mothers keep their babies naked in the sling or wrap, carrying them skin-to-skin, which keeps baby at a perfect body temperature. If so desired, you can keep a cloth diaper under her while wearing her. It is, of course, not a requirement to keep your baby naked in the sling. Even if she is wearing some clothing and/or a cloth diaper without a waterproof cover, you will know when she goes.

As a demonstration of how quickly infants learn by association, some mothers who spend more than a few days studying their babies' timing find that their infants learn to go in unusual places. One mother who started out by laying her baby on the changing table and making the "sssss" sound every time the little girl peed was baffled and discouraged when she later could not get her baby to go in the sink. She knew it was time for her baby to go, but the baby refused to pee in the sink. Then as soon as she lay her baby down on her back, she would pee. It finally dawned on the mother that she had inadvertently taught her daughter to pee when laying on her back rather than in-arms over the sink. A mother starting out with her 4-month-old son soon found that every time she placed him on the changing table and removed his diaper, he would immediately go—he associated the positioning, feel of cool air and diaper removal with a cue to eliminate. For these reasons, many EC'ers offer pottytunities at every diaper change.

Mothers who use their intuition to know when baby needs to go may only need to rely on timing to get started. Some may even skip Step 2 altogether and instead rely exclusively on the intuitive connection with their babies. Trust your instincts and abilities. If you feel, have a hunch or simply *know* it is time for baby to go, offer her a pottytunity. Most mothers sense other things by instinct and intuition, such as when their babies are tired, hungry or ill. In a way similar to automatically knowing when to respond to these things, you can help your child relieve herself at the right moment too.

As you observe your baby, you will likely begin to note that there are "toilet patterns" in relation to when she eats and sleeps. Many babies urinate at fairly regular intervals, depending on the time of eating and sleeping. For example, the "peequency" for newborns and small infants might be once every 5–15 minutes for a number of times after a feeding. As babies grow older, they go less frequently. A 3-month-old might pee every 15–20 minutes three or four times after nursing, and then the interval might increase to 30 minutes, or else baby might just pee once after 30 minutes and then not need to go again until she eats again. Some infants go during or soon after a feeding while others don't need to go until 10–15 minutes after nursing. Most need to go upon waking, especially first thing in the morning. A common pattern is to pee more frequently in the morning than in the afternoon.

In India, mothers non-coercively get their babies to poo first thing in the morning. "A physiologic aid for bowel training, called the gastrocolic reflex, may help predict when your baby will have a BM. A full stomach stimulates the colon to empty around 20–30 minutes after a meal. Best odds for a predictable daily BM is after breakfast. Another benefit of this daily routine is that it teaches baby to listen to his bodily urges. It's a physiologic fact that bowel signals not promptly attended to will subside, and this can lead to constipation."[6]

Always remember that whenever possible, timing should be based on baby's elimination timing and patterns. If you potty her every 15–20 minutes after feedings, it is because you have learned this from her. Even if you feel that potty visits are hit-or-miss based on an educated guess, your guess should be based on your observations and feelings about when your baby needs to go. And other factors can come into play here. For example, if baby is tired, ill or cold, she may go more often. If in warm surroundings or warm clothing, she may pee less frequently than usual.

Bear in mind that baby's timing and patterns will change from time to time as she grows and as her bladder capacity increases. Every so often, try waiting a little longer between toilet visits—maybe stretch it from going every 20 minutes to going every 30 minutes. If she does okay, use the new timing. If she isn't ready, go back to the earlier pattern for a while longer.

The key to learning baby's timing is to relate elimination to feeding and waking. An attentive mother will instinctively sense or eventually recognize a correlation. If you feed and put baby to sleep on a fairly regular schedule, it is usually easier to determine a regular timed pattern of discharge. Mothers who breastfeed on demand should bear in mind that continuous breastfeeding can at first make it tricky—especially for a beginner—to find a recognizable elimination timing pattern. This is especially true if you start with a tiny infant who is nursing and eliminating almost continuously during the first weeks of life—the bowel movements tend to be irregular for a while. A solution for this is to hold baby in a comfortable position over a receptacle, such as a small bowl or small potty while nursing her. Or you can sit on the floor or bed with both the potty and baby facing you, wrap your legs around the potty and wrap your arms around baby as you nurse her.

Finally, there are exceptions to every rule. Not all babies have a regular or predictable elimination pattern, so don't be alarmed or discouraged if you can't find a pattern. It can be a challenge for beginners to catch an elusive and enigmatic pee or poo. The first catches may seem like pure chance. Some mothers start out by relying on the clock. Using a timer can be helpful for this until timing becomes second nature. Others do really well the first day or week, then seem to lose the knack for a while. Some have an easy time with pees but not poos, while others do well with poos but can't seem to get their baby to pee for them for days or even weeks. Some babies have very irregular or infrequent bowel movements (breastfed babies might only poo once every 7–10 days). You may have to rely more on signals, body language, intuition or a combination of these to get in sync with your baby. And later you may find yourself using some or all of these to different degrees as your baby changes over time.

STEP 3: Select Locations and Receptacles

Select whatever locations and containers best suit you, your child and your situation. For the first few days or weeks, it is advisable to use the same place and receptacle(s) whenever possible so she learns to associate these with elimination. One of the most popular places is the bathroom sink. For peeing, you can also use the shower. Receptacles include a potty, small baking/ mixing bowl, plastic rectangular basin, toilet, bidet, pet bowl, food container, bucket, plastic sweater box, bedpan, chamber pot or any other catchall that works. For boys, you can also use containers with smaller openings such as a quart canning jar, plastic cup, bottle or (portable) urinal. If you seat your baby on a vessel, it should be "baby-bottom friendly" in terms of size, comfort and temperature. Whenever possible, containers should be rinsed or cleaned after each use and disinfected when needed. Use mild cleaning products that do not irritate baby's skin.

Some babies develop their own potty particularity or strong preference for a specific location or receptacle and refuse to go anywhere else. If your baby cries or arches her back, this may be the reason. The easiest way to find out is to "test the waters" by trying different locations and receptacles. Most infants don't have a preference and will gladly go anywhere peaceful and warm. Some are happy using a variety of receptacles. Baby's taste in receptacles may suddenly and inexplicably change one day, so be prepared to offer options. After a while, most children evolve to where they occasionally like a "change of scenery" and appreciate your putting their potty in varied and interesting places such as the back porch or balcony, in front of a window, near their books and toys, or in a special room.

You can also take your own preferences into account as long as your baby is content with your selection. For example, many mothers prefer the toilet since they can instantly flush the waste away without having to clean a receptacle. In addition, it is easy to hear when your baby goes in the toilet. If you use a training seat, it is convenient to carry with you when you go out. Sitting on the edge of the bathtub is a good place to potty and nurse simultaneously. It's also helpful with boys whose strong and unruly stream is hard to aim.

When going out or traveling, you can use a potty or other container in the car, plane or hotel. Explore your surroundings for clean and comfy pit stops. In urban areas, learn which places offer facilities. Use your discretion in public restrooms. If you are carrying your own potty, you can use the changing table, a counter top or toilet stall. If using the toilet, you can sit on the seat and let your baby sit on your lap for warmth, sanitation, comfort and security. If your baby is frightened by loud and unpredictable automatic flushers that tend to flush every time you move, cover the motion detector until you are done.

At home, I held my infant son over the bathroom wash basin when he had to pee. I aimed his penis downward so there was no mess or splashing. There was a mirror above the sink, and he enjoyed looking at our faces while we were waiting for him to go. Most babies enjoy the mirror, but like everything else, this is subjective. In some cases it may prove to be (or eventually become) too distracting for a baby to watch her reflection. I found it was a cozy occasion to bond and communicate while holding him close to me, gazing and smiling at each other in the mirror, having him pat my face and talking to him.

Some tactics work with some children but not with others. With every phase, parents find that certain approaches work well for a while, then need to be changed as their babies grow and mature. *There is not a fixed way to "do" infant potty training.* Be creative, try different things and do what works best for your family.

STEP 4: Find the Best Positions

The classic elimination position resembles sitting in a chair or squatting in-arms. For neonates, let baby lie flat on her back in your arms, with her head touching your chest or abdomen (depending on the height of your sink or receptacle). For both of these positions, hold baby's thighs in your hands, spreading the thighs slightly apart while aiming her over the sink or other potty place. Take care not to pull her knees up too high and also not to squish or otherwise apply pressure to her belly. As she grows, you'll need more arm space to accommodate her height, and you can cradle her in your arms by resting her back between your forearms and leaning her head against your chest. Most babies find this position relaxing. Many variations are possible. Whatever position you use, it is your responsibility to provide the following:

- comfortable, secure and relaxing position
- proper support for the neck, head and spine
- warm, hygienic and peaceful surroundings
- positive attitude

Caregivers with physical limitations can seek alternative ways to hold or support baby. If you experience back pain or if a young sibling finds baby heavy to hold in position, one solution is to seat and support her on a towel (for warmth and padding) which is draped over the edge of the bathtub. Another solution is to hold her in your lap while you sit on the toilet, serving as a warm human cushion and taking the weight off your back. A variation is to sit on the toilet and hold her between your legs. For this position, you can hold her in either a squatting or sitting position, with her back against your abdomen or thighs. You can face either way on the toilet; some babies like to face the back of the toilet while others prefer facing forward.

Some parents find it is easier on their backs if they squat or sit on a stool in front of the toilet and let the toilet support the weight of their baby. For this position, you can hold baby's thighs while resting your hands, elbows or arms on your knees or on the toilet seat. This allows her to avoid contact with the cold seat, relieves pressure on your back and prevents your arms from getting tired. You can also place a child's toilet seat over the adult seat and provide support in any of the ways already mentioned.

You can, of course, squat over any type of receptacle. Parents living in rural areas often enjoy squatting outdoors with baby in-arms.

If you are in a car, you can squeeze a bucket (ideally with a tight-fitting lid) or other container between your knees while you are seated and holding her slightly above the rim. For tired arms or to avoid straining your back, rest your arms on your thighs or against the side of the vehicle.

A simple position that can be used just about anywhere is to simply cradle baby in one arm while using the opposite hand to hold a small bowl under her.

Another popular position is to let baby stand while peeing and sometimes even while pooing—the latter being a temporary preference for some. This applies to both boys and girls. In the case of girls, it is usually short-lived and more likely if they have one or more brothers. Some boys don't like to stand for quite a while. One baby boy who would spit up when the slightest pressure was applied to his belly was not comfortable in the traditional squatty position. His parents used an "in-arms standing" position that applied no pressure to his belly, provided adequate support and was comfortable for all concerned.

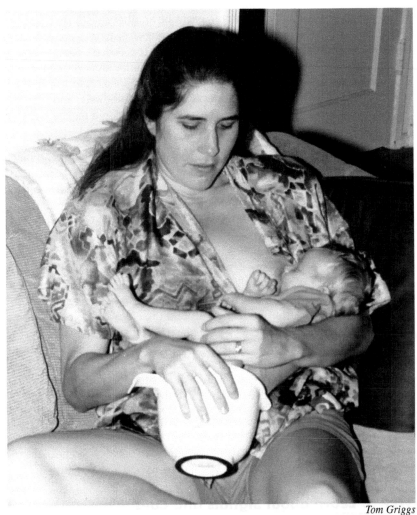

Tom Griggs

2 weeks old — Nursing while pottying.
Holding a small baking bowl under Sara allows her to nurse
uninterrupted while her mother becomes familiar with her
signals, timing and elimination patterns.

Some babies spit up in one position but not in others. Holding baby in a more reclined version of the classic position or else in the in-arms standing position might alleviate this. Jiggling her too fast or abruptly while switching from lying down to an upright position might be another cause. There are babies who work their abdominal muscles while trying to eliminate, and this extra pressure can cause them to spit up or even vomit. This doesn't seem to bother babies, as evidenced by their cooing and smiling during the experience, and it is generally not a cause for alarm. Children soon learn to distinguish which muscles they need to void the bladder and empty the bowels, and then the problem disappears. There are also babies who spit up on a regular basis no matter what, and you simply have to wait for this phase to end.

Girls are harder to precision-aim for pees in that the direction and range of the urine can be unpredictable, reaching a rather large area. Wiping girls after pees is more difficult too due to folds in the anatomy. With boys, aiming is essential since urination affects the penis and stream by lifting or spraying upwards, streaming at an angle to where they are pointed or even panning from side to side. One solution is to use your fingertip to aim him downward when the stream starts to rise. Another is to aim his body as best you can, then cup your hand to direct the stream, in effect using your palm as a splashguard. Or you can place a container at a slight angle between your thighs or calves and direct the fountain there. If he sprays the surroundings while using a potty, try putting his legs in front instead of around the sides of the potty. With a toilet or bucket, hang his bum deep enough so that the stream remains in the receptacle. If he can stand while peeing, see if he likes peeing into a bottle. Small boys, and even some girls, generally enjoy watching their stream, and this reinforces awareness. When old enough to sit well on a toilet, boys can straddle the seat further back and shoot into the bowl without assistance.

If you find that the positions depicted in this chapter are not right for you and your baby, gently experiment until you find one or more that work well for both of you. Bear in mind that a favorite position can one day be unexpectedly rejected by your baby, in which case you'll need to find an alternative.

STEP 5: Learn about Signals and Cues

The next step is for caregiver and baby to develop the ability to read and respond to each other's cues and clues. This can be done on various levels and differs from child to child and parent to parent. In this phase, you continue to teach baby to associate certain things with potty time and strive to learn her own particular signals.

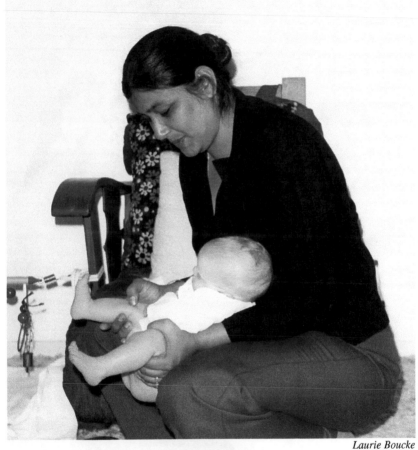

Laurie Boucke

3 months old — Bibiji demonstrates the classic in-arms
squatting position with Rob.

Dana Pace

3 weeks old — A position for newborns.
Newborn Adaline rests comfortably in her mother's arms.

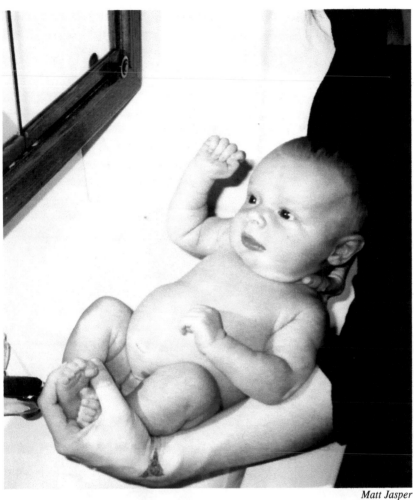

Matt Jasper

3 weeks old — Another position for newborns.
Some parents find it more comfortable to grasp baby's feet
and rest him on one arm while supporting his head with
the other hand. Here little Albion relaxes in this
laid-back pose. The position also makes it easy to
aim a boy's stream downward.

Jon Adams

6 months old — Supporting Hannah on a potty on the toilet.
Kim sits on a 4-legged stool to avoid back strain
as she holds Hannah securely on the potty.

Gunnar Dibbern

5 months old — Janus enjoys a beach pee.

Laurie Boucke

4 months old — Connecting with Dad.

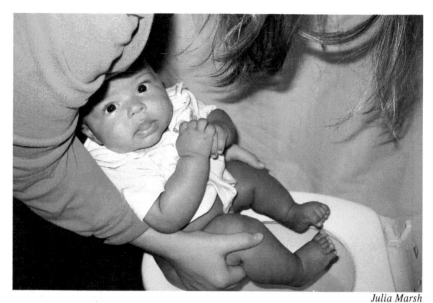

Julia Marsh

4 months old — Classic position over the toilet.

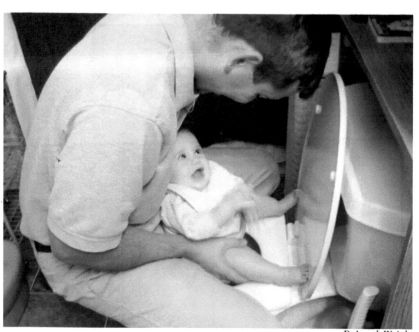

Deborah Wright

6 months old — Keeping it fun.

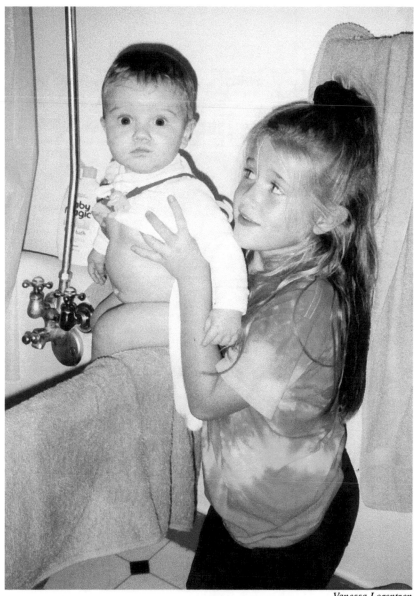

Vanessa Lorentzen

5 months old — Siblings can help.
Where baby's weight is a concern, one solution is to use
the bathtub rim as a support (works better with boys!).

Laurie Boucke

4 months old — In the Rocky Mountains.

Brett Cornish Scott

7 months old — After a nap, Colum is offered
an outdoor "pottytunity" by his mother.

Vanessa Lorentzen

4 months old — In-arms standing position.
Looking in the mirror is great fun for little Zion!

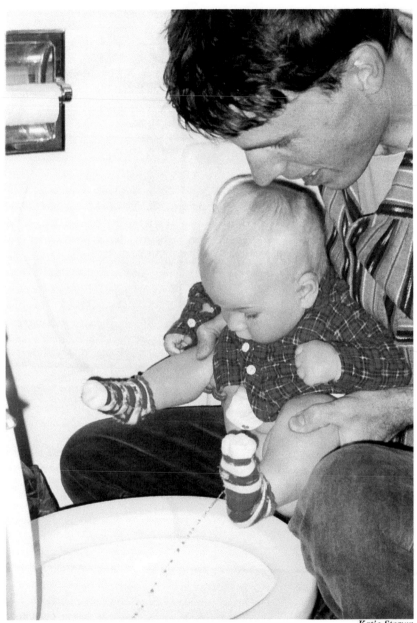

Katie Strawn

5 months old — Aidan is right on target.

Colin White

4 months old — Classic position over basin.

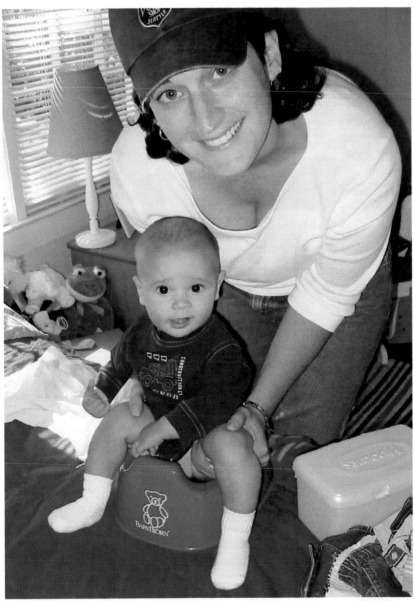

Mark Kayser

5 months old — Ben's mother holds him slightly above the cold potty
and stabilizes him by supporting his thighs.

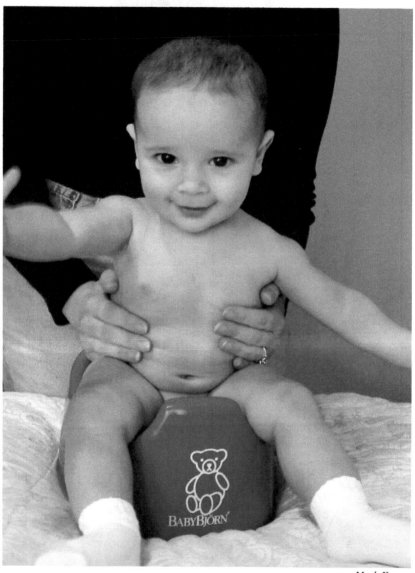

Mark Kayser

5 months old — Potty on bed.
Mother supports baby with her hands around his waist.

Elissa Van Marter

5 months old — Leggings make pottying and
changing little Alizabeth quick and easy.

Rawlinson, Pile, Herring
Potty covers keep baby warm and comfy.
The pee mat at the bottom helps protect carpeting in the home.

Signals from Caregiver to Baby

Pick a time when you think your baby might need to go. If helpful, you can refer to your notes for this. The important thing to remember is that a baby will not usually respond to your signals if she doesn't need to go.

When you think or feel it is a likely time, take her to her potty place and give your signal. If you do this for just a day or two, you will be amazed at how quickly she learns to associate your cueing with elimination.

The main types of signals that infants respond to are:

- vocal or verbal cues ("sssss" or "do you have to pee?")
- physical cues (in-arms position, location, receptacle, etc.)
- implicit/intuitive cues
- manual cues such as gestures or sign language

If you are consistent and fairly intense at first, your baby will associate your specific vocal, verbal and physical signals with toilet activity within a week or less. A signal as subtle as "feeling mama breathe" as you hold her against your belly can trigger elimination from an in-arms baby—inhale, then tighten and relax your abdominal muscles a few times.

If it's time for her to go but there is no response to your signal, try touching her feet or running a little water in the sink or bathtub. The sound of running water may prompt her to go. You can also try running a little water over her feet, dipping her feet in water or sprinkling a little water on her tummy. The water can be warm or else slightly cooler than her body temperature but not cold. If you think it is time for your baby to urinate but she is resisting, the sound, temperature change and contact with water will help her relax and release. If she still doesn't go, take a break, then try again in 5–10 minutes or whenever her natural timing suggests.

Another tactic is to give her something to suck (e.g., your thumb), chew on (e.g., a teething toy) or drink, and she may suddenly relax enough to go. In general, you should not have to signal baby for longer than 1–2 minutes. If there is no reaction, she probably doesn't need to go. Do not continue to hold her in position unless she is comfy, happy, relaxed and wants to remain there. If she resists and you cannot quickly distract and relax her, respect her wishes and try again later.

The concept of implicit and intuitive cues may seem unusual at first, but the ability develops naturally and without much effort as you practice more and more and learn baby's elimination needs. Manual cues (hand signals) can be started as early as you like and are discussed in detail in Chapter 5.

Signals from Baby to Caregiver

Baby's cues may be audible, inaudible, visible or invisible. Try to correlate her natural timing and patterns with her cues. The main types of signals that babies use are:

- body language
  If you observe your baby just before or during elimination, you'll start to notice physical indicators such as specific movements or facial expressions. Watch for her body language and natural timing to coincide.

- vocal cues
  Vocalizations that sometimes signal impending or completed elimination include grunting, fussing, crying and screaming.

- implicit/intuitive cues
  Some mothers perceive intuitive cues in the form of physical sensations, odors or sounds.

- manual cues such as gestures or sign language

For an in-depth explanation of baby's signals see Chapter 5.

STEP 6: Understand and Commit

After you have understood and instigated Steps 1–5, the next step is to make a further commitment to continue on a realistic and fairly regular basis with respect to your overall situation. Strive to observe and adhere to baby's natural rhythms whenever reasonably possible. If you do not have the opportunity to potty her throughout much of the day, try to do so at likely times. Even if you can only concentrate on it a few times a day, this can keep her elimination awareness alive.

Some parents start by making a halfhearted attempt, perhaps due to skepticism, self-doubt or fearing a lack of time to do it properly, only to be amazed and pleasantly surprised at how well their babies respond. Others have a difficult time synchronizing with their babies from the very start. It may take several days or even a few weeks to be able to coordinate with your baby's timing and signals. It's fine to ease your way into this gradually. There is no hurry. It is going to take time and practice. Your confidence will build as you start to make more and more catches. There is nothing complex or mysterious about infant pottying. *Whatever works best is the best approach.*

It is important to always remember that an infant will automatically go whenever her bladder is full. In no case should you direct anger at her if you arrive too late, nor should you feel guilty for not being on time. Both baby and caregiver need to be relaxed for this to work.

Expectations

A lot of parents start out expecting too much. Expecting too much too soon can lead to giving up. Time goals set us up for disappointment and feelings of failure if our child doesn't meet our objectives. In some situations, this leads to pressuring the child and ourselves, and is thus counterproductive. As one mother put it, "The biggest lesson parenting has taught me is not to expect but to discover."

Of course, certain basic expectations must be in place before you begin, such as "infant potty training is possible." Realistic expectations include an increase in communication, responsiveness and bonding along with a gradual gaining of control over the months.

It is normal to experience many misses and accidents along the way. Babies make the journey at their own innate rate, and the best you can do is to be there for them when they need you and when you are able to assist without yourself becoming too overwhelmed.

Each child is unique. There is no way to know at what age a child will be toilet trained or when a baby will begin to consciously signal her elimination needs. It is possible that she won't signal until she is nearing completion and that this might happen around the age of 24 months or older. If this is the case, you can use the other tools discussed in this chapter: timing, patterns and intuition. It doesn't matter how you figure out your baby's timing. The important point to remember is this: If a child doesn't give clear signals, you can still move forward as a team.

The fact that a child doesn't give overt signals or take the initiative to potty does not mean that she is unaware or that you have done something wrong. Rather, it is the pace and design of her natural development. If your baby doesn't get upset by going in a diaper, there is nothing wrong with this. Some babies just naturally aren't bothered by dirty diapers. Others are so busy all the time (especially once mobile) that they don't notice or care. And of course, many *do* care. It's an individual thing. By dropping fixed and rigid expectations and wishes, new channels of appreciation and communication will open.

Parents can easily fall into the trap of being too hard on themselves. It's easy to feel like you have failed when you miss one or more pees or poos. If you reverse the way you view this ("Is the glass half empty or half full?") you are more likely to appreciate your efforts. If you catch just one or a few pees a day, don't be discouraged. Every "catch" is one less diaper used. Start using misses as a chance to learn more about your baby's patterns, body language and other signals, or anything else you notice.

Take care that you do not become too obsessed with pottying. Keep a balance in your activities. If you get to the point that you feel you can hardly do anything else but potty your baby, you are trying too hard. If you find that you are constantly looking for signals or that you are imagining that every little movement or sound is a sign, you are overdoing it and headed for burnout. If you constantly worry about when you will finish, you will miss a lot of the "magic" and likely become frustrated. If you are thrilled at each little deposit in the potty and enjoying the closeness with your baby, you are gaining far more than potty progress.

Squirts and Spurts

Many infants urinate and defecate in 2–3 intermittent squirts and spurts. Once you're aware of this pattern, it's easy to notice. If possible, avoid diapering or dressing baby until she has truly finished going. If the wait between spurts is long and she is impatient, take a short break, then bring her back to the potty later. If she has diarrhea or a cold or is suffering from another ailment, do not expect to capture all the spurts and squirts until she has recovered.

There are a variety of ways the squirt phenomenon can happen. The "warning pee" involves letting out a few drops as a signal that more pee is about to follow. You'll either feel the warmth and dampness or see a small trickle of pee. This gives you time to take your baby to her potty place and demonstrates that babies *can* gain some bladder control early in life. Or you could be dressing your baby after she pees for you, and she might start to signal by crying. Try giving her the opportunity to go again before you finish dressing her.

Other manifestations include the "pre-poop pee" (starting to push the poo out first sends out a little pee) and the "post-poop pee" (whereby baby invariably has to pee shortly or several minutes after pooping, whether or not she peed before the poo). And some experience the dynamic duo or tandem pee and poo.

"Skid marks" can be caused by releasing gas or else by pooing in stages. The spotting can go on for several months. To avoid soiling extra diapers, use a small cloth insert to catch the poo smudges in her diaper in between potty visits. If she is a poop dribbler, try slightly longer potty sessions, or else come back for a second round after a short break. You can also try wiping. If you wipe her after what seems like the end of a poo, this might stimulate another spurt. If you don't wipe, you may end up waiting 5 minutes or longer—even up to 20 or 30 minutes—until the next spurt or "explosion" (newborns!) happens.

Diapers can accentuate squirts and spurts for a while. It is not uncommon for a diapered baby to go a little, then hold back when she feels the sensation of excrement (or urine) against her body. Her mother dutifully changes the diaper, then soon finds she needs to change baby again . . . and perhaps yet again. Babies who are allowed to eliminate freely into a receptacle sometimes learn to regulate their elimination within a few weeks or months, to the point that they have fewer but larger pees and just one or two poos a day instead of a continual stream of small poops. Some EC'ers believe the drips and dribbles stem from the days of wearing full-time diapers when a child only "went" a little at a time in the diapers without ever trying to "hold it," and without ever completely emptying the bladder or bowels in one elimination session.

Changes in Timing

Sometimes due to illness, experiencing milestones or any major life change, a change in diet, an emotional situation (e.g., the arrival of a new baby or an upset in the home), travel or a change in routine (e.g., moving, hosting out-of-town guests or spending the night outside your home), baby's elimination timing may fluctuate. Do not feel discouraged. A regular or recognizable rhythm will likely return once your situation is back to normal. The only time this will not be the case is when she outgrows one pattern and adopts a new one. Changing patterns will happen from time to time throughout infancy and toddlerhood. When this occurs, tune into your little one for clues, then observe and adjust to her new rhythms.

Mysterious and short variations in timing can occur when, unbeknownst to you, someone such as a grandparent or sibling feeds your baby. On other occasions, baby may happen to "find" some food and in this way eat between meals.

Travel can disrupt baby's regular routine, especially if she misses or is awakened from naps. Travel sometimes throws parents off schedule more than it affects baby's natural timing. If it's not too disruptive or stressful, it's fine to continue with infant pottying while traveling. If this proves too difficult, use a diaper on such occasions. I managed to persevere in cars and airplanes; at airports and train stations; on camping trips and picnics; at family functions; in department stores and other shops; in foreign countries and hotels.

Timing can change with the occurrence of developmental milestones such as learning to crawl, walk and talk. Teething can throw things off course for a while. Many babies pee more often while teething. For more details on all of the above situations, see "Potty Pauses and Potty Strikes" in the next chapter.

If you experience some difficult days, don't let it get to you. Keep an even keel and you'll find your way. If you are feeling frustrated, angry or guilty, perhaps you are trying too hard. You may reach a plateau and feel "stuck" for a while. *Infant potty training is not an exact science.* We adults tend to want things to progress logically and uninterrupted in a linear fashion, but infant pottying moves more as an ebb and flow with three steps forward and one step back. It takes trial and error, and improves with experience and practice. If you try this with more than one child, you may be more confident and relaxed with the next.

Going Out Diaper-Free

Some mothers don't dare take their babies out diaperless, fearing embarrassing accidents. It's perfectly fine to use diapers on outings. Going diaperless is a matter of preference and "what works best."

Potty your baby before departing and offer pottytunities at logical times when you are out. Devise a plan for finding toilet places, whether it be in public facilities or outdoors. Take your preferred equipment along—perhaps a portable potty or child's toilet seat—or just hold her over a diaper. If you are walking or cycling, become familiar with your surroundings so you can quickly find or improvise a toilet place. Your potty "route and routine" will soon become second nature and not require a lot of strategic planning.

Many mothers report that they are more attentive when they go out, "When I leave him in underpants, I find I am more responsible about taking him to pee before we leave, when we are out and when we get to our destination." Some feel more in tune with their babies—especially if wearing baby in a sling or other baby carrier—without the usual household distractions. Whatever the reason, they find that they have significantly fewer misses when outside the home. Amazingly, some babies will do their best to "hold it" when out and about or will refuse to pee if they are in a car seat. If this happens, don't make your child wait too long as it could cause a bladder infection. On the other hand, there are mothers and babies who temporarily disconnect from their elimination awareness when they are out, due to involvement with their surroundings.

If you are using a sling and want to go diaperless but would like some extra security, place a diaper or soft cloth under baby in the sling. No matter how you are transporting her, if so desired, it is fine for her to wear training pants or a diaper, either with or without a waterproof cover. The important thing is for you to feel relaxed and not worry about accidents.

Dress for Success

Use clothing that is quick and easy to remove. The way you dress your baby is a matter of personal preference and a lifestyle choice and can range from naked to bare-bummed; training pants to diapers; dresses to stretchy shorts or pants with an elastic waist; and from "open pants" to leggings with a T-shirt. Climate and seasons are factors to be considered. Although easier to implement in warm climates, infant pottying is used in all climates around the globe, including the coldest places on earth. Find ways to modify and adapt to your local climate. Here is a list of some of the most popular types of EC clothing:

- Homemade pants—use wool or warm fleece for winter and cool fabrics such as cotton knit for summer; trace around some baby sweatpants or PJ bottoms and use elastic in the waistband
- Prefolds—thick cotton diapers with an extra thick middle layer down the center
- All-in-one diapers—cotton diapers similar in design to disposables
- Fitted diapers—cotton diapers similar in design to disposables but requiring a separate waterproof cover over the diaper
- Pocket diapers—a waterproof outer cover and an inner lining of fleece or other absorbent material
- Homemade leggings (made from adult socks) or BabyLegs
- Wool knit pants with elastic waistband—for cooler weather; if helpful, turn inside out so seams don't irritate baby's skin
- Training pants—thick cotton underpants with an extra thick middle layer in the crotch area
- Chinese open pants—for home use and warmer weather

If you can't find what you need in local shops, search the Internet for terms such as "infant potty training" and "elimination communication" to find the latest links for IPT websites and online shops selling training pants, open pants, specialized IPT clothing, cloth diapers, woolens and other useful items such as small potties.

If you like to see before you buy or are anxious to meet other IPT families, the nonprofit organization Diaper Free Baby hosts playgroups in many places around the world. In addition to being able to check out clothing and potties, you can also see demos of how to hold and potty your small infant, ask any questions you have, and learn from more experienced parents. Check the DFB website at www.diaperfreebaby.org for local listings.

Keila Rawlinson

5-week-old Ross wearing his "I love EC" shirt and Babylegs along with a cotton prefold diaper secured by a prefold belt and a wool knit cloth cover.

Newborns

If you feel up to beginning on the first day, do as much or as little as you like. If you prefer to savor the day without dealing with EC, wait until you feel rested and ready. The age at which you start (first day, first month or later) is a matter of preference rather than necessity. You might find it less stressful to wait until baby goes less often (once your milk comes in, she may pee every 5 minutes for some weeks); gains more muscle tone and becomes less wobbly; and is awake for longer periods. You may want to give yourself time to recover from the delivery, to gain confidence in holding baby or to sort out any breast-feeding problems.

For parents wishing to keep their newborn out of diapers from the start, here are two scenarios to consider:

Holding Baby
Many parents want to hold their newborn as much as possible. Some enjoy skin-to-skin contact, and others prefer to clothe baby. While try-ing different potty positions, keep her warm and be sure to give her comfortable and adequate support, as many newborns are frightened if they feel like their bodies or feet are dangling. Keep a prefold or diaper under or around her. If she goes while you are holding her, make the "sssss" sound (or whatever basic signal you have selected) while she is going or immediately afterwards.

Laying Baby Down
Protect the mattress with a waterproof pad, wool blanket or fleece, then cover this with a soft, absorbent cloth such as a flannel sheet, cloth diaper or soft towel. When she starts to go, gently raise or pick her up so she does not wet or soil herself. Cue her as she goes or immediately afterwards, then gently replace the wet items with clean, dry ones.

Many newborns dislike being undressed. In terms of cleanup and disturbing baby, it's easier to have her excrete the meconium *on* a diaper rather than in a diaper. Parents who have caught the meconium with one baby but not with another report that it is easier to learn signals and communicate when starting with the meconium.

Some mothers nurse while pottying since newborns often go while suck-ling. Some hold their babies over tiny, comfortable (soft edges and at a warm temperature) receptacles, such as a plastic bowl held in their laps.

The first weeks can be very intense dealing with near-constant elimination. Even if you cue her just a few times a day when she goes and ease your way into catching a daily pee or poo, this is a good start. In other words, don't get discouraged before you even begin. And don't feel badly if you find that it's better to wait and start in a few months.

Don't worry about nighttime pottying unless you're awake anyway and find it easy to do. Interestingly, some mothers report that their infants wake up mainly to pee and poo, rather than to feed. Once they've done so, they will nurse, then go back to sleep or just look around the room for a while.

As baby consumes more milk, she will pee more often and in greater quantity. As her bladder grows, she will be able to retain more urine between pees. Watch for these two factors to come into play from time to time, and observe how they affect your infant's timing.

Premature babies

Preterm babies tend to be very sleepy. Some rarely wake up for anything for weeks or even a few months. They also intensely dislike feeling cold so it's important to focus on rest, feedings and comfort for a while.

If you want to work on IPT, concentrate on cueing and keeping her dry by pottying her when you change her; do this in a very warm room and with warm hands. If this upsets her, just keep her in a long T-shirt or gown with a prefold tucked between her legs and replace the prefold when she goes. Another option is to hold her against you while changing her.

If you are present when she goes, signal her to start establishing the cue association. You can also cue at each diaper change since the temperature change when removing her diaper is likely to make her pee anyway.

Other approaches include keeping her wrapped in a light wool blanket with a prefold or diaper wrapped around her or carrying her in a sling or wrap with a cloth diaper lining for protection.

Beyond these peaceful and minimal activities, it's best not to do anything until she is at or past her adjusted due date. Whatever you decide to do, remember that it is essential to avoid stress and frustration for both mother and child. Once she is developmentally ready to do more, try removing her diaper and doing some in-arms pottying in a warm room. If she's okay with this, you can proceed as you would for a full-term baby.

chapter 4

the
potty phase

The potty phase begins when baby can sit comfortably on a potty or toilet—at first with "loving live support," then later on his own—and continues until he completes toilet training. This chapter covers both unstable sitters (babies who cannot yet sit proficiently on their own and who need some physical support) and stable sitters.

Many parents start using a potty before their babies can sit well on their own. The coziest and safest way to assure that your baby feels comfortable and secure on the potty is to support him with your hands, arms and/or body. This will be reminiscent of the in-arms phase and will keep him steady and secure. It will also allow you to focus and notice the moment he goes.

It is not easy to find a potty that fits a tiny baby bottom since most potties are designed for toddlers. The most readily available is the BabyBjörn Smart Potty. If you use the toilet, BabyBjörn, Flip-N-Flush, Graco, Cushie-Tushie and others sell attachable child-sized seats that fit dinky bottoms.

The potty you select should be readily available. It's a good idea to have more than one or else to move it from room to room. This is in order to avoid any unnecessary delays. In many cultures, tiny children simply squat and go. The fact that they don't have to waste precious seconds looking for a potty or bathroom is one reason these children toilet train so young. Learning to go to a specific room (the bathroom) is something that can be accomplished at a later time.

Small children sitting on a full-sized toilet, even one with a smaller seat attached, need constant supervision and companionship. If left alone, they could fall off or into the toilet. Most need help getting on and off the toilet. A footstool or steps can be helpful in this regard and can also provide support for their feet while sitting on the toilet.

A common position is for the mother to sit on the toilet seat and hold baby in her lap, aiming him so that his elimination goes directly into the toilet. This way he is sitting comfortably and securely, using mom as a warm cushion. A variation is for mom and baby to sit facing the back of the toilet, with baby seated comfortably on or between his mother's legs. Some babies feel more secure facing the toilet tank rather than an open space at the front. In addition, they can place a toy or book on the toilet tank. (This applies to toilets that have a tank with flat surface at the back.)

Babies usually transition easily from the in-arms phase to a potty or toilet but if not, you can nurse your baby on or over the potty or hold him in-arms while squatting in front of the toilet or other receptacle.

Make potty time as easy and simple as possible. Avoid clothing that will slow down the process. Buttons, snaps, buckles, zippers and tight-fitting outfits can cause delay and anticipatory accidents. The idea is for baby to be free to go as soon as you know it's time or as soon as he signals.

Once he can sit steadily on his own, you may no longer need to physically support him. Although he is becoming less dependent on you, your presence, assistance and commitment are still essential. Never leave him alone at potty time, as he may decide to sample his own excrement.

As he becomes more aware of his environment and more able to explore his surroundings, he may at times resist the potty—a situation that arises with most methods of toilet training. Use fun and creative ways to keep him seated, while maintaining a balance between the following:

- Keep him happy and entertained at potty time.
- Don't make unreasonable concessions or use bribes.
- Don't leave him on the potty too long (30 seconds–2 minutes is fine).

Potty Comfort

Sitting on the potty or toilet should be as comfy as possible. Assess the situation and make any adjustments that will improve his comfort and level of contentment. If you live in a cold climate, for example, the potty or toilet seat is likely to be cold. Babies do not like being plopped onto a cold seat or undressed in a cold room. Feeling cold can cause them to dislike potty time and rebel, so always be sure he stays warm. Keep the potty or child's toilet seat near a source of heat such as a heating vent or radiator, or find another way to ensure that it is at body temperature or a little warmer. Other possibilities include placing a hot water bottle, heating pad, electric blanket, flannel diaper, cloth seat cover or other soft cloth on the potty. You can also warm it with your hands or thighs, place your hands between your baby and the cold seat, or hold him in-arms above the seat. If he's barefoot, be sure his feet stay warm too.

For most, sitting on a potty is relaxing and comfortable. It is certainly easier—since it requires less pushing—for a baby to poo into a potty or toilet than while sitting in a diaper seated on his rear end or while lying down. In addition, some mothers report that infant pottying relieves constipation and indigestion.

An open-door policy helps children feel relaxed about visiting the facilities. Familiarity with toilet use by others via live demos on the big toilet—dad for boys, mom for girls and siblings for siblings—creates a comfort level when small children are first introduced to the toilet. It is natural to want to imitate older family members. The mother of a 6-month-old boy explains, "He loves to go with visual encouragement. His dad demonstrates, his brothers demonstrate and he loves it. He will usually go while they are demonstrating, even if it's just a quick pee. It has shown me that he can go when he wants to."[7]

Selecting a Potty

There are many factors to take into consideration when selecting a potty for children under 1 or 2 years of age. Choose a suitable size for your child. The potty should be of the correct dimensions to fit his anatomy. Bear in mind the following when making your selection:

- height
- seat diameter
- seat shape
- stability
- portability
- transparency

Height

His feet should rest squarely on the floor for comfort, support, security and extra pushing power. If his feet cannot reach the floor and his legs stick out straight, this position can eventually reduce or cut off the circulation to his legs and feet, causing discomfort or other problems. The weight of dangling feet and legs can cause his rectal muscles to tighten, making pooing difficult or even leading to constipation. Once he's walking well, he can learn to get on and off the potty. The smaller the potty, the safer and easier this will be.

Seat Diameter

The seat should be of small diameter. Ideally, your child should be able to sit comfortably with a straight back at all times. Be certain that his buttocks does not sink into the potty, as this is not good for his spine and can be unhygienic. Smaller babies will need to be supported and held in place by their caregivers.

Seat Shape

Boys require a potty with a small, raised lip at the front. The lip directs the pee into the potty. If you are ever in a situation where a lipped potty is not available, you can aim him in the right direction.

Avoid using a potty with a relatively large shield or guard (urine deflector). The possibility exists that both girls and boys can injure themselves when sitting down or standing up. A flat potty seat without a shield is the safest shape for girls.

Stability

When baby becomes more independent, he will start to find his way to the potty on his own. Choose one that doesn't tip easily when he squirms or stands up. The BabyBjörn Potty Chair is ideal for this, since it has a high backrest and sits firmly on the floor, which helps it remain stable without spilling when he moves.

Portability

A small, portable potty is very useful as you can take it with you wherever you go and use it in restrooms (on the counter or diaper-changing station) or in the car. To avoid spilling while in motion, place prefold diapers or paper towels in the potty, or else use a non-spill bowl or a container with a tight-fitting lid. If none of these are available, place the full potty in a plastic bag until you can empty it. You can also take along an attachable toilet seat to use in restrooms.

Transparency

A transparent or semitransparent potty is useful in that you know instantly when your child goes. You can provide immediate positive feedback and know when he has finished. He is then free to leave. This type of positive reinforcement encourages him to use the potty on a regular basis. If you can't find a transparent potty, another way to get instant feedback is to feel the bottom of the potty. It will change temperature when baby goes—unless you are in a very warm room or the potty is too thick to feel the warmth.

Phases

Your baby may test and try different behaviors which result in temporary disruptions. A common scenario is for a baby who has made considerable progress to suddenly start to "hold back" on the potty, then pee in his diaper or pants as soon as you dress him. A baby who normally waits to be taken potty when he awakes in the morning may suddenly shift to secretly peeing in his bed in the morning. Some go through a phase of crawling behind furniture or into another room, rather than signaling you when they need to go.

As babies develop the ability to produce specific sounds or words, they advance from meaningless vocalizations to simple one-syllable verbalizations such as "da" to two-syllable or multi-syllable versions such as "mama." Next, more complicated sounds such as "caca" and "poop" are attempted. At this point, some babies are able to verbally tell you if they need to go or if they already went. It is not uncommon for a child around 12–15 months old to assume that a word such as "pee" or "poop" refers to both types of elimination. If your baby signals you by saying "poop" and you end up with a pee in the potty, consider this good progress. She will eventually learn to distinguish between the words.

Tactics

Here is a summary of IPT tactics. For toddlers, many of the tactics listed in Chapter 9 "Late-Starters" may also apply, even if your child started at birth.

- Potty in relation to feedings and meals (he may go while nursing or at fixed intervals after feedings).
- Potty before and after sleep. Note that some can "hold it" for a while after a nap and don't need to go immediately upon waking.
- Potty after misses/accidents.
- Potty at diaper changes (even if he's wet, he may go again when you change him).
- Potty before and after outings.
- Be sure both he and the potty or other receptacle are warm at potty time. Velcro a piece of thick polar fleece around the sides and cut a hole in the middle, use a T-shirt as a potty warmer cover, place your warm hands under his thighs as you hold him over the potty, cover the potty with a think cloth diaper or buy a potty seat cover.
- Let him nurse, suck your finger or drink from a cup as much as he wants when sitting on the potty. Some infants need to suck or swallow in order to relax and release.

- Use warm water. For example, splash warm water on his feet or belly or give him a warm bath. Warm baths can also relieve constipation.
- Touch or massage his toes and feet.
- Tickle him.
- Blow on his head, or let him blow bubbles or blow on a pinwheel while seated.
- Let him/her potty a stuffed animal or doll. If you have a spare potty, let baby and cuddly toy potty together.
- Let him hold or play with a toy or interesting object.
- Read to him, sing songs or play hand games with him.
- If he has a favorite color, buy a potty in that color.
- If he can't bear down properly on the toilet, find a way for him to squat or firmly plant his feet so he can push (e.g., with the soles of his feet against the toilet lid), or use a small potty instead.
- Put his potty in different and interesting places. One mother's suggestion, "We put his potty in a cardboard box. He can't fall, he can't crawl away, and a toy keeps him busy in his own little castle for a while."
- Let him practice the whole toilet routine including flushing and washing hands. He may enjoy waving bye-bye as he flushes the toilet or splashing the water while washing his hands.
- Say "Wait" or "Stop" if he signals or starts to go at an inopportune time such as while you are driving or when you are not near a potty. Some children can and will wait a bit longer for you. Be soft-spoken so as not to be abrupt or startle him.

The Transition to Going Diaper-Free

There is no fixed time for this. The best time is a matter of preference and of what is possible, practical and desirable with respect to your own individual situation. Being diaperless can be helpful or even indispensable for some, while for others it doesn't seem to make much difference.

Treat the transition to training pants, "undies" or going "nakey butt" as you would any other day. In Israel, the process of toilet training is called "weaning from diapers," and this is precisely what you are doing. You might want to start with a half hour or morning session, then increase the time over the days, weeks or months. Do not make a "big deal" out of the occasion. Some mothers start to feel and behave more seriously about potty training once they remove the diapers. Your baby will sense the change in your demeanor and may balk at responding to your signals. He may feel you are nervous or pressuring him—and he may well be right, even though you are unaware of the change in yourself.

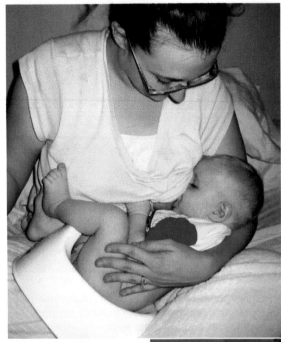

4 months old —
Nursing on the
potty.

Christine Puschkin

5 weeks old —
Nursing on an
infant potty.

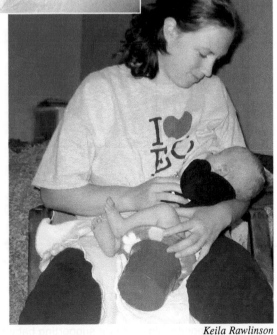

Keila Rawlinson

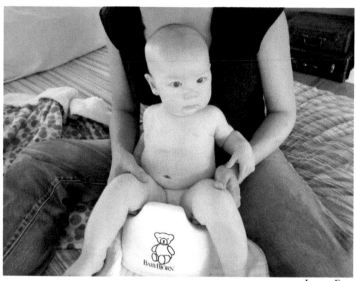

Lonny Frye

5 months old — Micah is secured by leaning against his mother and by her gentle grasp around his thighs. Note that her hands rest between Micah and the potty seat.

Gigi Kayser

6 months old — Sister supporting baby on potty on bed.

Craig Baas

7 months old — Zachary is secure, safe and having fun.

Jessica Bergen

10 months old — Johnathan in the back seat,
doing just like Dad does.

Lucia Wright

10 month-old twins — Imitation is fun and stimulates learning between sisters Moriah and Tsameret.

Maria Le

8 months old — Taking a break with Dad.

Deborah Wright

ASL sign for "toilet"   ASL sign for "finished"

14 months old — Annabelle was proficient at sign language
early in life and communicated her elimination and other
needs this way for many months before she could speak.

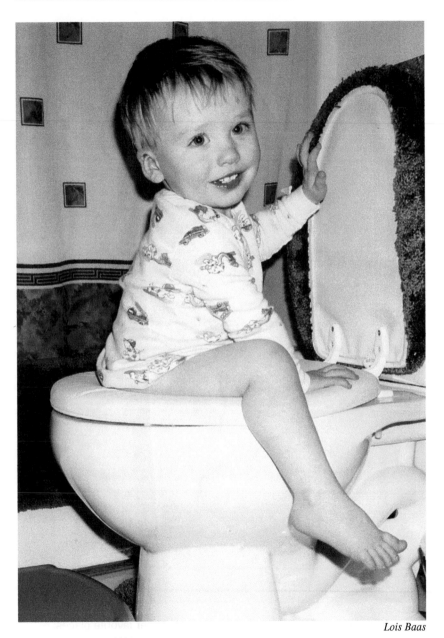

Lois Baas

17 months old — Zachary prefers facing the tank.
Sitting low allows him to aim into the toilet.

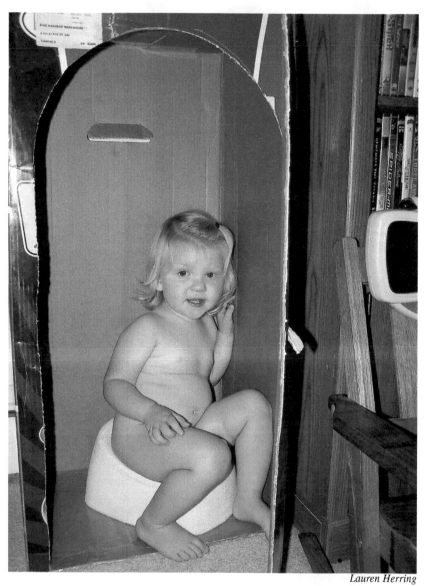

Lauren Herring

18 months old — Bree going potty in one of her favorite places:
her box. Her mother reported, "We call it her in-door out-house.
She likes to shut the door and be private."

Kevin Illige

20 months old — Aeron enjoys pottying with his bear buddy.

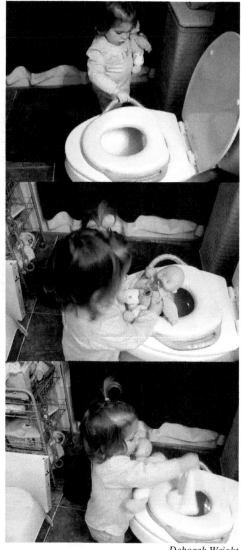

Deborah Wright

21 months old — Pottying baby doll.
Annabelle first installs her toilet seat, then potties her doll.
She finishes by wiping her doll and disposing of the wipe.

Making the transition to a bare bum can cause accidents at first. For example, if your baby is accustomed to wearing a diaper in his high chair and suddenly one day he is bare-bummed in the chair, the new and different feeling—perhaps from experiencing a chill when you seat him—may be enough to make him pee unexpectedly. If he is not accustomed to wearing training pants or underwear or to being naked or bare-bottomed throughout the day, he may initially interpret the transition as carte blanche to go in his pants or anywhere he happens to be. He may be used to the feel of a diaper, and it could take a while to adjust to the switchover.

Some babies make more of an effort to "hold it" when wearing a diaper or underpants—they need to wear *something* or else they pee everywhere. In this situation, the transition from diapers to pants may be fairly easy. Moreover, some mothers feel they are more tuned in without the safety net of diapers.

If you are worried about your carpets, one solution is to buy a fairly large, natural-fiber piece of remnant carpet and place it over your permanent carpeting. If your baby has accidents, you won't need to worry about your carpets. You can roll up the remnant whenever you like. If it starts to smell, let it air out in the sun. Or you can put a towel or mat under the potty so there is protection in the immediate area.

Graduation and Definition of "Toilet Trained"

In one sense, Westerners do not consider a child to be toilet trained until he can perform all toilet functions independently and without reminders—find the potty or bathroom, walk there on his own, pull down his pants without help, do the job, wipe, dismount, pull up his pants and remain dry all day and night. Taking all these factors into consideration yields the strictest definition of "toilet trained," and this might not be achieved until a child is 5 or 6 years old. No matter what means of toilet learning is used, most parents claim their children are toilet trained before absolute perfection per this strict definition is achieved.

In another sense, a child can be considered a grad at a much younger age, anywhere from 12–20 months, as long as you get him to the toilet on time and offer the necessary assistance. Per this definition, a child has reasonable control, is able to communicate most of his elimination needs, understands the concept of going to a potty place and may still need physical help and occasional reminders. In short, there are different definitions of endpoints in determining when a child is toilet trained and "because studies use different endpoints (independent control versus child indication of need with caregiver attending to the need), they cannot be compared directly."[8]

EC families refer to four levels of graduation:

- Level 1: Stays dry fairly reliably with mother's help
- Level 2: Signals fairly consistently; needs occasional reminders
- Level 3: Goes potty without reminders
- Level 4: Dresses & wipes self, stays dry all night

Genital Groping

Small children tend to occasionally grope and explore their genitals to some degree when sitting on a potty or toilet. A baby boy will typically touch his penis before or during urination. In fact, once he understands why he is on the potty and what he is supposed to do there, a small boy also figures out that touching his penis makes him pee sooner than just sitting there. It is not uncommon for a boy to use this trick to speed up the process so he can get on with other activities. For many boys, this is a passing phase. There is no need to be alarmed or to react with negativity or morality.

Every male, once toilet trained, touches his penis in order to urinate. This is a normal part of urination for all males. There is nothing sexual or perverted about it. It is conceivable that a little boy's discovery and groping of himself on the potty is in part a precursor to normal male toilet behavior in that the little boy will eventually hold his penis each time he urinates.

Once he has peed, his interest will often shift to other things. If he continues to grope himself, you can either let him off the potty (if he is finished), or if you know he has not finished using the potty, gently distract him. Examples of ways to shift his attention include playing hand games such as Pat-a-cake or Itsy-bitsy Spider, playing clapping games or placing a book, toy, radio, gadget or anything else of interest in his lap. A sibling, friend, caretaker or pet can make a sudden appearance to divert his attention.

Food Sensitivities

There is a correlation between food sensitivities/allergies and baby's elimination frequency (both pee and poo), misses, bedwetting and enuresis. Many babies become incontinent, go far more often than usual, lose their elimination awareness and stop signaling in reaction to wheat, gluten, soy, citrus, tomatoes, vinegar, strawberries, cow's milk/dairy, pineapple, tea and other foods. Breastfeeding mothers have found that if they cut out one or more foods from their diet, the elimination problems usually disappear within a few weeks. Some babies have a mild sensitivity to certain foods so that there might not be a problem if a mother has, say, a little wheat, but the more wheat she consumes, the greater the elimination complications. Here are comments from mothers:

- "My baby was dry at night even though she nursed several times throughout the night. Then I had an increase in wheat consumption, and she started waking up completely soaked. When I figured out wheat was making her incontinent at night and we eliminated it from our diets, she resumed her night dryness."
- "My child had tons of accidents from 8–13 months until I discovered she had a food allergy. Then we went from no catches to a near grad almost overnight."
- "I stopped eating wheat; he stopped pooping constantly. It was EC magic. We ditched dipes permanently a month later!"
- "The only time we have damp or wet pants is when my son has soy (and he's a grad)."

One wonders if food sensitivities/allergies might explain why some traditionally toilet-trained children have trouble with sphincter control for years (thus supporting the erroneous theory that kids are unaware, don't care and have no control).

Potty Pauses and Potty Strikes

Some babies go on potty pause or potty strike. The main reasons are usually physical, developmental or emotional—basically, when baby experiences discomfort, intense learning, distraction, upset or pressure (in these ways, a potty strike is similar to a nursing strike). Here is a summary of the main causes:

- physical discomfort due to teething, diarrhea, gas, constipation, urinary tract infections, cold temperature in the room or on the potty/toilet seat, the common cold and other illnesses, injury, food sensitivities/allergies, eating problems or anything else that causes him pain
- developmental milestones (learning to crawl, walk or talk, or mastering another major skill)
- emotional upsets stemming from the unwanted interruption of an activity, a change in schedule/routine, pregnancy, family strife or suddenly receiving less care and attention

A potty pause takes place while baby is working out an issue. It is not a conscious thing that a child does to be naughty or to manipulate you, whereas a potty strike can be a means of purposefully striking back at you for something that is bothering your little one. Strikes can last a day or longer, even up to a number of months, whereas pauses are usually less intense. In both cases, it is up to you to ascertain what is upsetting or distracting your baby.

Typical behavior for both pauses and strikes includes arching the back and straightening the legs, crying, screaming, holding back or refusing to sit on the potty. Note that these same behaviors can at times manifest for reasons other than a strike, such as misreading baby's signals or incorrect timing, in which case baby is simply letting you know he does not need to go. Be careful not to equate accidents with a potty strike—all babies experience numerous misses, and *many never pause or strike at all.*

If your baby is not feeling well, he might stop signaling and responding to your cues until he recovers. Viewed another way, *IPT can help you find out about your baby's other needs.* If he refuses offers to go several times a day, this could be a sign that something is amiss, and you can look for ways to comfort him. For example, teething can throw your baby off kilter and cause him to shut down for a while, plus there are the added complications that it may take days for you to even realize your baby is cutting teeth and that he will cut lots of teeth over many months. If he is not feeling well, he will need extra sympathy and understanding. Be sensitive to his needs. Do not view his refusals as rebellion or defiance. If you use force or punishment, it will backfire on you, and you could prolong the situation.

Developmental milestones tend to disrupt pottying for a number of reasons. Generally, as mobility begins to increase, so do accidents. Otherwise stated, during the learning of mobility, as mobility increases, bladder control decreases for a while. This is perfectly normal and to be expected. With mobility come freedom and independence. Babies are fascinated by their surroundings, and some have such a love affair with all the new discoveries that they lose interest in pottying for weeks or months. In this situation, continue to offer pottytunities at times that do not upset your little one. If life is too stressful, it doesn't hurt to use diapers again for a while until the potty interest returns.

Some activities put pressure on the bladder, and this pressure can cause babies to unexpectedly pee. For example, when baby is lying on his belly or attempting to scoot or crawl, he tends to pee without warning. When learning to stand and walk, new sets of muscles are contracting in the back and abdominal regions, again pressuring the bladder. One veteran mom and expert refers to this as the "learning to walk, don't bother me with EC phase" and explains:

"I'm watching my 9.5 month old learn to walk, and watching the accidents pile up with a relaxed eye. I've done this before and thankfully
have no worries, knowing he'll be more capable of ec in a few short
weeks. If you're out there watching your baby learn to crawl and walk,
and wondering why babies seem so surprised to see pee pouring out
of them when they get upright, let me explain. When baby is learning
to stand, there is a lot of muscular activity happening in the back and
stomach. Standing up, we have to keep our backs straight, right? Or
we'd bend forward and flop over. So we have muscles that pull our back
up. If these muscles are used to capacity, our backs arch. So what stops
baby from arching and falling over backwards? Stomach muscles—they
pull baby back forward. What does this do to the belly? Well, if you have
a partially full bladder and then tighten your belly muscles, this puts
pressure on the bladder and BAM, baby pees on the rug with that 'Gee,
where'd all that water come from' expression.

"Standing upright and walking demand extraordinary muscle coordination, concentration, and lots of trial and error. That alone would be
distracting enough. Add to that the muscular squeezing of the belly
and the urge to be independent and influence their environment, and
it's amazing any ec happens at all!"[9]

Learning the use and power of "no" is another milestone that can distract
for a while. Children seem especially fascinated and empowered when they
start signaling "no" or using the word "no." They like experimenting with the
consequences. Sometimes it's possible to learn the difference between a negative no and an affirmative no, although the meaning can change over time. If
need be, reduce pottytunities or take a break for some days or weeks until you
find a more receptive time for your child. One mother discovered that, for a
period of time, the older her baby got, the more often she would signal "no":

"At 6 months, Kate would signal 'no' very clearly and only signaled 'no'
when she didn't need to go. At around 7 months, however, she started
signaling when she didn't WANT to go. There were times where I was
sure she needed to pee, but she would arch her back and refuse, so I
decided to back off, even if it meant she went in her pants. Then from
9–10 months, she still occasionally signaled 'no' even though she needed to go—sometimes just to be mischievous, because she was tired,
sometimes just because she could or else (our latest discovery) in order
to get something. For example, she would often signal to go, then signal
'no' the minute we got to the toilet. We found out that 'no' often meant
'No, not until you give me a toy.' Even when we got up at night, in her
groggy state she signaled 'no' until we put a toy in her hand. Then she'd

pee and fall back to sleep. Around 11 months, she stopped signaling 'no' unless she really meant it and did not need to go."[10]

Here is what the mother of a 16-month-old said about the "no to everything" phase:

"I asked if she needed to go, and my daughter said, 'No, no, no!' (her current response to just about any question). Five seconds later, she RAN into the bathroom and peed. I've learned that she just likes saying 'no' and that often it means 'yes' or doesn't mean anything at all."[11]

Another mother thought her 21-month-old son was on strike for a while, until she figured out his meaning of "no":

"I learned that his 'no' didn't mean, 'No, I don't have to go,' but rather, 'No, don't take me. I can do it myself.' I also think he disliked me asking, 'Do you have to go potty?' after he had said 'poo.' If he didn't have to go, he wouldn't be saying 'poo' to me. So now if he announces his need to go, we just go, and I only help him as much as necessary."[12]

A solution for this phase is to avoid asking yes-or-no questions about pottying. If you offer options, "no" should not be one of the options. Instead, simply state that it is time to go and have a pee. If your child says "no," let him know that "no" isn't a choice. As one mother put it, "Pottytunities are never offered as a choice in our house. Even with my 5-year-old I have to tell (rather than ask) him to visit the toilet."

When experiencing an "I'm busy learning something else" phase, a baby's "brain power" is temporarily diverted elsewhere. At this time, children have better things to do than deal with pottying. If you don't respect their "space" and determination, they can turn hostile in an effort to get you to back off for a while. In other words, adults can be the catalyst that turns a potty pause into a potty strike.

There are many other things that can cause a potty pause and/or lead to a strike. Travel, moving house, hosting overnight guests, divorce, quarreling or other tension in the household, mama being pregnant, arrival of a new baby in the family, adjusting to a new nanny or babysitter, switching from the family bed to his own bed and room, dislike of or discomfort on a potty or toilet, dislike of a new toilet position or location, preference for one location only (perhaps in the bathroom where adults go), significant change in house temperature or noise level, construction in the home, receiving less care and attention (for example, at Christmas when you devote lots of time to shopping, cooking, guests, decorations, gifts, etc.)—all of these and more can trigger toileting trouble.

Strikes can start out for the same reasons as pauses but manifest themselves differently in that baby is sending an SOS message of discontent or
disapproval and is awaiting resolution. If you are going through emotionally
difficult times, your baby will sense this and may go on strike—a pee strike,
poop strike or both. You might have to wait until you sort out your own problems before resuming pottying. On the other hand, solutions can seem amazingly simple once you figure things out. For example, if your child has signaled
and you ask him to confirm, "You mean you have to go?" this might annoy
or frustrate him—why should he always have to confirm what he has already
told you? Or you may be offering too many pottytunities in a quest for potty
perfection and upsetting him this way.

One way to view communication with your baby is to see yourself as a
translator. You are the one who needs to tune in, read and interpret the meaning of his communications and to then do some troubleshooting and solution
seeking. Examples that have worked for mothers include letting baby sit on
an adult toilet rather than a potty; using different locations to cut down on
boredom; letting boys stand to pee; letting baby be diaperless for a while after
pottying (he may resent being put back in a diaper right away); or helping him
adjust to a new nap routine or to napping alone. If you're moving to a new
home, keep him close to you in a sling, wrap or baby backpack so he feels
secure and doesn't get in the way; try to maintain a fairly normal schedule;
talk to him about moving; and let him help pack boxes. Gigi Kayser, mother
of four EC'ed children, summed it up nicely: When baby refuses a pottytunity,
he is not saying, "No, I don't want to potty." He's really saying, "No, not *here*"
(wants a different location), or "No, not *this* way" (prefers a different position)
or "No, I'd like to do this *myself*" (wants his independence). EC is consensual.
It's important to make the distinction between a baby's protest of uncomfortable feelings that will be resolved soon with gentle encouragement and a
protest of not wanting to do this thing in this way right now. One is saying "I
feel discomfort," the other is saying "No, *stop!*"[13]

During a pause or strike, it is easy to mistakenly assume that baby has
forgotten everything he once knew about IPT. This is not the case. Your baby
is simply preoccupied or too busy doing other things. Try taking a break for a
day or longer and waiting it out to take some pressure off both of you, or else
cut down on potty visits and only make them at times when it isn't likely to
interrupt or upset him. By relaxing about the situation and letting go of your
expectations, you'll be happier, and he will get back on track when he is ready.

At some point with toddlers (this tends to work near graduation), it can
help to use an incentive for just a day or two—a sort of "brief bribe" that is
so short-lived that a child doesn't see it as a bribe because it only serves to

help the child break through a barrier. This can help with potty pauses and other related situations. One mother helped her son overcome a fear of pottying anywhere but on his own potty at home. She offered him a small treat each time he used a different place or receptacle. This help him transcend his inhibitions, and within a few days, he was relaxed enough to pee anywhere she took him, without the need for a treat. My niece experienced a potty pause with her toddler daughter and found that offering her a sticker each time she used the potty helped her regain interest within a day. This got her daughter firmly back on track, and she graduated in a few days.

Potty pauses and strikes are not unusual and should not discourage you from continuing. If after a sincere attempt you cannot find a cause, don't worry, this too shall pass. Interestingly, many mothers report that they experience a pause or strike just before graduation, and then suddenly everything clicks.

Some speculate that pauses and strikes might be cultural and only happen in Western societies. But it's more a question of perception. Westerners tend to feel upset, impatient or frustrated about accidents and to consider pauses or strikes a big deal, whereas mothers in other parts of the world simply laugh them off or tease each other about them. In short, they just view them as a normal part of the process instead of analyzing them and blaming themselves.

Longer-term setbacks can happen at any stage or even after what seems to be total completion of toilet training. This type of potty regression can happen to children using all types of toilet training and can result from emotional issues or medical problems.

Special-Needs Children

Children with medical conditions tend to have trouble with toilet learning due to developmental delays and/or the use of medication. There are babies with challenging medical conditions or disabilities who have had good results with infant potty training. These include spina bifida, cerebral palsy, Down syndrome, deafness, low vision, blindness, partial paralysis and other conditions that result in delayed development. Children confined to wheelchairs can also benefit. Although parents should expect toilet training to take longer in most of these situations, it is comforting to know that it can be done gently and at a child's own pace. Families will likely experience added stress at times, for a number of different emotional, financial or social reasons. The gentle, laid-back and part-time approach of IPT can help in this regard.

chapter 5

baby signals

The more you know about baby communication, the easier it will be for you to read her signals and be responsive to her "pees and cues." To get started, just relax, watch and listen. If you can't detect signals for a while, don't feel bad or guilty. You can be just as effective and responsive by using timing and patterns.

Just how important is communication? Infant development specialist Dr. Michael Lewis has found that the responsiveness of a mother to the cues of her baby is the single most important influence on a child's intellectual development.[14] Anthropologist Edward Tronick writes that infants possess self-directed regulating systems that take over if their communication signals have not been read, resulting in a system that is out of balance. When signals are missed, babies stop signaling and withdraw.[15] Ainsworth and Bell found that when a mother (or other primary caregiver) is unresponsive, her baby eventually loses interest in regaining contact with her and turns inward.[16] Although none of these experts specifically referred to elimination communication in their studies, there is no reason to discount or diminish the importance of this type of communication in the overall repertoire of signals a baby transmits.

Tuning in does not mean that all you think about is baby's elimination. It is an awareness in the back of your mind that your baby needs to go every once in a while. Watching for signals becomes second nature, and your conscious focus remains on other things most of the time.

If you work with more than one baby, you'll need to make allowances for differences in temperament and timing. This means you'll need to respond appropriately to each baby's individual cues, personality, physical abilities, needs and limitations.

If you learn and reinforce signaling, your child will at some point begin to communicate about pottying in one form or another—firstly after the fact, then during and eventually before she goes. Her cues may be audible, inaudible, visible or invisible. Try to correlate her natural timing and patterns with her cues. The main types of signals that babies use are:

- body language
- vocal and verbal communications
- implicit/intuitive communication
- manual cues

Baby Body Language

Your baby makes facial expressions and uses other body language just prior to or while going. Through careful observation, you can learn to recognize her body language. For example, she may use her eyes to point towards the bathroom or squirm as you approach it. If you are walking past and she needs to go, she may lean or throw her weight in that direction. These are attempts to point before she can indicate with her arm, hand or finger. Some body language is extremely subtle and hard to decipher. There are mothers who swear that their infants do not signal at all. If you are in this situation, use the other forms of communication for now, and watch for body language to become apparent as she matures. Be prepared for signals to change over time. Also, some body language is so blatant that it can be misunderstood. This happened with my son; while nursing, he would sometimes twist, grunt, turn red in the face and struggle at the breast. For a while, I assumed it was a problem with nursing rather than a plea to be taken to the bathroom.

The list below contains examples of both spontaneous and learned body language signals. Your baby may use just one, a few or several or even her own unique cues not mentioned here.

Behavior:
- slows down or remains still and silent momentarily ("quieting")
- quickly changes mood from smiling and happy to grumpy or sullen
- stops or refuses to nurse, pops off and on the breast, perhaps with a special "look"
- becomes animated, lively, energetic or hyper
- bites or gnaws your fingers, clothing, nipple or other body part
- when in sling, wrap or other carrier, wriggles or kicks to get down
- assumes special posture
- stirs or is restless in sleep, sometimes with head rocking
- awakes

- gets excited when looks at potty or bathroom
- throws a fit if signals ignored
- suddenly stops or loses interest in an activity (including babbling)
- releases tiny amount of pee as a warning (day or night)
- bangs head on potty or toilet
- undoes own clothing fasteners
- removes diaper
- pulls down pants or undresses
- stands with feet apart, looking down before or during elimination
- hides or goes to private place to be alone

Eyes:
- stares into the distance at nothing ("faraway look")
- looks or stares at bathroom, potty or other toilet place
- looks down just before pushing out a BM
- twitches eyes or bats eyelids
- looks at your hand, then towards bathroom, as you sign "toilet"
- stares at own crotch or genitals

Face:
- has look of concentration on the face
- assumes blank, hard, piercing, dreamy or imploring expression
- has a thoughtful look or expression
- turns red in the face/flushes
- pulls faces, grimaces or wrinkles face
- looks uncomfortable
- makes a special facial expression before or during elimination
- tenses throat, chin and/or face
- flares nostrils before and during pushing
- twitches mouth or blows raspberries
- smiles before pooing or when you give cue to go

Abdomen:
- tenses abdominal muscles
- contracts abdominal region when "pushing"

Whole Body (Physical):
- squirms, wriggles or twists body
- arches back
- tenses or stiffens body
- shivers
- squirms to awaken you at night
- squirms in your arms as you walk past or towards toilet place

- leans towards toilet place as you walk past it
- climbs into or stands up in your arms or lap
- taps, grabs, or pulls self up on your leg
- moves (scoots, wiggles, crawls or walks) towards toilet place
- looks back at you at least once as moves towards toilet place
- crawls towards you
- crawls from carpeted area to linoleum or wood floor
- stands in a funny or special position
- squats and turns quiet or concentrates (often in a corner or behind furniture)

Legs:
- wiggles leg(s) or foot/feet
- engages in unique leg position or movement
- kicks or pumps one or both legs in the air (sometimes frantically)
- pushes against you with legs
- kicks you
- pushes up to standing position in your lap
- squeezes legs together

Breathing:
- changes rate of breathing
- takes a sudden deep breath
- breathes heavier or exhales loudly

Buttocks:
- passes gas
- assumes special buttocks posture
- pats diaper, butt or pants
- contracts/pumps anus (BMs)

Arms and Hands:
- points at or touches self (points at diaper, groin or bottom; places or holds hands between legs; places hand on head or face; rubs face or nose)

- points at or touches mother (reaches for you; pats, taps or slaps you; hits you on the head; pulls your hair; scratches you)
- points at or touches toilet, potty, etc. (points at bathroom, potty or other toilet place; reaches for or grabs potty; pats or bangs on toilet or potty; plays with toilet lid or potty)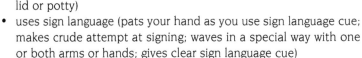
- uses sign language (pats your hand as you use sign language cue; makes crude attempt at signing; waves in a special way with one or both arms or hands; gives clear sign language cue)

Genitals:
- grabs or looks at crotch area
- pats genitals
- points at genitals
- pulls on penis
- scrotum contracts or swells slightly before urination
- penis wiggles shortly before urination
- penis becomes slightly erect

There is also body language that tells you when your baby does *not* need to go or when she does not *want* to go. The most obvious signals are arching her back and straightening her legs, or shaking her head "no." However, there are times where these forms of communication are used to "test the waters" or in playful gesture rather than as a means of true protest. As always, it is up to mother to be the great communications expert and figure out the meaning. If your baby arches and stiffens when you know she has to go, try to distract her so she can relax. For example, scoop her into your arms and cuddle playfully, then retry pottying her.

Vocal and Verbal Communication

Before they can speak, one of the ways infants communicate is to make vocal sounds. This does not imply that every sound a baby makes contains a message, but an attentive and discerning parent will soon learn which sounds have meaning. Grunting invariably signals defecation, while crying and fussing can indicate a number of different things. There are different types of cries consisting of different pitch, volume, intensity and duration. There are also different types of fussing. As an example, in a recent breakthrough, *Dunstan Baby Language* discovered five sounds or "words" voiced by babies (usually while fussing) from birth to approximately 3 months old, such as the utterance "neh" which means "I'm hungry."[17] It may take a while to figure out exactly why a baby cries or fusses, or what a particular cry or sound means. Elimination needs should be considered a possible cause. Most small infants will fuss if they need to go and cry if they are in a wet or soiled diaper. This instinct is often suppressed early in life. The more attentive and responsive a parent is to baby's vocalizations from birth, the better for all concerned. In fact, many IPT families report that their babies become less fussy and are more content once parents start being responsive to their elimination needs. In this way, IPT can serve as a tool to help parents interpret and diagnose fussiness—not just for elimination needs but for other needs too.

In an effort to *announce* that they need to go, some babies vocally summon their caregivers by fussing, crying, screaming, grunting or making a unique sound such as a little yelp. Parents of babies who vocally signal are especially fortunate since this type of signal is so easy to detect—that is, as long as they are paying attention and are responsive.

In societies where infant elimination training is the norm, babies typically signal to be pottied. They are also in constant physical contact with their mothers or caregivers, co-sleep, are breastfed and are immediately taken care of or soothed if they cry. In these intimate ways, signals and responses are coordinated by and between baby and mother. "There is extensive scientific evidence that the accepted Western caretaking style repeatedly, and perhaps dangerously, violates the adaptive system called crying that evolved to help babies communicate with adults." In addition, it has been found that there is little or no colic in many of these traditional societies.[18] It is tempting to ask if making babies wear their waste contributes to colic in the West, due to dirty-diaper discomfort or to withholding elimination in an effort to avoid this discomfort. In both situations, cries for help go unheeded.

Another sign to watch for could take place as you walk past the bathroom or other "pot spot." Listen closely and you may hear her signal you.

To summarize, some of the most common vocalizations and verbalizations occur when baby:

- fusses
- cries, screams, squeals, yells, gurgles, coos, chirps or babbles before, during or after elimination
- grunts before or during defecation
- makes an imploring sound such as "eh, eh, eh" or "uh, uh, uh"
- makes a special, unique toilet sound (e.g., "pfff")
- laughs before pooing
- sighs or whimpers

- gives learned toilet cue such as "sssss"
- utters own sound (e.g., "eeew" or "ba") before or after pooing
- says "mama" while looking intently at you
- says "pee" before or after pees or poos
- says "poo" before or after poos or pees

There are also vocalizations and utterances that tell you your baby does *not* need to go, or that she does not *want* to go. The most obvious are screaming, crying and saying "no."

Crying can communicate other things with respect to elimination too. Many babies cry before, during or after pottying for some weeks or months. Here are common causes:

- **Before:** uncomfortable due to a full bladder or gas; overwhelmed by all the new digestive sensations she is experiencing
- **During:** uncomfortable position or receptacle; feels cold; resents interruption from play or sleep; accustomed to going in a diaper; can't relax and release; illness; gastrointestinal disorder; digestion problems; dyschezia; bladder infection; injury; foreskin separation in uncircumcised boys; hernia; upset when scooped up abruptly at potty time; wants to nurse; upset by stressed parent
- **After:** letting you know she is done; anxious to get off potty

And of course there are plenty of situations where crying and fussing have nothing at all to do with elimination. For example, a child might awaken early if she doesn't feel well or might be awakened by something before she is fully rested and cry when you try to potty her. At these times, it usually helps to nurse her for a while. If you think she needs to go and if you keep her warm and comfortable, she might not mind nursing over a potty or other receptacle.

Implicit/Intuitive Communication

Many mothers report that their babies send out pee signals on an intuitive level. The most common sensation is a feeling of spreading warmth or wetness as if their babies were peeing on them. Some refer to these imagined pees as "phantom pees." One couple calls this phenomenon a "chi pee" (per the Chinese word for "energy") as they notice their baby has a warm burst of energy when she is about to pee. Others smell urine, hear the word "pee" in their minds, dream their babies need to go, or subtly feel a full bladder in their own bodies. But in all these situations, when they check their babies, they find that they are clean and dry. When the mothers then hold them in position to go, the babies respond by peeing. Some mothers report the same with defecation—a warm sensation or the smell of baby poo precedes the actual movement. But not all babies communicate in this way. Some families have reported that while one child communicated intuitively, a sibling did not.

Intuition is a subliminal phenomenon that is always functioning in your subconscious. For scientific-minded folks, it is like DSL, constantly streaming in the background, and you just have to tap into the current to access it.

For some, implicit and intuitive communications are difficult to detect since they are not visible or audible. Many Westerners do not believe there is such a thing as telepathic communication. Others believe this type of communication exists but that they are not able to achieve it. If you feel this way, don't worry. You can be just as responsive by using timing, patterns, body language, vocalizations and even "guessing." One day you may be surprised to suddenly hear or feel something that tells you "it's time" and your intuition will kick in. Another way to view it, your guessing might just be your intuition kicking into gear. If you all of a sudden think your baby might need to go, act on it rather than ignoring it, and you may be pleasantly surprised.

Manual Cues

Early gestures and manual signals include pointing at an object, extending an object toward the mother and openhanded reaching toward an object.[19] Babies can start moving their hands in a crude mimic of sign language as soon as they develop some hand coordination.[20] In comparison with the progress of learning a spoken language, sign language can be learned somewhat earlier in life. The mean age at which signing children make their first recognizable sign is 8.6 months—although some have reported starting as early as 2 months— whereas most infants do not purposefully utter their first intelligible word until 24–25 months.[21] Some report this happens much earlier too. Of course, babies can haphazardly pronounce several short words long before this time, but to make the direct connection between a specific word and concept generally takes longer.

Parent and child can define their own particular manual cues or use ASL (American Sign Language) or another sign language—many countries have their own. To the untrained eye, when an infant first uses the ASL sign for "toilet," it may resemble a wave rather than an intentional sign, but a parent can usually distinguish between a "toilet wave" and a "bye bye wave." Be ready for your baby to at first practice the hand coordination of signing at times when she doesn't need to go.

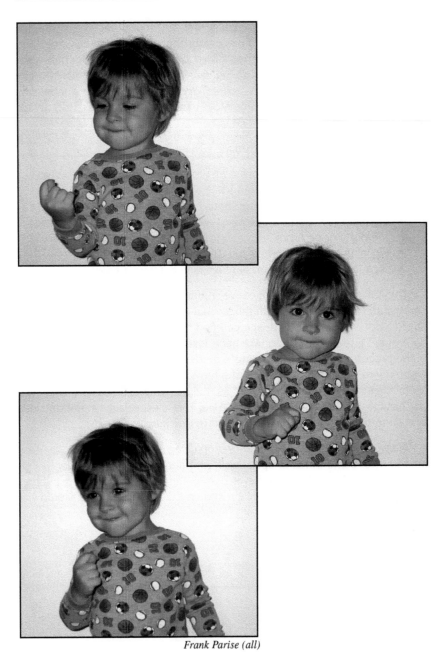

Frank Parise (all)

2-year-old Jack making the ASL sign for "toilet."

To make the American Sign Language sign for "toilet," face your palm to-wards your baby. Make a fist and place your thumb between your index and middle fingers (this forms the letter T for "toilet"). Then twist or shake your hand back and forth a few times to indicate "toilet action" such as, "Do you need to go?" or "Shall we use the toilet?" You can reinforce the sign by say-ing "potty" or "toilet" while signing. Most parents use a combination of sign language and words.

Here is a way to gradually introduce sign language:

- Make your potty sign when asking her if she needs to go, when seat-ing her on the potty/toilet or while she is going.
- Reinforce the sign by saying "potty," "pee pee," etc. while signing.
- Sign and say "potty," "pee pee," etc. as you point or walk towards the potty or bathroom.
- Signal her in silence when you think she may need to go.
- Sign "potty time" or equivalent while in a different room.

The ASL sign for "toilet" can convey different meanings, depending on the context and time line. They can range from a child telling you in advance ("I have to go"); to asking where she can find the potty or toilet ("Where's the bathroom?"); to asking you to take her ("Take me there"); to telling you she is in the process of going ("I'm peeing"); to identifying a potty or toilet ("That's a potty"); to letting you know that she has just gone ("I peed"). Another very useful sign is "finished" or "all done" as it allows your child to let you know if she has finished or if she needs more time. This is especially helpful with kids who go in squirts and spurts as opposed to one surge.

Many children who sign in infancy stop using sign language once they are able to utter some words or speak well. And don't worry if your baby has no interest in hand signals. Some never sign, preferring communicating in other ways. I didn't know about manual cues when EC'ing my son, and we did just fine!

chapter 6
nighttime

In terms of nighttime, it is important to do what works best for the family as a whole. Staying dry at night often takes longer to accomplish than staying dry during the day. The degree of difficulty of staying dry at night depends on your baby's elimination frequency and patterns, as well as on your diligence and ability to be in tune with your little one. At night, there is the added stress of waking, and the consequences of this should be weighed and considered.

Some parents find it easy to get up at night, while others find it extremely difficult. You'll soon ascertain whether or not it's a good idea. If you and baby don't find it too unsettling or tiring, carry on pottying at night. If it makes you negative or worn out during the day, or if disturbing your rest at night makes you susceptible to illness, it is better to sleep through the night. If your little one protests being pottied at night, it might be wise to "let sleeping babies lie" for some nights before trying again. If it goes well most of the time except for phases where his patterns change or when he is ill—he may temporarily nurse and pee a lot more at night—don't worry about getting up during those times.

Nighttime pottying is not essential in the early months. In most situations, if you devote time to pottying during the day, it won't slow down the process if you go off duty at night for a while. It is possible that baby will simply outgrow bedwetting as his capacity and control increase.

If you want to potty at night, keep the bedding and clothing dry and clean, even if you have to change them at night. This encourages baby to remain dry. In the event of accidents, quietly and nonchalantly clean up, with as little fuss and disturbance as possible.

Many babies remain dry all night only to be left to wet their bed or diaper in the morning. Babies generally need to go as soon as they wake. Bear in mind that they often wake up before everyone else in the house. Remember to base the "first thing in the morning" pee on *his* timing rather than yours. If you do not take him to pee immediately upon waking, it will probably be difficult for him to wait more than 1 to 5 minutes before he goes. The result will be a wet bed or diaper, not because he wet it during the night but because no one made the effort to potty him when he woke up. As he grows and his bladder gains more capacity, he will be able to "hold it" somewhat longer after waking. Don't wait too long, though. Even most adults need to relieve themselves first thing in the morning.

If you pee him just before he goes to sleep at night and then potty him as soon as he wakes in the morning, there is a good chance he will stay dry all night. The reason he can remain dry all night is because certain hormones cause urine production to decrease at night. His kidneys produce less urine while he is asleep than during his waking, active hours. If you let him eat something with a high liquid content such as watermelon before bed, you can expect him to need to pee during the night. Babies who nurse or drink a lot before bed or during the night are also likely to go once or even several times at night, especially when they are very young. If your child is old enough for no liquids before bed, try to gradually move the time of the last intake earlier and earlier until he can stay dry all night.

How do you know when to pee your baby at night? Many stir, kick, cry, scream or otherwise (partially) wake at night if they have to go. As with day-time signals, nighttime signals can be either blatant or subtle. Many babies are restless in their sleep. They might toss and turn, with or without sound effects such as grunting, or perhaps just turn their heads from side to side. They might roll over or raise their rear ends in the air in an attempt to get the pressure off their bladders. Mothers often assume that if babies wake at night, it is to nurse, and they quickly offer the breast. But many babies stir or wake at night to pee. Through observation, you will know if this is the case. Some are adamant about fussing and waking you and will even refuse to nurse before they have relieved themselves. Others will eliminate then drift back to sleep without any nursing. And of course many will want to nurse themselves back to sleep after going.

But what if you aren't forewarned at night? Perhaps your baby doesn't squirm or wake before he pees. Maybe he went to bed hours before you, and you aren't present when he stirs or whimpers. Perhaps he just wakes up and lies quietly waiting. Or maybe he is a deep sleeper and sleeps through just about anything. If your baby wets the bed and you want to do something about it, figure out the optimal time to take him for a "preventive pee" at night and see if he will go for you.

As a general rule, do whatever is the least disruptive at night. You can let him go in a portable receptacle (bucket, potty, plastic bowl, etc.) kept near the bed, or else take him to the sink, toilet, shower or bathtub. You can also let him pee on a diaper, a cotton changing pad with a waterproof backing or anything else that works in your situation. A newborn can be placed on a diaper, towel, or other soft cloth on your chest or on the bed. After he pees, just toss the wet item into a container and replace it with dry one. If helpful, the pottying can be done while nursing.

Keep him warm and comfortable. Darkness or dim lights, silence or quiet surroundings, gentle and minimal movement while changing bedding or clothing can all be helpful. Some babies only half wake up to go, keeping their eyes closed the whole time, then fall back into a deep sleep in your arms after peeing. If yours likes to wake up slowly, respect this tendency and let him wake at his own pace. There is usually no need to fully wake baby or otherwise disturb his slumber, as illustrated by this tip from one mother: "I wondered for a time, if by taking Zachary to pee in his sleep I might inadvertently train him to potentially go in his sleep. I was concerned at his being so relaxed that he slept through my toileting him in response to his restlessness or when I took him preventively before my bedtime. But he began to awaken more and more on his own, and would cry out and get up on his knees while waiting to be taken to the bathroom. And when he could sign, he would also wave the ASL toilet sign as I arrived. My experience with Zachary led me to conclude that my attentiveness at nights led to his learning to awaken fully on his own to go."[22]

If he is awake after he goes, nurse him back to sleep. You may soon find that both you and your baby remain in a light stage of sleep while taking care of his nighttime elimination needs. Do whatever lets you both fall peacefully back to sleep.

It can take a few nights to become accustomed to a nighttime routine and isn't unusual to meet with a little resistance at first. One mother discovered that candlelight mesmerized and relaxed her baby—he stared at the glow, and out came the pee. Try different strategies such as rocking baby in your arms, nursing him over a receptacle or nursing while walking around. Or it might be helpful to nurse him for a few minutes, then pee him and then nurse him back to sleep. Some smaller babies will only go while being nursed. After some nights, you'll get into a routine and will both grow accustomed to staying more relaxed. And as always, be prepared for the inevitable changes over time.

An important factor in the nighttime equation is clothing. Avoid lots of layers and fasteners. Find something that is super fast and easy to remove with as little fuss as possible. A pajama top, long-sleeved T-shirt or sweater might

Thembi Butler

3 weeks old — Dad helps Sophie with a sunrise wake-up pee.

be all you need for warmth. Smaller babies who don't move much can sleep on prefolds or cloth diapers. If diapering, fitted diapers are excellent in terms of keeping the bed dry.

But using diapers at night can actually encourage bedwetting for some, especially once a child has reasonable daytime control. This is particularly true with toddlers since having to remove a diaper adds to the time and complexity of using the potty or toilet independently, and this may be enough to discourage the attempt. Also, association with diaperlessness and/or the power of projection can have a positive effect on nighttime pottying with both infants and toddlers. One mother ran out of disposables and told her infant son not to pee in his sleep; another mother forgot to diaper her son one night. Both were happy to find their babies dry the next morning. They never diapered at night again and their babies stayed dry. Another mother found that when her baby was diaperless at night, he remained dry, but whenever she diapered him at night, he wet the diaper. Once she noticed this pattern, she stopped diapering him at night. And let us not forget how disposables suppress feelings of wetness that might otherwise wake a child at night and encourage him to use a receptacle.

Diapers can be especially uncomfortable for boys. If your boy cries at night for no apparent reason, his discomfort could be caused by diapers restricting penis movement and swelling/expansion during a nighttime erection.

Once your child begins to walk, use one or more nightlights in strategic locations. Place the potty near the bed. Invite him to wake you when he has to go, even if you are co-sleeping. The thought of you waking up to accompany him might be just the encouragement he needs.

If one parent remains at home with baby during the day, it is helpful if the other parent takes on the task of getting up at night whenever possible and reasonable. Some fathers are glad to make this sacrifice, while others flatly refuse. Each family has to weigh their total situation in order to determine who does what, if anything, about nighttime pottying.

If you want your baby to be diaper-free at night but are worried about your mattress and bedding, there are a number of ways to protect them. Natural wool is one of the best solutions since wool is water resistant, doesn't grow bacteria or fungus, absorbs a lot of liquid before feeling wet and is a natural deodorizer. You can let baby sleep diaperless by placing a sheepskin rug (short-haired is preferable, to reduce the risk of suffocation and also for cleaning purposes), wool blanket, mattress pad or fleece blanket under soft and natural material such as a cotton or flannel sheet. If the wool starts to smell after some days, let it air out in the sun. If you ever find mildew on the wool, thoroughly clean it asap. If you don't want to use wool, try cotton changing pads with an absorbent core and waterproof backing.

By using the right materials to protect your bed, you will not have to worry about nighttime accidents. This will allow you to be relaxed while your baby enjoys sleeping diaper-free. This in turn will make it easier to pee him in the middle of the night since you won't have to unnecessarily disturb him or spend time removing a diaper. There is a chance that having a diaperless baby in bed will (at first) keep you on high alert and cause you to lose sleep, in which case you can use a diaper. If you use a cloth diaper without a waterproof cover, or if your baby pees through a disposable diaper, your bedding and mattress will be protected by using wool or other absorbent materials.

Sleep position can make a difference at night. Some mothers report that they have a lot more misses when their babies sleep on their stomachs, perhaps due to pressure on the bladder. Food sensitivities/allergies can contribute to bedwetting too. See "Food Sensitivities" in Chapter 4 for more.

It's common for children (usually toddlers) to use potty signaling to engage in bedtime stalling tactics. Some will summon you when they don't have to go. Others will purposefully release just a few drops into the potty and hold back the rest, then signal again once they are back in bed. If you want to discourage potty stalling, make the visits after bedtime less attractive by pottying in a dimly lit room with no toys and then put him back in bed as soon as he has finished. Or if he has just used the facilities and signals again, tell him that he already went and that's it's time to go to sleep. Another option is to be firm about offering only one single pottytunity before bed (perhaps while reading a book or telling a story), then put him to bed; if he starts to sign again, explain that he just went, that he is fine and that it is now time for sleep.

If you are not getting up at night and baby pees most nights for a year or longer, it may be wise to reassess the situation and change tactics as a means to help him avoid long-term nocturnal enuresis (bedwetting at night after the age of 5 years). Enuresis is an elimination disorder that can last for years. In fact, adults in their twenties have been found to still be incontinent. There are a number of treatments available, but none are guaranteed to work. If your baby is showing repeated signs of enuresis, it might well be worth the sacrifice to get up and potty him as a gentle and natural way to combat the problem before it progresses into a true elimination disorder. It would of course be preferable for him to learn to stay dry all night at a relatively young age, rather than going through years of the embarrassment and discomfort of bedwetting.

Nighttime regression after staying dry for a month or longer can be caused by emotional factors. "Children's brain patterns change if they are overly tired, stressed, or depressed, preventing the sleeping brain from detecting signals from the bladder and awakening. The problem can be expected to disappear as soon as the child is back on an even keel. Urinary tract infections, sleep apnea, diabetes mellitus, and seizure disorders can also cause sudden bouts of bedwetting. See your pediatrician if your child begins bedwetting after having remained dry for a month."[23]

chapter 7

parental attitude

Parental attitude plays a tremendous role in a child's ability to learn and is key to IPT. The importance of patience, attentiveness, responsiveness and a relaxed approach cannot be overemphasized.

Practice *The Three C's*

Be calm, confident and communicative. Strive to be relaxed and as stress-free as possible. For example, if you worry about the opinions of others, be discrete by taking your baby to the bathroom and closing the door for privacy. Most will assume you are just changing a diaper. Have confidence in yourself and in your baby. Some parents feel insecure at first, The many steps you take along the way are like the pieces to a jigsaw puzzle. With determination and loving interaction, you will gradually complete the big, beautiful picture. Never forget that EC is more about the "C" than the "E."

Customize Your Approach

Different people with different babies need to take different approaches, per the expression "Different strokes for different folks." Capitalize on all your strengths. Combat your weaknesses and convert them into strengths. If you are laid-back, your casual demeanor is a true asset, but you may need to strive to be more structured and consistent. If you are a perfectionist, your abilities to be punctual and organized will prove to be extremely helpful, but you also need to unwind and appreciate yourself. Be objective rather than subjective. Practice reacting to a puddle of pee on the kitchen floor as if it were a puddle of water. Nonchalantly wipe it up as if nothing has happened. Do not feel you have failed or let down your baby.

Most parents feel excited and extremely pleased with their babies after getting them to go on cue. Your natural reaction is the best reaction. If you are exuberant and want to verbally praise or thank your baby, that is fine. If you are less outgoing and prefer to just state what happened, that is fine. Or maybe you'll express your joy for a while and transition to being nonchalant. If you have more than one child and feel less enthusiastic with the second or third, this is fine. The important thing is to let the child know that you are aware he has responded. He will sense that you are pleased and be encouraged to continue his behavior.

If you start to feel overwhelmed, slow down and just take things one day at a time. The process is similar to slowly but surely progressing through school:

Kindergarten
These are the first really fun days, when you discover what a joy your little one is; spent perhaps partly with baby on your belly, in a sling or lying next to you; learning timing and how to read and respond to each other's signals.

Elementary School
This is the in-arms phase, consisting of many days of standing by the sink, tub, potty or toilet; holding, cuddling and coaching; listening, learning and laughing; adjusting as baby's timing changes.

Junior High School
Moving into the potty phase and then gaining some independence by becoming mobile is where it can get a little rough for a while, with both of you trying to establish who knows best and perhaps sampling a taste of rebellion.

High School
This often begins around the time of learning to walk, setting out on the road to true independence; at times a battle of wits with plenty of ups and downs, it may seem to last forever for some, but all in all a fun and interesting time where character and personality blossom.

Graduation
The day of graduation arrives rather suddenly. It is almost unexpected after all your efforts, and looking back, you are amazed at what you have accomplished with your little one.

Be Reasonably Consistent

A frequently asked question is: "If I'm not consistent on a regular basis, will this confuse my baby?" As long as you are fairly regular for one or more potty sessions each day, you will not confuse your child. A typical scenario is to have a fairly regular morning and/or evening routine but a nonexistent or chaotic daytime schedule. You may be constant and punctual first thing in the morning and before bedtime at night, but you have a job or other children and must deviate from your desired or ideal scheme in order to attend to other duties. Many mothers keep their babies apprised of the situation, "I can't get you to the potty while we're out driving around (or working in the office or whatever applies to your situation) so you need to use diapers in the afternoon."

What *is* confusing is to be erratic and irregular, only pottying baby when it is convenient for you. Those convenient times will dwindle until they disappear altogether. In addition, once baby senses that you aren't really serious about communicating and working together, he will stop signaling you. Find a balance between the following:

- The more regularly and faithfully you potty, the more likely your child will be diaper-free at the earliest moment possible.
- It is better to occasionally take a break—and not consider this a failure—and tend to other family members or tasks than to wear yourself out or direct anger and frustration at your child.

In other words, be as consistent as possible but not to the point of becoming stressed, obsessed, exhausted or frustrated. Sometimes we try too hard and make too big a deal out of EC.

Avoid the No-Nos

Avoid damaging and counterproductive behaviors per these no-nos:

- no punishment
- no pressure
- no negativity
- no coercion
- no shaming
- no competition with others
- no obsessing
- no perfectionism
- no rushing toilet learning
- no attachment to time goals

Do not punish, blame or shame baby if you arrive too late or if he accidentally goes on the floor, furniture, etc. Just clean up and move on.

Your baby must never feel under pressure to perform. This means that you cannot be in a hurry. If you find you do not have the time to correctly and peacefully potty him on some occasions or if you're feeling exhausted, take a break and go back to diapers for a while.

Every one of us occasionally experiences a "bad day." The difference between a good day and a bad day is often not so much the things that happen but our attitude towards them, whether we can smile or laugh about them. Babies sense when we are upset. They detect our mood in our behavior, facial expressions, tone of voice, body movements, muscular tension and breathing. If you experience multiple misses and find that baby's elimination is "out of sink" (sync), don't become distraught. IPT takes many months, mishaps, cuddles and laughs to complete.

Babies also have the occasional "off day" where they may not give their usual signals or where their timing is off. No blame or guilt should be assigned. Pay close attention and strive to resynchronize as soon as possible. This could take a number of days.

It is important to avoid all feelings of competition and showing off. You should not compare what you are doing with any other child, and you should not ever attempt to get your child to "perform" for anyone. It can be tempting to try to impress others by giving live demos with your adorable and amazing baby, but this can backfire. Your baby is so in tune with you and his potty routine that he may sense a disruption in communication or be distracted by the presence of others.

It is equally important that you avoid obsessing and seeking "potty perfection." Parents who are too hard on themselves and their babies reduce their chances of doing well. They tend to experience burnout and give up.

IPT is *not* about rushing toilet learning. Another way to set yourself up for problems such as feelings of failure is to set time goals. Your child will progress at his own rate along with your gentle and relaxed assistance.

Above all, enjoy your baby. No matter if parents start at birth, in infancy or with late-starters or multiples and practice this full time or part time, EC can be harmoniously integrated with all other aspects of parenting. Just remember to always **KEEP IT FUN!**

chapter 8

part-time pottying

Working parents and other busy families can find ways to combine EC with their tight schedules. If you manage your time well, pottying doesn't need to be overly time-consuming or to unduly take away from family activities. Be consistent, even if it is for just one or a few sessions a day, preferably around the same time each day. Some part-timers are successful with bowel movements, but rarely catch any pees or vice versa. Getting every pee in the pot would be far too time consuming, stressful and restrictive for all concerned. In this sense, it can be said that everyone does part-time pottying for a while.

The best times to implement part-time pottying are:

- first thing in the morning
- after a nap
- before or after a feeding
- before bed at night

If parents are able to find a trustworthy and reliable caregiver (nanny, babysitter, older sibling or grandparent) who will continue during the day, this will of course be a bonus. Parents should give their caregivers explicit training and detailed instructions. They should require frequent feedback in order to be certain the caregiver has the right attitude and approach, is comfortable with EC, and does not feel stressed or direct anger at baby.

If you need to send your child to daycare, look for one that is willing to potty your baby at least a few times a day. Be prepared to give instructions and a brief demo. Daycare centers usually put toddlers on the potty throughout the day anyway and might be willing and even delighted to do the same with an infant. If you cannot find a daycare that will do this, go for the next best thing, which is to find one that is diligent about quickly changing diapers. Potty your baby before leaving her at the center and tell her what to expect: "The ladies here will potty you," "The people might not know when you need to go, so dont feel bad if they are late," "The people here don't use potties but will change you really fast," "We'll get back to the potty after daycare," and so forth.

Siblings and Multiples

Older brothers and sisters can be a great help. It is of course necessary to teach an older child the exact procedures needed to keep baby safe, content, clean and healthy. Siblings helping siblings increases family bonding and closeness. Where twins and other multiples are concerned, parents need to be extra vigilant about keeping a healthy balance in all their activities. This may mean fewer potty visits and more diapers for a while.

It is possible to potty train two or more young children at the same time. There are two scenarios for this. The first involves families who start at the same time with both an infant and a toddler. A child 2 to 4 years old who has not yet been potty trained is likely to be encouraged to work on potty learning alongside her baby brother or sister and vice versa. Older children tend to be more enthusiastic about potty learning if they are in the company of someone else going through the same process. They may well feel responsible to set an example for their baby sibling.

The second scenario involves twins or even triplets. IPT is used by many families with twins. Most of the basics apply. Here are the essentials for working with twins:

- It's best to first recover from the birth and establish nursing, then slowly ease your way into IPT. To get started, watch for body language, listen for vocalizations and focus on maintaining their elimination awareness. When you feel ready, start gradually with just one or two sessions a day until the children get accustomed to it. Then gradually increase over the weeks and months.

- Don't set lofty and unrealistic goals. It is absolutely fine and commendable to do part-time pottying from start to finish.

- Since you are doubling the potential for stress, work on staying as relaxed as possible. If you can't potty perfectly, it's no worse than the other imperfections you will experience with your children.

- Dress them in clothing that is quick and easy to remove. Chinese open pants can be very helpful at home.

- Have at least one potty for each child. It's even better if you have two potties in multiple rooms.

- Do joint potty sessions whenever practical. One reason for this is that if you signal one child, the other may also respond.

- If you observe one using the potty, be sure the other sits on her potty too. Children enjoy imitating each other, so it's likely that if one goes, the other will soon do the same.

- For misses, instead of immediately cleaning up after one goes, try to get the other child to the potty on time.

- Twins develop and progress at their own individual rates, so variation is to be expected and respected. They may be polar opposites in many ways such as elimination patterns or degree of concern about staying dry, so that one may be months ahead of the other during the entire process, including graduation.

For more advice and a detailed testimonial about twins, see Part 2, Chapter 6, "Twins!"

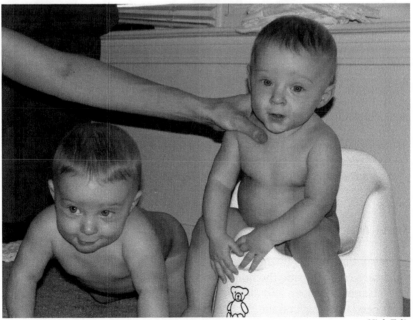

Nick Felix

5-month-old twins Oscar and Titus taking turns on the potty.

John Lamela

6-month-old twins Tressa and Wyatt making a start with IPT.
Their mother Julie took an interest when Wyatt developed
severe diaper rash at 6 months. Tressa finished potty training
at 22 months and Wyatt was done at 27 months.

Time Management

Savvy time management is essential. You will need to carefully prioritize
child care, work outside the home, housework, mealtimes, family life, social
life, leisure time, sleep and all other aspects of daily life. Regular potty sessions need to be high on the list of priorities, even if only possible a few times
a day. Obviously, the more regular and diligent you are (without overdoing it),
the better. Finding a reasonable and harmonious balance is key.

Shivalila

An 11-year-old helps potty 4-month-old Kanoa.

If helpful, post a list of priorities on the refrigerator or elsewhere. Using a timer as a reminder to take baby to the bathroom may prove beneficial. And, as always, remain sensitive and responsive to your internal clock. When necessary, elicit the assistance of others.

Multiple Caregivers

Most babies do fine with multiple caregivers. Caregivers can of course include family members, such as siblings, grandparents, aunts and uncles. You can divide the day into shifts; or else at times when the whole family is present, let everyone be in charge of a particular aspect of the routine (holding baby, removing pants or diapers, cleaning up if there is an accident, dressing baby, etc.), making it a family undertaking or assembly line.

In the early weeks of life, infants have no fear of strangers. If you want to train a nanny or babysitter, it is easiest to begin this before the child develops a fear of strangers or a sense of shyness. This is not to say that you cannot have multiple caregivers once a baby is older. Many families have no problem introducing an attentive newcomer to care for their child.

If a baby proves to be truly upset by being held by a certain person, do not force the issue. Try introducing her to another caregiver and see if this helps. If not, you'll need to wait until she is more open to being held by others. Sometimes a caregiver will be hesitant to potty your child. Baby will sense this hesitancy, and it may cause her to not want to work in this respect with a particular caregiver.

Homeschooling

Homeschooling and IPT are very compatible. In fact, having a baby around the house is a homeschool project in itself. Kids learn to handle interruptions and how to get back on task. Siblings that nurture one another in childhood gain life experience for their future parenting skills.

Here are some tips and tactics for combining IPT with homeschooling:

- Schedule your day so that one or more family members share potty responsibilities at fixed times each day, such as lunchtime or during breaks, or brother in the mornings while sister gives her full attention to her studies and vice versa in the afternoons.

- Keep a potty nearby so you can continue teaching while pottying.

- Have the kids work on an assignment while you potty baby.

- If baby has a preferred potty place, homeschool near that room or place so you can resume teaching asap.

- When a child takes a bathroom break, let baby accompany him for a potty break. Be sure the older siblings know to potty baby first.

- Encourage the children to watch for potty signs when your focus is fully engaged with school instruction.

- Lead by example. Because IPT is never 100% perfect, children learn early on that "one does one's best" while keeping a cheerful attitude through thick and thin.

- Keep a pile of durable board books near your potty station so that siblings can entertain baby at potty time. As one mother put it, "Potty time at my house became a path to literature and the love of reading. We also did a lot of singing while pottying."[24]

- Elicit IPT help from a nanny, relative or friend if pottying baby proves to be too disruptive to the academic work.

Vanessa Lorentzen

A homeschooling break allows Hollis to potty his baby brother.

Unexpected Extended Interruptions

Sometimes parents meet with unexpected circumstances and must devote a lot of time and attention to helping a sick relative, sorting out financial problems or recovering from an illness or injury. Such events can result in long and unintended interruptions in pottying. The good news is that if you have spent a minimum of a month or two pottying your infant, a reduction or temporary cessation in the time you spend at it does not necessarily mean she will forget all that she has learned. Parents who have had to take a break due to unforeseen circumstances have been pleased to find that their baby still remembers how to potty after a break of some days, weeks or even a month. There is no formula for knowing how long a baby can remember, but some families have reported taking a break of up to a month or longer, only to find their babies anxious to pick up where they left off. Again it must be emphasized that each child is different—some will retain things longer and better than others. While it is not advisable to take time off, it is comforting to know that all may not be lost should you be forced to take an extended break.

Erratic Pottying

It is not advisable to use part-time pottying if you are going to do it in a haphazard and erratic fashion. Do not repeatedly start, stop and restart for no apparent reason such as being lazy, irresponsible or a procrastinator. It takes long-term and consistent commitment. Taking an occasional break for illness or if you need a little time off is okay as long as it doesn't happen repeatedly. But if you frequently feel disenchanted or apathetic about EC and cannot stick to a fairly regular minimal schedule, it may be better to go back to full-time diapering. And no guilty feelings, please! EC is not for everyone.

What to Expect

By using part-time pottying as described in this chapter, baby will maintain her natural awareness of elimination and will learn and remember how to release upon receiving your cues. She will be able to benefit from this ability whenever you are available to potty her. This will help prepare her to transition to underwear, continence and independence in due course.

chapter 9
late-starters
6 months & older

Late-starters are also good candidates for IPT. There is not a fixed age at which a child becomes a late-starter, but the term generally applies to children over 6 months old. The closing of the first window of learning around 6 months may be in part related to the start of exploration and independence resulting from new motor skills such as learning to sit without support, to pull up to a standing position, and to reach for and manipulate objects with both hands. In any case, it can be tricky or different to begin with a child who:

- has missed the first IPT sensitive period or window of learning
- has been trained to go in a diaper
- has used disposables and can't associate the feeling of wetness with elimination
- has lost awareness of his elimination functions
- has developed an ego and a will of his own
- is mobile and active. When he learns to crawl or walk, he will become more independent and naturally want to explore his surroundings and focus on new and exciting things. If he is not familiar with potty sits or his "toilet muscles," he is not likely to understand why he is being detained on a potty and is thus not likely to want to remain there.

Once babies pass the first window of opportunity around 6 months, some still remain receptive for a while. Others close down and then open up again, but there is no way to know when this might happen. And it is possible that some babies remain in a constant state of readiness. Their behavior might be mislabeled as "high needs," "colicky" or "fussy," or they may have unexplained tantrums. In the meantime, all they can do is await the day that someone finally responds to their needs. It's not uncommon to hear the following, "My baby caught on within a few days!" Perhaps the same could have been said many months or even some years earlier.

Except for a few simple and logical modifications, all the IPT principles apply. For example, if your child is mobile, he won't be lying down for the observation phase, and if he is verbal, you can communicate back and forth with words instead of sounds or sign language. Peruse these late-starter tactics, then sculpt and hone the best strategy or "recipe" for your child and situation:

Late-Starter Tactics

- Make potty time fun. For example, read books with your child, including books on potty training, or let him play with a favorite toy.
- Potty at likely times such as upon waking, in relation to meals and drinks, when you change him, after accidents, and before and after outings.
- Always change wet or soiled clothing as soon as possible.
- If you are using disposables, switch to cloth diapers without a plastic cover so you can change him asap when he goes, learn his timing and patterns, stop him from feeling comfortable when wet, and help him learn the cause-and-effect of elimination.
- If your child resists the potty or toilet, try to relax him, then offer again. Give him something to drink, tickle him, touch his feet, dunk his feet in water, or splash water on his feet or belly. If he can't relax, don't force him to remain seated. Just try again later.
- If he refuses the potty or won't remain seated, try the toilet with an attachable child's seat instead, facing forwards or backwards.
- Talk to him about pottying ("Pee goes in the potty") and let him help clean up (empty the potty or wipe the floor). It is normal for late-starters to sit on the potty for a while, then get up and go on the floor. If he seems clueless, don't despair, he will eventually catch on.
- When your child is old enough, take him shopping and let him help select a potty.
- Use training pants. They are far easier to use than diapers and protect your busy baby's bottom and genitals.
- Offer him diaper-free time at home. This can be in undies, a cloth diaper without a cover, in training pants or bare-bummed. Many have found that it's much easier to clean up a little puddle from the floor with a cloth, or to pick up a poop with some toilet paper, than it is to change a diaper.
- Let your child help shop for undies. For girls, pretty undies might be the catalyst that motivates a girl to stay clean and dry. Boys might be inspired to keep their favorite "character" undies dry.

- Use an open-door policy by letting your child accompany you, dad (fathers are especially helpful with boys) or siblings to the toilet.
- With boys, try target practice by having your son aim at something floating in the toilet (examples: Cheerios, bits of toilet paper or store-bought targets designed for this purpose) or outdoors at his favorite target (examples: a tree or a rock, perhaps with an actual target on them). He can also have fun drawing patterns in the dirt or snow, playing pee games such as seeing who can shoot farther, or crisscrossing streams with dad or a brother.
- Get siblings involved. They can teach by example, inspire, entertain and assist in many ways. Some siblings are better at "reading" their younger brothers or sisters than adults.
- If you use praise and it encourages him to go on cue, celebrate! If he rebels against praise, just state what is happening when he goes.
- Use trial and error to find what works for you, always remembering that each child and each family situation varies from the next.
- For parents starting with children who are already walking, any time your toddler has an accident, calmly tell him what he did and that pee/poo belongs in the potty. Supervise as he cleans the mess, then accompany him to the potty, toilet, hamper or laundry room.
- Expect some resistance and fooling around by toddlers. For example, when they go through the phase of saying "no" to everything, their "no" does not always really mean "no." If you ask your toddler if he needs to go and are met with a resounding "no," this response may sometimes have little to do with your question. Try asking in a different way such as, "It's time for dinner. Let's potty first so we can be dry at the table," then head to the bathroom with him.
- Sometimes offering a choice works well, as opposed to offering yes-or-no options. If your toddler is squirming or holding himself, or you otherwise simply *know* it's time for him to go, give him a choice such as asking (a) if he would like to go and use the potty in the bathroom or (b) if you can bring it to him.
- Patiently answer any and all questions your child may have about pottying, even if you've already explained the same thing many times.
- Constantly explain what is going on and what you are doing. Try to engage him in conversation, "Shall we try the potty?" Or if he is in a no-to-everything mood, adopt a "don't ask, do tell" approach, "I think you have to pee. Let's go read a book together while you try."

- If your child dislikes reminders or talking about EC, don't say anything at all about it. Instead, every hour or so comment out loud (so he can hear) that you really need to pee, and then head to the bathroom. If he follows you and uses his potty, don't comment or praise him unless you feel this will encourage him.
- If independence is a big issue and your child doesn't want to be asked if he has to go, let him take charge of potty time.
- If he can "hold it" fairly well and enjoys pottying in different locations, let him choose where to go. He may like moving his potty to different rooms, on top of chairs or to the backyard.
- Go with the flow of your child's natural learning process. A common scenario at first is for toddlers to let you know they went *after* they have gone in their pants or diaper or on the floor. This is part of the learning process, and your child will eventually learn to inform you beforehand.
- Be creative. Adopt the motto "*Whatever Works*" and proceed with an open mind.
- Review "Tactics" in Chapter 4, as many of them also apply to late-starters.
- Join online discussion groups dedicated to EC.
- Consult parenting books and look for more ideas. Read through the *positive* tips and advice offered for conventional training and test some of these to see if they work with your child.
- Watch potty-training DVDs or videos together, then talk about them at potty time.
- Do not expect immediate results. Many parents feel frustrated if their children don't care about staying dry, forgetting that they taught them to go in a diaper in the first place. It takes considerable time to unlearn this. Give yours a while to make the connection.
- Never compare your child's results with another in a competitive or judgmental way, or you risk experiencing negative and detrimental feelings.

If you're skeptical, test your child's "pot luck" for a few weeks, then assess if you want to continue. If you get no results after 2–4 weeks, you can either simply carry on or else take a break and try again in some weeks. Even if he doesn't appear to know what is going on, it is still fine to potty him as long as you are both happy and comfortable with it.

chapter **10**

doctors &
other experts

Until recently, entrenched, trendy and unproven theories about readiness and letting baby dictate when to toilet train coupled with instilling fear in those who go against the grain and begin toilet training in infancy discouraged many from trying, completing or even learning about infant potty training. But those days are over. We are experiencing a generational shift and a new era where parents have more options available and can freely consult about infant pottying with their doctors and pediatricians.

Dr. Karin Susskind, family practitioner confirms this. "Some parents ask me if they should tell their doctors about their plans to practice infant-based potty training and I say: Absolutely. That is a terrific idea. Most likely you'll get a very excited response if the doctor is familiar with it. If the doctor is not familiar with it, I recommend you educate your doctor. A good time to bring this up would be predelivery."[25]

Testimonials by medical professionals about personal experiences with their own children and patients can be found in this chapter as well as in these other chapters:

- Dr. Rita Messmer, a psychologist in Switzerland—Part 1, Chapter 14, "Sensitive Periods"
- Dr. Lauri Nandyal, a family physician in Ohio—Part 2, Chapter 9, "A Physician Speaks Out"
- Dr. Randy Mont-Reynaud, a psychologist in California—Part 3, Chapter 1, "Vietnam"
- Drs. Min Sun, Ph.D. from China and Simone Rugolotto, a pediatrician in Italy—Part 3, Chapter 2, "China"
- Dr. Sarah Buckley, a family physician in Australia—Part 3, Chapter 5, "Australia"

The International Board for Assisted Infant Toilet Training, or AITT Board, was founded in 2007. The goals of the Board are to conduct study and research on the topic of assisted infant toilet training and to educate and support parents and medical professionals who use or know families interested in IPT. The mission is carried out through research, writing for medical journals, community outreach and keeping tabs on current resource information.

Favorable Written Medical Opinions

1958 – Report by J. W. B. Douglas & J. M. Blomfield

The authors conducted a survey and reported in their book *Children under Five* that in 1958, 60% of English mothers started to "pot" their infants during the first 2 weeks of life; 25% started between 2 weeks and 6 months; 15% started after 6 months. By the age of 1 year, 47% had completed toilet training; at 18 months, 83% were finished. They also stated that "Neurologists generally consider that 6 months is the earliest age at which myelination is sufficiently developed to support voluntary control."[26]

1971 – Report by Thomas S. Ball, PhD

Mrs. Lela Humphries devised her own infant potty learning approach for catching BMs and used it with her three children who were born between 1947 and 1956. She stated that while she was feeding her first son, she noticed that each time he had a bowel movement it was during a feeding. "I could always tell by the facial expression when the movements were going to occur." At 6 weeks of age, she would unpin the left side of his diaper, and the instant he made his facial expression indicating an impending BM, she would pull the diaper to one side (without actually taking it off) and place the potty between her legs, directly under her son's buttocks. She left the diaper draped over his front in case he peed. "His position was the same as if he did not have the pot under him. He did not make any kind of fuss." She reported that her first two sons completed bowel training reasonably well at age 6 months and bladder control around the age of 14 months.

Her third son had Down syndrome, but this didn't deter her. Although she kept no records ("never once thinking they might prove useful"), she recalled that he would scoot to the bathroom door and whine to be put on the potty before he could walk, and that at 16 months he started walking and would head to the bathroom when he had to go.

Dr. Thomas Ball explains that her approach can be interpreted within the framework of operant conditioning as "toilet training by reflex. The baby does not get used to eliminating in his diaper and does not feel comfortable doing so, [and] therefore will fuss to have the potty placed on his buttocks. The same applies to a child that eliminates in a diaper for two or three years [and] does not feel comfortable on the pot, but wants his diaper." This is what makes conventional toilet training difficult for many. Diaper changing involves "physical handling with much tactual stimulation and, in many instances, pleasant social interaction. These consequences to soiling diapers serve to reward incontinence; it is no wonder that many children actively resist giving it up."[27]

1978 – Comments by Gersch & Ravindranathan, MDs

Two doctors endorsed the deVries study of the Digo (Kenyans who finished toilet training at 6 months, see Part 4) via letters to *Pediatrics*. Marvin Gersch wrote that the merits of the deVries article demonstrate, among other things, that "our previous thoughts of toilet training were incorrect; training can be accomplished and has been accomplished at a much earlier age."[28] S. Ravindranathan also sanctioned the observations and conclusions of deVries when he wrote, "Not only does this bring about closer mother-infant interactions, contact, and communication, but it also eliminates future attempts at unnecessary coercive methods on a reluctant toddler."[29]

1985 – Study by Smeets, Lancioni, Ball & Oliva

In this study, three girls and one boy started between the ages of 3–6 months. The parents used toilet learning 3–4.5 hours a day several days a week. To get the attention of the baby, the parent held or tapped the potty, or else called or touched the child while holding or tapping the potty, in order to be sure the baby looked at the potty before being placed on it. If the baby went within about 3 minutes, the adult displayed pleasure and approval; otherwise, the baby was removed from the potty. This phase of the study was completed when a baby had at least 18 BMs on the potty plus 8 out of 10 consecutive training days without any bowel accidents.

The next phase established a relationship between potty reaching/grabbing and both types of elimination. The potty was located 30 cm from and slightly to the right front of the baby. Upon spontaneously signaling or reaching for the potty or else when the mother knew it was time to go, the baby was guided to grab the potty and then sit on it.

All four babies completed training before they could walk, between the ages of 8.5–10.7 months. However, the endpoints or definition of completion here would not be acceptable to all Western families since "At the end of the program, the babies were not yet required to hold their eliminations longer than a few minutes and still needed assistance on taking the appropriate position and dressing and undressing."

"In essence, the conditions were arranged such that the visual and tactile stimuli of the potty could develop into a natural and functional event between two already chained behavioral links, the state of distension associated with straining (the first link) followed by stool expulsion associated with physical relief and praise by the mother (second link)."

It is important to note that no negative side effects, such as tantrums or eliminating immediately when removed from the potty, were reported and that "the potty manipulation, as it was used here, was markedly different from other procedures in which the mother places the child frequently on the potty in accordance with a fixed daily regimen."

The study reached the conclusion that "the maturational explanation for the success of currently advocated delayed training methods should be reconsidered."[30]

1990 – Commentary by Paul Fischer, MD

Dr. Fischer debunks the American view that a child must be both "psychologically and physiologically 'mature' before successful toilet training can occur. . . . There has been almost no research to document these theories. They are no doubt nonsensical to much of the world where 'potty training' begins shortly after birth." Concerning the Western approach to toilet training, he continues, "By 2 years of age we expect children to have mastered running, speaking, and a variety of social skills. It is amazing that we continue to feel that such children are often not old enough to control a couple of sphincter muscles!"

Fischer's Pakistani wife and mother-in-law started infant pottying with their 2-week-old daughter and reported that by age 3 months, she "obviously understood the association of the time, sound, and body position with voiding and defecation. By 1 year of age she was out of diapers both during the day and at night."

He states that people in much of Asia and Africa find the Western version of toilet training to be "primitive and unsanitary." Concerning the premise that infant potty training can lead to psychological problems, he states, "I can only speculate that this stems from attempts to use negative reinforcement with 18-month-old children who have had no prior conditioning. This is certainly not the case for the millions of children around the world who are trained in the first year of life."[31]

1997 – Book by Charles E. Schaefer, MD

In his book *Toilet Training without Tears*, Dr. Schaefer discusses various methods of toilet training, including what he calls the "early approach" for babies between 3–15 months of age. He discusses the method of toilet training used in the USA in the 1920s and 1930s, noting that this was a conditioning process based on learning by association. He emphasizes that child development experts and pediatricians of the day coerced parents into adopting the wrong parental attitude and that this is what has given early toilet training a reputation for being harsh, rigid and punitive. Schaefer advocates a positive and unemotional attitude as well as a nonpunitive and noncoercive approach. After years of analytic and cross-cultural studies, "we now know that the age at which a child is trained is not the cause of later emotional and psychological problems; rather, it is the parental attitude that is used during the training period that will determine the long-term effect of toilet training."

Schaefer also gives infants credit for having some ability to control elimination. "Although it is not known exactly when a child can attain this kind of muscular control, studies have shown that some infants between three and six months can learn this skill very successfully, provided their caregiver is observant of the signs that indicate a need to eliminate and then acts promptly to put the child on the potty." He also says that babies are able to gain complete voluntary bladder and bowel control starting around the age of 15 months or later and that it is unrealistic to expect complete control before this time.

The early approach in his book is based in part on the 1985 study by Paul Smeets et al. and includes potty reaching and potty grabbing. Schaefer states that the goal of elimination conditioning is "to establish a close relationship between your baby's body signals and his defecation on the potty." Conditioning is based on associating the feel of the potty against the buttocks. Mothers base potty visits on baby body signals and elimination timing. For these, Schaefer urges extensive record keeping for weeks. He covers a lot in the 20 pages devoted to the topic, including advantages and disadvantages as well as do's and don'ts of the early approach.[32]

2000 & 2002 – Studies by Bakker & Wyndaele, MD

Physiotherapist E. Bakker and urologist Jean-Jacques Wyndaele of University Hospital Antwerpen conducted a study to "evaluate changes in the onset of toilet training, the attitudes of parents and the results of training during the last 60 years in Belgium." A questionnaire was completed by 321 people who had toilet trained 812 children. The findings indicate that voiding problems have increased in recent years and suggest that a major change in the way parents toilet train their children compared with the approach used 60 years ago may contribute to the apparent increase in lower urinary tract dysfunction among children.

"Most authors are convinced that the development of bladder and bowel control is a maturational process which cannot be accelerated by toilet training." But their findings contradict this theory, instead indicating that "the age at which bladder and bowel control were achieved showed the same differences among the groups as the ages at the onset of training."[33]

One of the findings of a different questionnaire that was completed by 4,332 parents was that children who did not have a UTI started potty training much earlier than those who had a UTI. The early start was before 18 months. It was also found that postponing the onset of the training after 18 months and using methods such as asking the child to push to provoke voiding probably increase the risk of later problems with bladder control.[34]

2004 – Article by Rugolotto, MD & Sun, PhD

In this report, pediatrician Simone Rugolotto and his wife Min Sun started caregiver Assisted Infant Toilet Training with their son at age 33 days in a Western family setting. During the first two days, the mother made observations of the infant's bowel movement schedule and the cues he provided, from which she learned when to assist him to eliminate in the bathroom. During the elimination process, the infant was held in an in-arms position, with close contact between the infant's back and his mother's chest. Meanwhile, she gave vocal signals to prompt her son to eliminate—"tutu" for bowel movements and "shhh" for urination. Successful bowel training was completed at 5 months. At the beginning of the 7th month, she helped him use a toilet seat reducer and a potty. Occasional accidents (less than 10 during the first 19 months) occurred only during episodes of diarrhea or when the parents did not pay attention to his signals. Cues for defecation differed from those for hunger, fatigue, sensory irritability and the need for other types of attention.

Overall, her personal observations and sensibility to her child's needs were the most important factors, and her acquired ability to associate the need to defecate with timing and cues was pivotal. Initially, she dedicated nearly one hour per day and paid full attention to all the child's needs whenever possible. However, when she understood the child better and when this task was shared by other caregivers (e.g., the father), the necessary time investment decreased.

This case report shows that assisted infant toilet training is possible in a Western family setting if the caregiver properly learns the infant's natural elimination timing and signals.[35]

2007 – Article by Rugolotto, Ball, Boucke, Sun & deVries

There is a surging new interest in benign assisted infant toilet training (AITT) in Western countries. The facts that bladder sensations are processed at the cortical level in infants and newborns and that children in Africa can be toilet trained much earlier than those in Western countries counteract the assertions of Brazelton that infants under 18 months cannot be toilet trained.

Recently, some studies such as those by Bakker & Wyndaele have demonstrated that the incidences of constipation, stool withholding, stool toileting refusal, enuresis, and late bladder control increase as the start age for toilet training increases. Moreover, a delayed start age also means that freedom from diapers does not begin until the age of 36 months or later. In contrast, past generations that started toilet training well before 18 months were out of diapers much earlier.[36]

2007 – Survey by Ball & Boucke

This small study covers a survey of 65 households and 75 children who used assisted infant elimination training in the United States, Europe and New Zealand. Some mothers initiated training as early as shortly after birth. Assisted bowel control was typically achieved before the children could walk and sometimes within the first few months of life.

None of the parents reported that their child or children met the criteria for stool toileting refusal (STR), although five did experience stool withholding due to constipation, brief periods of stress (a family trip or moving) or the occurrence of a milestone in development (learning to walk). Prior to this, no data on STR has been available for children whose instruction was started during the first year of life.

This study lends support to the notion that toilet training initiated before age one may help prevent extended periods of STR. That demonstration, alone, should be sufficient to arouse the dormant curiosities of critics who do not hesitate to reject an alternative approach that they have never bothered to examine. At the very least, it presents 75 contradictions to the cliché that, with early training, it is the parent who is trained, not the child.[37]

2008 – International Survey by Rugolotto, Sun, Boucke, Calò, Ma & Tatò

The aim of this study was to investigate toilet training among children who started IPT in the first year of life in the United States, Canada, China, Italy and some other countries. A total of 298 eligible participants were asked to fill in a questionnaire, and 286 questionnaires were completed (participation rate of 96%).

The mean toilet training completion age that yielded an ability to stay reasonably clean and dry with some assistance was slightly less than 18 months. Those who initiated toilet training during the first 6 months finished earlier than those who started between 6 and 12 months. The completion age did not differ between girls and boys.

Over 90% of the respondents reported that their children gave elimination signals. Those children whose caregivers recognized their signals had a significantly earlier completion age than those who did not. Children with regular elimination patterns had an earlier completion age. Those who used disposable diapers had a significantly later completion age.

Many more things were explored. The main conclusions are that IPT as currently practiced is (1) noncoercive, (2) based mainly on elimination signals and (3) without notable side effects in the short term. It offers another option of toilet training to motivated caregivers who want to meet infants' elimination needs with a more sensitive approach.[38]

2012 – Study of IPT in Vietnam by Duong, Jansson & Hellström

This study of Vietnamese mothers' experiences with toilet training children from birth to 2 years of age was conducted by interviewing 47 mothers seven times (newborn, 3, 6, 9, 12, 18 and 24 months). The interviews were analyzed using qualitative content analysis.

"According to tradition, diapers were used only rarely. The mothers used a whistling sound at certain times to remind their children to eliminate and frequently checked for signs of need. With this process, all children used the potty by the age of 9 months. At the age of 24 months the potty training was completed, and most of the children managed the whole process independent of help."[39] The study concluded that IPT with good outcomes is possible and can be achieved through ongoing communication between parent and child.

2013 – Prospective Studies on Assisted Infant Toilet Training by Boucke, Sun, Rugolotto & Ball

Two studies were conducted in 2010-2013. Both were prospective studies, meaning that data came from interviews done in realtime every 2-3 months with parents, so that minimal or no recalling of past information was involved. Study families were located in North America, Western Europe, Australia and New Zealand. Interviews were carried out in English, German, Italian and Spanish. Data analysis of these studies will be submitted to medical journals over the course of a few years for publication in 2014 and later.

Parents were of Caucasian, African and Asian backgrounds. The studies included families with twins, a family with male partners, new-to-EC families and experienced EC'ers (more than half of the participants had already used it with 1-3 babies).

For the first study, the interviews all started at or before age 3 months and continued to age 12 months. Interviewers were mainly nurses (RNs), some medical doctors, a psychologist, a Ph.D. and some IPT experts including the author of this book. Interviews for 87 babies were completed.

The first study demonstrated that IPT is effective and beneficial in infancy and that it is well-liked by interested parents. No side effects were reported. The study confirmed that it is important to observe and respond to infant elimination communication whenever possible, as long as this does not cause disruption in the family. The main types of baby signals reported were vocal and verbal communications, body language and manual cues. If parents perceived no signals but felt it was time for their babies to go, most used audible cues, positioning and/or location to prompt their little ones. Determining when to communicate was based mainly on babies' natural timing, elimination patterns and parental hunches that it was time to cue their babies.

The second study consisted of two parts, A and B. Part A used self-report questionnaires completed for the most part in realtime at ages 15, 18, 21 and 24 months. For Part B, parents stayed in touch until their children had completed both daytime and nighttime toilet training. Part B is still ongoing for some of the parents at the time of publication of this edition. Further details of this study will be reported in medical journal articles that will be prepared once all children have finished both daytime and nighttime training.[40]

Commentary by Pediatricians

1993 – Interview with Dr. Leah Lamb, FAAP

Board-certified pediatrician Leah Lamb lived abroad for several years and has witnessed IPT many times. She has practiced pediatrics in California, Texas, Idaho and Colorado.

Q: *Have you observed the use of infant potty training firsthand?*
A: I've closely watched many women in India and North Africa and also friends in Europe complete the training.

Q: *As a pediatrician, do you endorse this method?*
A: I think it takes a special kind of mother—the kind of mother who is very interested in bonding and in being receptive to her child's needs. I think the onus is on the mother to want to create a certain kind of closeness with the baby so she can be able to respond to the infant's signals.

Q: *Do you think it's a good method, a safe method?*
A: Without question, but as I mentioned, it takes a special kind of mother to bond closely enough and pay special attention to her baby's signals in order for the training to be successful.

Q: *Some doctors and psychologists think toilet training should not be started in infancy. How do you respond to this?*
A: They are referring to punitive, heavily enforced toilet training where there is a lot of negative pressure put on the child in order to perform. The method in this book is very different. This is a really gentle method, a mother-child dyad, bonded interaction. The parent/caregiver works with the baby, listening to his cues and signals. It's gentle and it's kind. I don't see that it would have any negative effect on an infant at all.

Q: *Do you agree that as long as the parents have the right attitude that there cannot be any psychological harm?*

A: I don't think any psychological harm can result. Basically, the child is responding to behavioral conditioning. The sound that the mother makes, coupled with her being in tune with the baby's signals, will result in the child either urinating or defecating on cue.

Q: *Do you think an infant is aware of its elimination process?*

A: Yes, absolutely. Babies know when they are eliminating. They make certain sounds, become still or their faces turn red.

Q: *If children are aware of the elimination process, why is it so hard to potty train a baby if you start the training later, around 2 years old?*

A: They may be aware of their elimination, but they are also aware of everything else around them. By definition, a toddler is very involved in exploration, and if he is more interested in exploration, a toy or a book, he is going to ignore the physiologic call to evacuate. In terms of interrupting his exploration, he may not pay attention to his physiologic prompts at that point.

Q: *Do you think that perhaps a 2-year-old child has already been trained to use his diapers as a toilet and really isn't concerned with toilet training?*

A: Human beings are the only animals that soil themselves. I think babies don't particularly like wearing diapers. They cry when they are wet or dirty.

Q: *Can you comment on the American medical school of thought that teaches that a child cannot be toilet trained until certain nerves and muscles are developed—not before the age of 2, in general.*

A: If you are looking at the traditional method of potty training, a child isn't considered trained until he can walk to the toilet, pull down his pants and evacuate by himself. That is what we in the West traditionally consider to be potty trained. There is a lot of pressure to be toilet trained, although less now than a generation or two ago, but infant potty training is a whole different thing. It is not the old militant-style toilet training of the West. Instead, it is a method where the mother is responding and tuned into her baby's internal, physiologic schedule, and the child has assistance and an advocate who helps him accomplish going to the bathroom. You're not expecting a child to do it on his own early in the process.

Q: *In your professional opinion, is the information provided in this book medically correct and sound?*

A: Yes. This book explores both sides of the physiologic question. Is the child mature enough at age 9 months in order to urinate and defecate on cue? They do it, but they do it with *help*, and I think that's the main thing that needs to be clarified. This is an interactive process between a mother, or a father, and a baby. The parents have to be involved and bonded enough to the baby in order to correctly pick up and act on his signals.

Q: *Do you think the method is just a matter of "catching" the child at the right moment? Some people claim that it is the parents who are toilet trained and not the child.*

A: The parent and baby are working together as a team. In this sense, you could say that the parent has to be trained, although I hesitate to use the word "trained." If a parent is bonded and closely enough in tune with a child's signals, the parent can pick up when the child has to go to the bathroom. As to "catching" the baby at the right time, you have to "catch" him at the right time. That's the whole point, that you are catching him when he has the urge to evacuate.

Q: *Do you agree that a more accurate description of "catching" baby's elimination in the potty is "being there for your baby to go potty when he needs you"?*

A: Exactly. Women in underdeveloped countries don't find this surprising. If you ask them, "How do you know your baby has to go?" they just know. They support the baby and help him accomplish his task.

Q: *How do you reconcile traditional medical teachings about neurological development and an infant's responding to cues before that development has been achieved?*

A: Traditionally in Western AMA thinking, a child really doesn't have, as they say, the ability to respond. We physicians are taught that the neural maturation that allows for complete toilet training occurs somewhere around the age of 2 years. However, if the child is tuned in and sensitive to prompts in a nonpunitive way, he will respond. It's behavioral conditioning, and the child will "go" for you.

Q: *A lot of people in the USA don't believe it's possible to toilet train a child in infancy. Even when you give them a live demonstration with a tiny baby, they still don't believe it.*

A: They don't believe it because toilet training in this country implies a toddler bopping off down to the bathroom, pulling down his pants, jumping up on the potty and going. That isn't what this method is about. This method is about a parent and a child interacting and accomplishing a task together. In Western culture, we separate our children from us. We don't sleep in the same room with them, and there is much more emphasis on individuation and privacy. The child is seen as a separate entity. With this infant toilet-training method, you're going back to a more natural state where the mother and child are as one unit, where they are interrelating with each other. This method is for people who are very in tune with their babies and who are looking for a unique connection with their child.

Q: *In this country, we only consider a child to be toilet trained when he is totally independent.*

A: Yes. I think we have to be careful about the definition we use. It's the infant-mother interaction in getting the child to evacuate. I would back away from calling an infant "toilet trained" because the term "toilet trained" implies a certain image in the West. With infant potty training, it's something really different. The mother helps the child, and the child knows what is going on and responds. In India and Africa, most families don't use diapers.

Q: *Have you in your travels seen small children, soon after they learn to walk, independently walk to their "toilet place" and use it?*

A: Yes, but the societal and cultural standards are a little different. If you just have to toddle to the edge of the compound to go to the bathroom where it is acceptable to go, that's very different from finding the bathroom, getting onto the toilet and going. It's a different environment. We have to be sensitive to these differences when we use the technique in America. The basic premises are the same, but the environment is different. It requires an adult who is sensitive, and primarily this is the mother in the infant stage.

Q: *Some Westerners who aren't very familiar with infant potty training claim that it is too time consuming for parents.*

A: In terms of time, potty training takes time no matter how you look at it. You're going to take time changing diapers, or you're going to take time interacting with your baby and responding to his signals. So you are going to spend time dealing with the evacuation from your child, one way or the other. This is just a different method. Millions of third world kids can't be wrong. It certainly works, and it's a matter of whether you are interested in something different, something innovative for the baby.[41]

2000 – Video by Dr. Barbara Gablehouse

In her DVD *The Potty Project for Babies*, Denver-based board-certified pediatrician Barbara Gablehouse states that 85 percent of the world's babies are toilet trained by one year of age and stresses that those babies have the same muscles and the same ability to control those muscles as our babies. She suggests that toilet training be approached as a skill and that we simply need to give our babies the opportunity to practice toilet sitting, just like tummy time to practice rolling over or floor time to practice crawling. "What if we thought of it like learning that the tub was for bathing, the high chair was for eating, and the car seat was for traveling? We don't wait until our children ask or give clues that they are ready for a bath or for a ride in the car. We teach them that these activities, which are a part of everyone's daily life, occur in a specific place. We don't make a big deal out of these places: tubs, car seats, highchairs. Why in the world do we make such a big deal about using the toilet? Why do we wait until the more difficult toddler years?"[42]

With practice, positive reinforcement and time, babies learn bladder and bowel control. "Like all of your baby's learning, repetition is crucial for successful early toilet learning."[43]

2007 – Commentary by Dr. Simone Rugolotto

Dr. Rugolotto, pediatrician and neonatologist at the University of Verona, Italy, has personal experience with infant elimination training. The fact that assisted infant toilet training is a common practice in Asia and Africa "shows that toilet training in early infancy is possible and without major side effects. Babies can clearly communicate their needs, and we can help them to eliminate in a gentle way, by bringing them to the bathroom and using a potty, in a more natural and comfortable manner than eliminating in a horizontal position into a diaper. Babies do have control over their bladder and bowel functions; otherwise they would eliminate feces and urine continually, which obviously does not happen. More particularly, the elimination process is an active one, and we can see all the efforts made by infants during this activity. When they are not able to retain feces and urine any longer, they feel discomfort, give signals (e.g., cry), and if nobody helps them, they let the process happen in their diapers.

"Infant toilet training has many advantages and should be supported by current pediatric knowledge. Some of the possible advantages are: an easier approach to independent toilet training during childhood (children will accept the potty more easily than children who have never used it before); less cutaneous rash (due to less contact between feces or urine and skin); and a closer bond and better understanding between mothers and their children (when effective attention is given to a specific need instead of the usual pacifier or bottle). We are not aware of any side effects of assisted toilet training if practiced in a nurturant environment with mutual understanding and without pressure or coercion. No evidence-based medicine is available on this topic. Unfortunately, no randomized controlled studies have been done on early-versus-late toilet training, and I hope that in a few years some will be performed to give a new option to children and parents."[44]

2007 – Commentary by Dr. Natalya Davis, FAAP

Dr. Davis, a board-certified pediatrician practicing in New York, has also had personal experience with infant elimination training and reported: "There are many reasons to practice EC. It increases parent-child closeness, bonding and communication, not to mention infant comfort. However, as a pediatrician I have come to realize that the self-awareness EC fosters and the gradual accumulation of knowledge the infant receives about elimination are key. Placing an infant on a potty early in life teaches him about his muscles of elimination and proper receptacles in addition to improving hygiene. The process also preserves early self-awareness of elimination and fosters that awareness, just as it preserves and fosters communication between the parent and infant.

"Elimination should really be viewed as another facet of a child's development, but unfortunately Western medicine does not yet recognize it. The American Academy of Pediatrics encourages parents to wait for the child to be entirely ready developmentally and physically before commencing toilet training. Nothing is as all-or-nothing in pediatric development early on as toilet training according to the AAP. In every subject save one—elimination—my Western pediatric training holds to the same mantra: development is a gradual process composed of infinitesimal steps along a continuum allowing improvement of an infant's skills. There may be bigger jumps at times as well as setbacks, but the pathway is still clearly a gradual progression.

"Development is necessarily a continuum. From infanthood babies are encouraged to have tummy time to strengthen their neck muscles, given ample floor room for first rolling, then crawling and finally walking and running. Also babies are encouraged to feed themselves first by hand, then using a spoon and fork. Proficiency is gradual, and teaching with successively more difficult tasks begins at birth. Newborns cannot formulate words, but that does not preclude parents from talking to them and encouraging them to mimic, then to utter syllables, words, and eventually sentences as they grow older. So too with elimination, development should be gradual with successively more difficult tasks. A parent begins the process supporting the infant completely. As communication improves, the baby's role increases. Encouraging elimination communication early on is the first logical step toward eventual independent toileting.

"Parents often ask me about toilet training. Unfortunately this conversation usually occurs around age two, sometimes as 'early' as 18 months. In stark contrast to my comfort in discussing gradually improving a child's skills in other areas of development, I am not always comfortable advising on toilet training infants. This is due to my education on toileting (or lack of it) as a pediatrician in this society. My pediatric training does not even offer EC as an option. It is as if no other possibilities exist. In fact, I discovered infant potty training independently, outside of my medical training and have used it with my own child. I know it can work, as I have experienced for myself, and it should be portrayed as a valid option by the medical world.

"Excuses by the rare privileged physicians who are aware of EC and its possibilities include the busy, hectic world of the parent. But we are not too busy (hopefully) to allow children to practice self-feeding and other skills before they can be proficient at them. Why should toilet training be any different? Can it be done in a busy society with working parents? Certainly. Development does not halt when parents are at work and are too busy for their children. Diaper changes take time and effort. There is no reason why including a potty trip into one's daily routine should be impossible."[45]

Commentary by Psychologists

2003 & 2005 – Books by Dr. Linda Sonna, PhD

Dr. Linda Sonna, psychologist and author, has written two books that provide much hope for spreading the word about infant potty training. In *The Everything Potty Training Book* and *Early-Start Potty Training*, Dr. Sonna emphasizes that if parents have the time and energy, it is best to begin during early infancy. Otherwise, she strongly recommends beginning shortly after babies can sit up by themselves. She considers it unfortunate that most parents wait until the toddler years, when children typically resist sitting still due to their mobility and high energy level, and resist following directions as the longing for independence increases and autonomy struggles intensify. While working on her book, she determined that standard recommendations from professionals rest on a single 40-year-old study conducted by T. Berry Brazelton, a "paid spokesman for Pampers disposable diapers. That study was too flawed to yield any trustworthy conclusions."[46]

"Brazelton warned that to begin before children had achieved adequate sphincter control was likely to create psychological difficulties that might well translate into a significant delay in skill acquisition, and he attributed chronic problems with bedwetting to premature training efforts." Sonna has not found any evidence to support these claims. "While some children do self-train virtually overnight if nothing is done until close to age three, habits of wetting and soiling are well entrenched by then, and many youngsters require a lot of time and have considerable difficulty. It is no longer unusual for children age four to still be in diapers.

"As a result of all of the warnings about the need for toddler readiness, the myth that younger toddlers (and some older ones) lack sphincter control began winding its way through the pediatric community. Amazingly, the knowledge that infants in fact have sphincter control was lost in two short generations."[47]

"In actuality, potty training does not pose any special risk to children's psyches. Teaching youngsters to use the potty is like teaching them to do most anything else. They need to be shown what to do and how to do it. . . . Harsh treatment of children is uncalled for and can traumatize them regardless of the issue; there is nothing special about potty training" in this respect.[48]

2007 – Commentary by Dr. Thomas S. Ball, PhD

My journey toward the recognition of the true significance of early infant toilet training began in the back wards of a state facility for the developmentally disabled. The custodial treatment of these profoundly disabled individuals was based on the unchallenged assumption that they were totally incapable of learning self-help skills, including toileting. Then, in the early 1960s, reports began to emerge regarding the development of a totally innovative training approach based upon Skinner's and Breland's work in operant conditioning. These reports seemed incredible—until I witnessed, firsthand, evidence to the contrary. Thus, operant behavior-shaping of self-help skills had resulted in a radical reassessment of the learning potentials of severely disabled people.

Several years later, I was fortunate enough to encounter in the person of Lela Humphries. Lela, a modest and unassuming teacher at the Forest Meadows Development Center in San Rafael, California, had toilet trained two normal boys and one Down syndrome child before they could walk. In the context of general American culture of the time, this was an unheard of achievement. For me, it was immediately apparent that her methods were highly consistent with the operant conditioning model of learning. In fact, for the most part, they were based almost entirely upon the selective reinforcement (reward) of spontaneous (emitted) behavior. Here was my second encounter with what should have resulted in a radical reassessment of the learning potential of a group of human beings (babies under one year of age).[49]

Anatomy 101

Urination and defecation involve the use of both voluntary and involuntary muscles. As the name suggests, "voluntary" muscles are those over which we have conscious control, while "involuntary" muscles are not under our conscious control.

A child who begins toilet training in infancy can learn to control the voluntary muscles of the urinary bladder and bowels at the earliest moment possible. By the time he gains full control of these muscles, he is thoroughly acquainted with a grown-up toilet routine.

The main muscles involved in going to the toilet are the sphincter muscles. These help control both the bowels and bladder. They are circular muscles that constrict an orifice. In a normal contracted condition, they hold the orifice closed. In order to allow the orifice to open, the sphincter muscles must relax.

The ileocecal valve and puborectalis muscle play a role in defecation. "The colon is equipped with an inlet valve (the ileocecal valve) and an outlet valve (the puborectalis muscle). Squatting simultaneously closes the inlet valve to keep the small intestine clean and opens the outlet valve to allow wastes to pass freely. The sitting position defeats the purpose of both valves, making elimination difficult and incomplete. The sphincter muscle, commonly regarded as the outlet valve, is actually not capable of preventing incontinence. It involves voluntary effort and is only for short-term emergencies. Maintaining

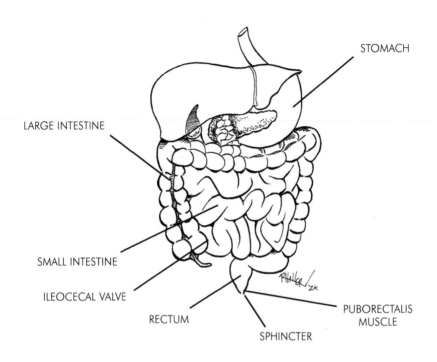

STOMACH

LARGE INTESTINE

SMALL INTESTINE

ILEOCECAL VALVE

RECTUM

SPHINCTER

PUBORECTALIS MUSCLE

continence requires the continuous grip of the puborectalis muscle. This grip is not released in the sitting position, so it must be forced open by straining." Infants of every culture instinctively use a squatting position for elimination as this is the way the human body was designed to function. Squatting makes elimination faster, easier and more complete by relaxing the puborectalis muscle.[50]

Doctors and medical books typically state that the sphincter muscles mature between 20 and 24 months of age. It is mainly on this basis that many have never considered the possibility that a child can start potty learning before 1 or 2 years of age. They do not take into account the many babies whose muscles develop before 20–24 months and do not consider the fact that infants are able to release urine and bowel movements upon association with a signal. The very first time your infant responds to your cueing, you will see that your infant does indeed have some control over his "toilet muscles." Many medical professionals also do not consider societal factors such as acculturation, support, parental devotion and lifestyle choices.

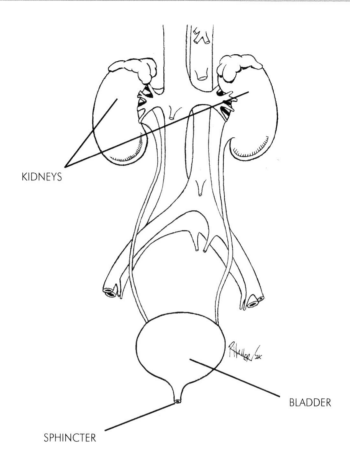

KIDNEYS

BLADDER

SPHINCTER

Medical Conditions

Some infants under 6 months suffer from a gastrointestinal disorder called dyschezia or uncoordinated stooling. The symptoms are: crying for 20–30 minutes by a healthy child, straining excessively, turning red in the face and screaming when trying to defecate. Although these symptoms are distressing for all concerned, the good news is that infants with dyschezia just need time to learn how to relax and release BMs and will eventually outgrow the condition. Parents assume it is constipation, but if the stools are soft and free of blood, it's likely dyschezia. "These infants have not yet coordinated the increase in intra abdominal pressure with pelvic floor relaxation so they are unable to enjoy easy defecation. Crying is the infant's attempt to create intra-abdominal pressure before they learn to bear down more effectively for a bowel movement."[51] Holding baby in the in-arms squatting position can help with this condition until he eventually learns how to pull his legs up to relax the pelvic floor and release the stools.[52]

Constipation means infrequent, hard stools. Grunting and straining do not necessarily indicate constipation. Exclusively breastfed babies are never truly constipated since breast milk is a low residue diet. Almost all of the milk is absorbed and used, which results in infrequent stools but not constipation. It is more common among bottle-fed infants, babies eating solids[53] and children over 2 years old. Since painful bowel movements can lead to potty refusals and withholding, it's a good idea to check regularly to see if the stools are soft. There are many causes of constipation.[54] Stool withholding is a possible cause since a child typically contracts the perineal muscles while the bladder and rectum are constricting. Stool toileting refusal (STR) occurs when a child uses the toilet for pee but refuses to poo in the toilet for at least 1 month.[55] Stool withholding and STR rarely occur when using infant pottying.

Treatments for constipation include commonsense diet modifications, gentle tummy massages, squatting rather than sitting to poop, warm baths (for minor cases) and medication. If constipation persists, discuss the matter with a doctor.

Babies are especially vulnerable to urinary tract infections (UTIs) because the fecal matter in their diapers can introduce bacteria into the urethra. Girls are more at risk because their urethras are short and straight, providing an easy means for bacteria to enter the bladder, the ureters, and even the kidneys. A bladder infection can cause loss of bladder control, frequent and/or painful urination, pain just above the pubic area or on the side, fever and lethargy.[56] IPT babies rarely suffer from UTIs since (a) diaper use is reduced and eliminated relatively early in life and (b) EC parents are diligent about changing soiled diapers in a timely manner. Moreover, if an EC baby does contract a bladder infection, his parents are likely to discover and treat the problem in the early stages.

Another medical situation where IPT can be of help is if your child needs to take a urine test to diagnose a medical condition. In some facilities, this is done to babies by using a catheter. You can avoid this painful and traumatic procedure by letting your doctor know that your baby can pee on cue for you. Request to use an adult collection bag or container instead of a catheter.

Enuresis (also called nocturnal enuresis), is the involuntary release of urine after the age by which bladder control should have been achieved. According to Western medicine, voluntary control of urination is usually present in children by the age of 5 years. For children younger than 5 years, the term bedwetting is used to describe the inability to control urination at night. Three processes that alone or in combination can cause enuresis are:

- lack of arginine vasopressin (AVP), a hormone that slows down urine production
- low functional bladder capacity or overactivity of the bladder (uninhibited bladder contractions)
- inability to awake upon sensing a full bladder

In 2005, Canadian researchers reported an association between the early achievement of developmental milestones and early nighttime bladder control. They found that babies of immigrant mothers in Canada achieved earlier milestones and nighttime bladder control than Canadian babies, suggesting that parental intervention, cultural attitudes and earlier training can result in earlier development. They also found a co-occurrence of bedwetting, motor/speech development (indications for a possible delay in motor development for boys and in language maturation for boys and girls) prematurity and behavioral problems and concluded that bedwetting "could serve as an early noticeable indicator for potential delays in some spheres of child development."[57]

Parents should also be aware of harmless nonmedical situations that can influence pottying. For example, physical positioning can affect cueing and serve as a clue to puzzling accidents, especially with newborns. If you know your baby needs to go but he does not respond to your cues and instead pees the moment you finally lay him down, this could simply be due to his anatomy. The sphincter muscles automatically clamp shut when there is pressure on them. There is more pressure on the sphincters in an upright position which means that babies have more sphincter control in an upright position. When you lay your baby down, the muscles tend to relax and release the contents of the bladder. If you know it's time for him to go and he is holding back, try reclining him or putting him down briefly to help him relax those muscles, then offer another pottytunity.

In a more general sense, IPT can serve as a diagnostic tool for a variety of conditions and states of mind of babies. For example, when pottying her baby, one mother noticed an abscess on her child. Her doctor diagnosed a perirectal abscess and repaired the problem. Or, as earlier discussed, if a child fusses, cries or screams at potty time, this can alert parents to look for a possible cause such as teething, illness or injury and then allow parents to focus on the problem and find ways to soothe their little ones during times of distress and discomfort.

chapter 11

diapers

Even though the terms "diaperless" and "diaper-free" are often used when referring to EC, diapers are a part of EC in Westernized societies. While some parents always diaper in between potty visits, others strive to only use diapers on occasions when they are too busy or too tired to potty, or when accidents can be disruptive and troublesome, such as on trips or outings, when baby is ill or during times of stress. Either way, families gradually reduce diaper use over the months while enjoying sessions or sometimes even days of diaper freedom along the way.

Your decision to use cloth or disposable diapers will have an impact on your baby's comfort and health as well as on your potty progress. It can also impact the environment and your finances. These findings illustrate these points:

- A child spends about 30 minutes a day eliminating and being changed. He should not have to be stuck in diapers for all the other 23.5 hours a day. [58]
- A baby spends around 25,000 hours in a diaper and needs 6000 or more diaper changes.[59]

Most EC'ers prefer cloth diapers to disposables for a number of reasons. They prefer keeping baby in cotton and other natural fibers. They tend to be more vigilant about pottying and changing babes in cloth and find that infants wearing cloth are more aware of elimination too. Some have found that their babies will "go" in disposables at night but will "hold it" when using underwear or cotton diapers. Since many EC parents are likely to stay at home with baby or arrange one-on-one care in order to have someone reliable available to potty baby—or expeditiously change dirty diapers—they do not often feel a need for the conveniences of disposable diapers. They also tend to believe that using cloth diapers is better for the environment than using disposables.

IPT does not in any way exclude the use of disposable diapers for parents who prefer them. It's a matter of lifestyle choice. All types of diapers can work just fine. The "bottom line" is to reduce and then eliminate the use of diapers sooner rather than later.

Remember to keep a harmonious balance between pottying and all your other activities. Don't be so fanatic about trying to reduce or cease the use of diapers that you lose your perspective or neglect your family or important duties. It is better for your baby to "go" in a diaper or have the occasional accident than to be around an uptight or exhausted parent obsessing about potty perfection.

Cloth or Disposable Diapers?

There are convincing arguments on both sides of the cloth-versus-disposable-diaper debate. Manufacturers and marketers present compelling cases for the superiority of their respective products and the inferiority of their competitors' diapers. Parents need to consider and weigh the facts in relation to their own particular circumstances and lifestyle, then make an informed decision. There are situations where parents may prefer to use one type of diaper but are forced to use another. Don't worry or feel guilty about not being able to use a particular type of diaper if it jeopardizes the health or well-being of your baby or causes you to lose sleep at night.

Some of the main factors to consider when choosing diapers are cost, health, convenience and environment. The environmental impact of diapers is covered in Chapter 12.

Pro-Cloth & Anti-Disposable Arguments

- Cotton is natural and soft and lets baby's skin breathe.
- Cotton diapers are far cheaper to purchase than disposable diapers since only a few dozen cloth diapers are needed as opposed to thousands of disposables. Your savings increase if the cloth diapers are reused with any future children you may have.
- With cloth diapers, you avoid chemical gels, dyes and other possible synthetic irritants. The sodium polyacrylate a.k.a. super-absorbent polyacrylate (SAP) in disposables absorbs urine and stores it as a gel next to baby's skin. For sensitive babies, this chemical can be toxic. It can also stick to infants' genitals. Some of the other ingredients of disposables are heavily treated pulp/cellulose, polyethylene, glues, dyes and synthetic perfumes. The toxic chemical dioxin may also be present.[60]

- There is an array of different types and styles of easy-to-use cotton diapers, including prefolds and flushable refills to use as liners/soakers; fitted or pocket pullups; all-in-one diapers (flannel diapers with attached waterproof covers); and biodegradable diapers. Side snaps and Velcro fasteners make these quick and convenient to use. Covers are available in cotton, wool, fleece, nylon and breathable poly knit. Bamboo diapers are another option.

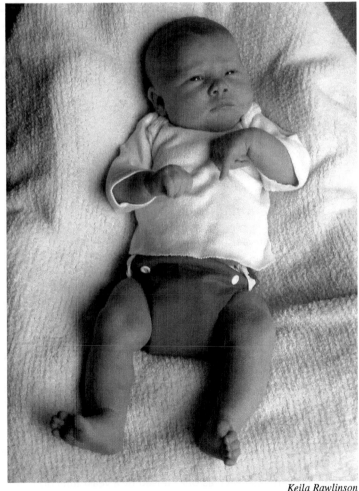

Keila Rawlinson

4-week-old Helen wearing a waterproof cover
with snaps adjustable at the sides.

- Good diapering practices (changing and laundering) can make cloth the equal of disposables in terms of staying dry and avoiding diaper rash.
- Parents don't need to make frequent trips to the store since they only need a fixed supply of cloth diapers.
- Diaper liners catch stools so you don't have to rinse the entire diaper after each poop.
- The word "disposable" leads parents to believe they can dispose of dirty diapers without any effort or bother, yet baby's skin usually needs cleaning with each change of a diaper, and it takes hundreds of years for disposables to decompose in landfills.
- The chemical dryness of disposables lets parents delay changing diapers under the false pretense, "As long as it feels dry, it's all right for baby."[61]
- The feeling of dryness of disposables delays the learning of cause and effect and can add months or as much as one to two years to toilet training a baby who wears disposable diapers full time.
- A cotton diaper has a multitude of handy and baby-friendly uses, including serving as a washcloth, towel, light cover, cushion, sunshade, bib and toy (peekaboo).

Pro-Disposable & Anti-Cloth Arguments

- Child-care centers usually require disposables.
- Disposables are more convenient since you can just throw them away and forget about them.
- Using disposables drastically reduces laundry.
- Disposables are adapted to fast-paced living where parents feel "time challenged" due to work or other reasons.
- Baby feels dry due to the absorption of moisture by disposables.
- Some newer styles change color or let children feel "cool when wet" when they pee.
- For some, disposables may be healthier for the skin and reduce or eliminate diaper rash since they keep baby dry.
- Bad smells are less offensive than with cloth diapers.
- Parents can get away with being lazy about changing diapers.
- Babies and parents are less likely to awake in the middle of the night if baby pees in an absorbent disposable diaper.
- With a severe rash such as one caused by a yeast infection, disposables may be the only way to ensure baby stays rash-free. Since yeast is resistant to hot water and detergent, cloth diapers can continually reinfect baby.

How I Made Use of My One Disposable Diaper

When my youngest son was born, I was given a free sample disposable diaper along with a lot of other sample baby products. Since I preferred cotton diapers, I had no use for the disposable diaper . . .

. . . that is, until one day when I was a passenger on an airport shuttle van. My baby and I were stuck in the van longer than expected. I knew he had to go, but he was still too small to use a potty, and there was no "toilet place" for him to use in the van. I whipped out my sample disposable diaper, opened it up, held him over it and gave the signal to go. He pooed on the diaper from a safe distance above, keeping his little bottom nice and clean. When he was finished, I folded up the diaper and later disposed of it at the airport. That was the only time I used a disposable diaper.

Diaper Rash

The term "diaper rash" refers to a variety of rashes that occur in the area of the body covered by a diaper. Genetics and hygiene contribute to the occurrence or lack of diaper rash. The different types of rash have different causes, but all are exacerbated by wet skin. Causes include:

- friction (typically where moist inner thighs rub together or where elastic rubs the wet skin)
- skin bacteria (bacteria begin to form as soon as baby wets or soils a diaper or underwear)
- irritated skin (typically resulting from skin contact with soaps, detergents or lotions)
- allergic reaction (can affect more than just the diapered area)
- psoriasis (a skin disease that affects more than just the diapered area)
- yeast infections

Most parents have found that diaper rash can be relieved by letting baby be bare-bummed at times. Exposing skin to air is a natural and gentle way to let it dry and be free of irritants.[62]

Diaper rash can be a blessing in disguise if it leads parents to try infant pottying and gives baby the gift of early emancipation from diapers. Families practicing IPT on a fairly regular and consistent basis rarely encounter diaper rash since their babies are rarely in wet or soiled garments.

Diaper Bulk

Imagine an infant, developmentally ready to turn over for the first time ever, being denied this joy for days or weeks whenever she is wrapped in diaper bulk. Or being deprived of the freedom to simply grab her toes whenever she wants, except during diaper changes. Babies love to do all sorts of things with their feet and will touch, grab, hold, gaze at and play with them constantly, often pulling them in front of their face, if given the chance. This early natural behavior must have a purpose, yet is limited by wearing diapers. How about the joys of wiggling and squirming and of being able to twist and bend as far as your little body, joints and muscles will allow without restriction. Or feeling, exploring and being touched on that whole sensitive area of your body, from waist to thighs, that is otherwise often "out of bounds."

More sophisticated coordination can be hampered too. Parents who let their babies go diaper-free during some or all of the day report that their children scoot, sit, crawl, squat and walk sooner than when swaddled in diapers. Here is what some parents have to say about diaper bulk:

- "When my baby has a diaper on, it slows her down. Without the diaper, she scoots all over the place, and earlier than our other children did since they always had diapers on."
- "The first time my son pulled himself up onto his knees and into a sitting position, he was not wearing a diaper."
- "For us, the diaper bulk restriction was most noticeable with sitting. It is *so* hard to sit on a big lumpy diaper!"
- "Jutta was able to roll over onto her tummy and then back onto her back about 3 weeks earlier without diapers than with diapers—at around 15 weeks without the diapers."
- "Katherine sits more gracefully, instead of just plopping down on a padded bum. Instead, she gently lowers herself down from standing."

By reducing diaper use, you are not only advancing toilet learning and helping the environment. You are also giving your baby a head start in physical development.

chapter 12

environmental issues

Perhaps not a day passes without some scary gloom-and-doom environmental statistics being paraded in front of us or forced down our heavily polluted throats. Everything, it seems, is bad for us, bad for our health, bad for the world, bad for the atmosphere and bad for . . . baby!

While the selection of a preferred toilet teaching technique is certainly not a life-and-death issue, there are consequences beyond convenience to consider. Many concerned families are first attracted to IPT when they learn how environmentally sound and beneficial it is, and in this respect it's true that "You can make a difference."

Even for those who are "turned off" by environmentalists, bored with apocalyptic predictions, dislike radical environmentalist tactics and resent the erosion of our freedoms and bank accounts via legislation instigated by certain environmental organizations, there is no denying the environmental damage caused by conventional toilet-training methods. Using an environment-friendly means of potty training does not involve donating money or otherwise supporting any particular group, since there is no environmental movement promoting this method. Instead of donating dough to a cause, families using IPT actually save a considerable amount of money on diapers, laundry, water and other costs.

An average baby uses 6,000 or more diapers by the time conventional toilet training is completed—and the quantity is increasing among families who delay longer and longer. Whichever type of diaper is used, tremendous amounts of resources are required to manufacture and clean or dispose of them. Although it may be more convenient in some respects to use traditional diapering methods for two to four years, the detrimental effects of "full-time diapers" (whether disposable or cloth) on the environment cannot be denied. By lessening or eliminating the use of diapers, you can conserve natural resources, decrease pollution and reduce your carbon footprint.

Water

Tremendous amounts of water are heated and used to clean the following:

- cloth diapers
- dirty baby bottoms, hands, legs and other body parts
- wet/soiled baby clothes, bedding, towels, mattress covers
- caregivers' hands after changing diapers

Water is polluted by laundering cloth diapers and manufacturing disposable diapers. Flushing disposable diapers down the toilet clogs sewer lines, creates tons of extra sludge each year and wastes large amounts of water.[63]

Trees

More than one billion trees go into the manufacture of disposable diapers in one year.[64] It takes the pulp from one tree to make 500 to 1,000 disposable diapers.[65] At that rate, you save 10 to 20 trees per child by using IPT.[66]

Manufacturers of disposable diapers claim that the tree population is actually increasing thanks to them. The fact that tree farming is profitable encourages the planting and careful management of more and more trees as the demand increases. This, they say, results in more trees being planted than are cut down. No rare or endangered trees are used to make disposable diapers.[67]

Landfills

Nobody thinks twice about making a mountain out of a landfill. And this is what appears to be happening all over the Western world, and in particular, the USA. Although the statistics vary and there is no way to determine exact figures, it must be evident even to the most environmentally disinterested that disposable diapers take a lot of space in landfills. Diapers are the third most dumped consumer product found in American landfills (after fast-food containers and newspapers).[68] The number of disposable diapers used in a year in the USA is staggering, somewhere around 27 billion.[69] This translates to more than five million tons buried in landfills each year. The annual cost to taxpayers for disposal of disposable diapers is around half a billion dollars.

Groundwater can become contaminated by viruses carried in the human feces and urine from disposable diapers. Flies and other insects drawn to the diapers can also spread viruses and bacteria. The most common diseases that are currently spread via diaper waste in landfills in Western countries are:

- enteroviruses (diarrhea and other intestinal diseases)
- rhinoviruses (influenza, common cold, etc.)[70]

In lesser developed lands, the situation becomes more hazardous to the health. More than 100 different intestinal viruses can be excreted in human feces, including hepatitis and—via vaccines passed in urine—polio. Although disposable diapers are used in far greater quantities in Western compared to third world countries, the use of disposables is gradually increasing in the larger cities of many nonindustrialized and developing countries. Finally, traces of the toxic industrial contaminant dioxin can be found in some disposable diapers. This can be harmful to both baby and the environment.

Biodegradable?

So-called biodegradable diapers are made of cornstarch-based plastic, biodegradable elastic, wood pulp and rayon, and they are chemical free. However, biodegradable disposable diapers don't solve the landfill problem. They have been shown to decompose in two to five years in a laboratory, but in fact take much longer (up to 500 years) to decompose in a landfill, due to compaction and lack of sunlight, water and oxygen.[71] Although they may decompose faster than standard disposables, they still use the same space in landfills, and the health risks are the same. The only way for biodegradable diapers to be environmentally effective is to have them processed by a sewage plant.

In terms of the environment, gDiapers are a better option because they break down in 50-150 days. They are plastic-free and breathable. They consist of a washable cotton cover and a snap-in waterproof liner that holds absorbent inserts that are flushable, disposable and compostable. The liners use SAP to keep babies dry. SAP reduces the chances of diaper rash for most but causes rashes (due to the chemicals) for others. Some parents improvise their own substitute liners.

Diaper Services

Diaper services are not a very environmentally friendly solution to pollution. In some ways, use of a diaper service merely passes the problems on to someone else.

Many of the services use large amounts of toxic chemicals, including chlorine bleach and other polluting agents, to get diapers as white as possible. The diapers must be collected and delivered, requiring fuel and adding to traffic congestion and air pollution.

For parents who prefer to use a diaper service, here are some positive points to ponder. Less electrical energy is used this way since the diapers are washed collectively.[72] Cloth diapers can be reused, and this spares trees. Plastics and other unnatural materials are not present in cotton diapers. Using a diaper service is cheaper than buying disposable diapers. You don't need to make frequent trips to the shop to buy disposables since you only need a fixed supply of cloth diapers. You will reduce your weekly garbage pile and cut down on waste going into landfills. Last but not least, you can send the laundry out for someone else to do.

So What?

Despite the statistics cited in this chapter and the fact that a widespread educational campaign could greatly benefit the environment, environmental groups have, for all intents and purposes, remained indifferent to the idea of reducing or eliminating diapers through infant pottying. IPT is not an "easy sell" in this regard. There are no frightening or heart-rending photos and no videos of endangered species that can be used to outrage the population in order to extract large donations or allow the media to sensationalize the topic.

Another disinterested group consists of parenting magazines, even those advocating a natural lifestyle. Both mainstream and alternative parenting magazines find IPT too much of an "inconvenient truth" to promote. In addition, magazines lack the courage to include much more than a brief mention of it, preferring to remain loyal to lucrative advertising "diaper dollars."

On an individual level, parents may think, "So what? Who cares about these environmental statistics?" One baby's worth of diapers may not seem to matter. But when the diapers of many thousands of babies are compiled, compacted or cleansed, the toll on the environment and our natural resources is staggering. It is our children and grandchildren who will have to deal with the mess we are making. One effective way to cut back on pollution and depletion is to reduce or eliminate the use of diapers. Since environmental groups have so far not embraced the cause and the media and parenting magazines only occasionally broach the topic, the role of individual responsibility takes on tremendous importance here.

chapter 13

dispelling the myths

This chapter presents a compilation of counterarguments to some common myths and misconceptions. Skepticism can be tough to handle. If you are facing negativity and resistance, you may find it helpful to read and reflect on the ways these myths and rumors can be dispelled.

"It's about Potty-Trained Parents" . . .

When people first hear of infant potty training, one of the common retorts is that it is the parents who are potty trained, not the baby, thus implying that baby has nothing to do with the process. The naysayers do not realize that adult and child communicate, work together as a team and thus undergo reciprocal learning and reinforcement. They do not understand that an infant has some control over elimination and that, when acknowledged and encouraged, this ability improves gradually over the months with the help of an attentive caregiver, until total control is eventually achieved.

Does the fact that a baby cannot take care of his needs such as eating and dressing mean we should ignore those needs? Of course not. Then why should a parent be criticized for taking care of baby's elimination needs in a loving and different way?

If learning to recognize when baby is tired or hungry is a form of training, then in this regard, learning to read and respond to elimination signals could also be considered parent training. When viewed from this positive perspective, parents are proud to be considered "trained."

"It's Purely a Matter of Catching" . . .

Some argue that EC is just about "catching" pees at the right time, and that it's merely a matter of luck. Luck is indeed part of the equation, especially at the start, but certainly not the whole equation. For the first few days or weeks as you are learning to communicate with each other about elimination, it might well be a question of "catching" baby's waste in a receptacle, but once a cue association is established, it's mainly matter of communication, responsiveness and teamwork.

Many parents use the word "catch" in a positive sense. If someone says "I caught 5 pees today" that means "I got 5 pees in the potty or toilet instead of a diaper." There is thus a difference between a "conscious catch" or a "cued catch" as opposed to a "lucky catch." There might be some luck involved at times, but in the long run, it's the communication and teamwork that result in the most catches.

"It's Impossible" . . .

Upon first hearing about infant pottying, some assume it's fake or just a passing fad. The denial is so strong that some refuse to believe toilet-training accounts coming from their own mothers. Such a defeatist attitude guarantees failure. Even Dr. Brazelton agrees that it is possible, as evidenced by his opening statement in a 2005 syndicated article: "Can babies be toilet-trained in the first year? Of course!"[73] He has seen it firsthand abroad. In many societies, families *know* it is possible. The combination of their history and confident attitude go a long way towards making it possible. The testimonials and cross-cultural studies presented in this book demonstrate not only that infant potty training is possible but also that it is prevalent and has been the norm for generations in many parts of the world.

"Babies Have to be Naked All the Time" . . .

There is absolutely no requirement for nakedness or going "nakey butt." These are nothing more than options and lifestyle choices. Some parents find that their children learn faster if they are able to spend some "nakey-butt time" at home, while others experience the opposite.

The terms "diaper-free" and "diaperless" may at first seem to imply that diapers are not used, but once parents become familiar with the basics, they realize that most families use diapers, training pants, underwear or other clothing in between potty visits.

"You Have to Constantly Monitor Your Baby " . . .

No way should an EC parent constantly monitor a baby. The only time this should happen is during an hour or two of the observation phase at the start. You do not need and should not attempt to be present for every elimination.

"You Have to Continuously Carry Your Baby " . . .

This is not a requirement at all. While some parents elect to "wear" their babies in a sling, rebozo, or other carrier and feel it helps with their EC progress, many do not carry their babies and do just fine too.

"Baby Isn't Ready" . . .

Baby *is* ready! Western medicine teaches that children are not physically or psychologically ready to start toilet training until they are 18 months or older (Europe) or 2–3 years old (USA). Both theories have been disproved by billions of families around the world. In other societies, parental communication, constructive expectations, training and guidance are the keys to readiness and eventual success.

Some claim that infants aren't ready for toilet training since they cannot speak, walk to the potty, undress or seat themselves unassisted. But these prerequisites are irrelevant where infants and IPT are concerned. As one mother put it, "It's like saying a baby is not ready to learn to walk before he can tie his shoes."

"It's Dangerous" . . .

Those who declare that IPT is harmful have never met or observed a family using it and have no idea what it entails. Instead, they read accounts that refer to a different, coercive and outdated method of early toilet training. Furthermore, children's psychological problems, if any, usually stem from their overall relationship or a lack of communication with their parents rather than from one particular aspect or phase. The relatively few Western doctors who have remained skeptical after witnessing IPT abroad have either not given it serious consideration ("far too primitive for a modern lifestyle") or else believe parents are incapable of dedicating the time and patience needed. To categorically dismiss infant pottying due to the latter view is tragic and belies the strength, devotion and love of those who want to use it.

"It's Too Time-Consuming" . . .

IPT is as time-consuming as you let it be. It can be done on a part-time basis. It should not reduce the time spent helping baby with other tasks. Parents are advised to establish and maintain a healthy balance in all that they do. Good time management is key. Perfectionists need to let go of unrealistically high expectations. IPT emphasizes that a relaxed parental attitude is essential and warns against "overdoing it" as this can lead to negative reactions, burnout or giving up. Many parents find that IPT is less time-consuming than full-time diapering since it is quicker and easier to catch elimination in a container. Many also find that IPT lends itself to "multitasking."

"It Takes Just as Long" . . .

A favorite argument used to discourage families is to claim that EC takes equally as long, or even longer, than conventional methods. This is generally false if EC is done correctly and especially if all the years of diapering involved with conventional training are included in the equation. Even more important, infant pottying is not about competition or finishing at a certain age.

"Wearing Diapers Is Part of Being a Baby" . . .

Some parents feel that wearing diapers is part of being a baby and that IPT is a way to "rush baby to grow up." They want baby to be a baby as long as possible, and this includes using diapers. What they don't realize is that most IPT parents *do* use diapers for quite a while. When, where, how many and how often diapers are used is a matter of preference and choice.

There have been, and still are, far more babies in the world raised without diapers than with diapers. In societies where IPT has been the norm for centuries, babies are "babied" and coddled much more than in industrialized countries where full-time diapers are used, since IPT inherently involves lots of physical contact and cuddle time with your baby.

Babies are born with the ability to communicate about elimination. The fact that some parents choose to recognize and respond to a baby's elimination communication does not mean their baby is being forced to grow up in a hurry. Any tool that enhances communication between baby and caregiver is valuable. A baby who goes in a receptacle is just as much a baby as a baby who goes in a diaper.

Finally, those who use the "pushing baby to grow up" argument are proud and thrilled if their own babies attain milestones such as walking or talking early. They don't feel they have pushed their babies to grow up, so why do they attack families who help their babies learn a different skill early in life?

"It's Too Inconvenient" . . .

With relatively few exceptions, toilet training is by definition inconvenient no matter when you start. Many parents lapse into a fast-food mentality about it. They want it fast, they want it now and they want it to be easy; otherwise, they opt to put it off for as long as they can. Now that disposable diapers are more absorbent than ever and, through the use of super absorbent gels, give babies the feeling of being dry the moment they pee, many are delaying potty training even longer. Daycare centers abound with children ages 3 and 4 who have not yet begun, and disposables have increased the largest size to size six.

Each time baby poos, and frequently when he pees, something must be done. Parents can do that "something" immediately before the fact or else sometime after the fact. Either way, elimination requires attention, time and energy. Many EC parents find that it is easier and more hygienic to potty their babies and empty a container than to let their babies go in a diaper and then have to change and clean their babies and take care of dirty diapers.

"It's for Parents' Convenience" . . .

In a letter to the editor in *Mothering* magazine,[74] a reader argued that helping baby avoid going in a diaper is a matter of convenience for caregivers and is "Victorian" in its "repressive, antilife aspects." Readers of this book will note that none of the text or testimonials refer to infant pottying as "convenient." It has been repeatedly emphasized that it takes dedicated, devoted, patient and diligent caregivers to work closely with baby. Granted, mothers appreciate not having to clean many diapers, but this is also beneficial for baby since avoiding contact with waste is far more hygienic and comfortable than sitting in a soiled diaper. In addition, many babies dislike being held down for diaper changes, and the battles resulting from this tend to increase over time.

The word "repressive" refers to excluding something from the conscious mind. This book repeatedly refers to the stimulation and encouragement of baby's awareness of elimination functions, as well as to the symbiotic relationship of mutual benefit to baby and caregiver that develops. Indispensable elements of this close relationship include bonding, intimacy, communication, caring, patience and respect.

For those who care to see things from a different viewpoint, the convenience argument is reversible—and certainly the way mothers in many other societies view the issue. Diapers are used for parents' convenience. We force babies to wear diapers because it's easier to leave them in diapers than pay attention and quickly respond to their signals. Parents can and often do delay changing a diaper until it is convenient to do so. The washing machine, disposable diapers and diaper services have liberated women a great deal. Liberation from hand-washing diapers has led to babies' imprisonment in diapers. (This argument is *not* intended to instill guilt in anyone using a different method.)

"It's Unhygienic" . . .

The idea of babies going diaperless leads some to conclude that these babies pee and poo all over the house. While some diaperless babies have occasional accidents indoors, infant pottying does not involve letting children eliminate whenever and wherever they please. With IPT, waste typically goes directly into a receptacle without first being smeared on baby's skin or handled by caregivers.

"It's Obsessing about Bowel Movements" . . .

This is another ridiculous argument that has nothing to do with reality. Again, it is offered out of ignorance, by those who are referring to a different method of toilet training or to their own strange hang-ups. There is no obsessing about bowel movements. Instead, caregivers are attentive and, when possible, watch for signals from baby in order to know when to potty him. There is certainly nothing wrong or obsessive with monitoring and being receptive to baby's signals and natural timing.

"Freud Says" . . .

Sigmund Freud's famous but outdated postulation that early toilet training leads to the development of the anal character traits of orderliness, cleanliness and miserliness has never been proven. The theory is good fodder for gossip but nothing more. The influence of toilet training on personality is debatable at best, with many psychologists believing that Freud's list of character traits are the by-product of other child-rearing practices or the child's upbringing as a whole. In any case, his theory was based on a different, old and harsh toilet training method. See Chapter 14 for a description.

chapter 14
history & theories

Toilet Training by Early Man

It seems plausible that in the earliest of times, baby's elimination was managed from birth. In warmer climates where clothing was not needed, it was easy to observe and anticipate elimination timing. Small babies were held and carried at all times since it was too dangerous to leave them on the ground or unattended. This made it easy to notice and immediately act on baby's signals. There were no elaborate home furnishings to worry about and little concern if a baby peed on anyone since no one wore expensive clothing. All this allowed for a relaxed, casual and natural approach.

It seems likely that the first substantial use of skins, furs or plant material to catch infant elimination would have been with populations migrating to cooler climates where babies needed to be clothed for warmth. Clothing infants made it more difficult to be responsive to elimination cues since it is not as easy to notice when babies go or need to go, plus it another step (undressing) to the procedure.

Western Attitudes 1400–1800

In 1472, the first medical book ever published was about the care of children. Author Paolo Bagellardo discussed the problem of bedwetting "not only up to the age of five or six, but sometimes even into puberty"[75] and offered an array of sometimes strange remedies.

Before the 1800s, personal and public hygiene was not an issue. There was no plumbing and no such thing as a bathroom as we know it today. Toilet training was of little concern to parents since babies were swaddled much of the time, and people believed a dirty child was a healthy child. There are no references to toilet training in child-rearing manuals of the day.[76]

Well-wrapped swaddling clothes served as both a babysitter and a diaper. Babies could be ignored and left alone or bundled in a corner for hours since the swaddling prevented their moving about the room or house. Babies were changed infrequently. Their bottoms were wiped and powdered with the dust of worm-eaten wood (the baby powder of the past) but rarely washed with soap and water. Soiled and wet swaddling cloths were dried by the fire, often without a washing, then reused. At the end of the 17th century, philosopher John Locke recommended putting babies in a "pierced chair" placed over a chamber pot after meals and leaving them there until they urinated and defecated. This was the precursor to the potty chair which appeared in the 1940s in the form of a small armchair in which a baby could be strapped until he finished his business.[77]

"Early Toilet Training" Method (circa 1840–1950)

In the 19th century, cleanliness became a virtue. Toilet learning was begun at the age of 3 or 4 months, and babies were held over the chamber pot at set times throughout the day.[78] A method known as "early toilet training" was used in the United States for over a century, until the 1950s, and even longer in Europe. Today many Western medical professionals are only vaguely familiar with this method of early toilet training and mistakenly assume that infant potty training is the same.

As the names imply, both early and infant toilet training are started in infancy. Although there were some positive elements to early toilet training, such as the fact that experts and parents recognized baby's ability to learn about elimination early in life, the negative aspects have, unfortunately, come to be associated with and attributed to any form of toilet training in infancy. Methods advocating an early start are labeled "severe." Since none of the negative aspects are a part of infant potty training, it is helpful to compare the two methods. The table overleaf provides a comparison.

Writings on "Early Toilet Training"

The writings on early toilet training are extensive. A short selection of what some American and European experts, authors and publications had to say about it in their day follows. (A much larger and more detailed selection can be found in earlier editions of this book at libraries.)

Early toilet training	Infant potty training
based on the fixed timing of the mother or nurse	based on baby's natural elimination timing
little or no attention paid to baby's signals	based on observing and responding to baby's signals
sometimes recommended the use of punishment	punishment forbidden
advocated use of suppositories and enemas	suppositories and enemas never used
method unnatural	method natural
method baby-unfriendly	method baby-friendly
method inflexible	method flexible
method harsh	method gentle
method strict and rigid	method casual and relaxed
approach negative	approach positive
approach one-sided (adult in control)	approach cooperative ("teamwork")
baby sometimes treated as an object	baby always treated as a feeling, thinking human being
baby sometimes strapped onto potty for long periods of time	baby held in-arms in phase 1 and sits on potty without restraints in phase 2
baby sometimes left alone on potty for long periods of time	baby held in-arms in phase 1; has short potty sessions with parent present in phase 2

1894 & 1903 Luther E. Holt, *The Care and Feeding of Children*
A baby is usually ready to start training by the age of 2 months. "A small chamber, about the size of a pint bowl, is placed between the nurse's knees, and upon this the infant is held, its back being against the nurse's chest and its body fully supported. This should be done twice a day, after the morning and afternoon feedings, and always at the same hour. . . . in a surprisingly short time the position is all that is required. With most infants, after a few weeks the bowels will move as soon as the infant is placed on the chamber." Holt claimed that using suppositories would result in success within 2 months.[79]

1913 Francis Tweddell, *How to Take Care of the Baby*
"The training of a child's bowels should begin at about the second month, and can be done in the following manner. A small pot is placed between the nurse's knees, and on this the baby is seated, taking care to support his body firmly, and to brace his back against the nurse's chest . . . if this is kept up with regularity, and the baby is in good health, he can sometimes be trained in this respect as early as the age of three months. . . . The training of the bladder is not so easily accomplished, but a great deal can be done by the practice of holding a child over the pot about a dozen times a day. In many cases, this is so successful that by the end of the first year diapers can be dispensed with entirely during the child's waking hours."[80]

1914 Mrs. Max West, *Infant Care*
Mrs. West wrote the first in a long series of U.S. government publications (by various authors) entitled ***Infant Care***. "In order to do away with the need for diapers as early in life as possible, the baby should be taught to use the chamber. This training may be begun by the third month, or even earlier in some cases. It should be carried out with the utmost gentleness, since scolding and punishment will serve only to frighten the child and to destroy the natural impulses, while laughter will tend to relax the muscles and to promote an easy movement. In order to be effective, the chamber must be presented to the baby at the same hour every day, usually just before the morning bath, and it must be presented persistently each day until the habit is formed. Much time and patience will be required on the part of the mother."[81] Her 1921 edition advised starting bowel training even earlier—as soon as a mother recovers from delivery—and stated that babies should finish by the end of

the first year. It also recommended: "One device for teaching the baby not to wet is to put him into drawers very young, discarding the diaper much earlier than is usually done. The warm, thick diaper constantly suggests to the baby the idea of wetting and no doubt retards his training in this regard. He will not like the feeling of the wet, cold drawers, and there will be nothing about them to suggest wetting, but rather the reverse."[82] The last edition of *Infant Care* to advocate early training was published in 1951.

1919 C. L. Hull & B. I. Hull, in *Pedagogical Seminary*
The authors collected data on children ranging from 9–31 months and refer to two distinct processes, "the first the power to relax the sphincters at will initiating micturition; the second the power to inhibit spontaneous tendency to such relaxation while in situations inappropriate for micturition."[83]

1921 L. Pouliot, *Hygiène de maman et de bébé*
"It is stated that the newborn urinates almost every time he is undressed, a few seconds after making contact with the air. Knowing that he will urinate, place him in a crouching position above a chamber pot and support his buttocks. This position will induce urination. After some days, the newborn will have made a strong association between the two sensations: the flowing of urine and contact with the chamber pot. He will become accustomed to urinating only in his pot—that is, except during his sleep—and you will have made him clean from his earliest weeks."[84]

1930 H. Litchfield & L. Dembo, *Care of the Infant and Child*
"Many psychologists and behaviorists are of the opinion that an infant can be trained at three months. It is our belief, however, that the reports of infants so trained are somewhat exaggerated. We have not been fortunate in seeing these infant prodigies. It is our opinion that if an infant is trained between the ages of six and nine months its mother is entitled to award herself a blue ribbon."[85]

1930 M. L. Faegre & J. E. Anderson, *Child Care and Training*
"[Bowel] training may begin as early as the sixth week, if the baby is in good physical condition." Concerning "the dry habit," the authors write, "Beginning not later than one year of age, watch the child for several days and note the time it urinates. Place the child on a vessel near the time you have noted and keep a record of the number of times you are successful in anticipating his needs."

The authors recommended a casual, relaxed approach and suggested the child be "taught a simple word, gesture, or grunt to indicate his needs, as soon as he realizes the possibility of control, which is usually between the twelfth and nineteenth months, and cautioned some may not be completely trained until he is 2½ years old."[86]

Infant Toilet Training in Modern Times

Dr. Benjamin Spock became America's child-rearing guru in the 1950s. He recommended a gradual introduction to toilet training around 6 months, once a child could sit with stability. In 1962, Dr. T. Berry Brazelton introduced his readiness theory that claims that a child isn't ready to toilet train before achieving certain communication and motor skills. He warned that early toilet training could cause psychological problems and convinced Western pediatricians that babies cannot have any control before they are 18 months or older (even though he had seen the opposite in other cultures). No proper medical studies back his theory, yet Western medicine continues to follow his guidelines to this day.

In the 1970s, disposable diapers gained widespread use, and the diaper industry grew into a huge money-making enterprise. This made it even easier to delay toilet training. In the 1990s, thanks to a shrinking world via travel and the Internet, information about IPT became more readily accessible to everyday parents.

Over the centuries, the simple and natural method of infant toilet training has hardly changed at all in nonindustrialized parts of the world. It is still the norm for millions of families in Asia and Africa. Some developing countries undergoing industrialization have only slightly modified it to coincide with modern living standards while others have started to use disposable diapers.

Sensitive Periods

Maria Montessori brought the concept of sensitive periods to prominence in the 1960s. A sensitive period is a critical period during development, a time when a child is naturally and optimally receptive to learning a specific task and when a particular event has its greatest consequences. In 1997, Swiss author Rita Messmer encouraged parents to be aware of their children's sensitive periods and recognized infancy as a sensitive period for infant potty training.

"Let's consider people in Africa, the Americas and Asia who traditionally carry their babies on their backs in a sling. Although the babies are usually naked in the sling, they do not pee and excrete on their mothers. The mothers are very tuned in to their babies' elimination needs. A baby signals through his behaviour when he has to go. The mother then quickly swings the baby from the sling and holds him out to the side where he takes care of business. After that the baby is put back in the sling on his mother's back, and the mother carries on with her work. If, occasionally, a mother gets wet, the other mothers laugh at her and she is regarded as a bad mother. The advantage for these people is that the child is naked, so a mother is able to develop a much better feeling for her baby's bodily functions. The babies are quickly cleaned with a little water, and there is no real fuss about anything. Moreover, toilet training never reaches the degree of importance and complexity that we give it in the Western world.

"After reading about these experiences in other cultures, I wanted to give it a try with my own children. I found very quickly that the opinions of many psychologists and pediatricians couldn't be right. When my son Stefan was almost three months old, I held him over the toilet and told him to pee. He was still too small for a potty, couldn't sit on his own, so I did what indigenous women do, but instead of aiming him off to the side, I just held him over the toilet. I hardly finished speaking when a little fountain sprinkled from his penis into the toilet. At first I thought this may be a coincidence. But when the same was repeated over and over, I knew it couldn't be sheer coincidence. I also found that every time I removed his diaper, he seemed to be waiting to be held over the toilet.

"It is clear to me that this sensitive period ends sometime around the fifth month. After that, babies want to go on eliminating in the place they learned to do it and are used to. This could mean that, during the sensitive period, they learned to eliminate in a diaper no matter where they are, and they want to go on doing it this way.

"Many child-rearing books insist that a small child can't control his bladder and warn that early training is useless and harmful. In cases where the sensitive period has been missed, I agree with the psychologists. Early toilet training can be problematic, especially if pressure is used against the child's will and imposes parents' unrealistic expectations of cleanliness. Pressure and control are never the way for children to be toilet trained. There is no moral or pediatric reason for children to be toilet trained early. Such ambitions do more harm than good. "But by being aware of this sensitive period, we can make things easier for ourselves and our babies by letting our babies be in control of their own elimination."[87]

Attachment Parenting

In the early 1980s, pediatrician William Sears coined the term "attachment parenting" ("AP") which refers to the intuitive, high-touch and responsive parenting style he advocates. He defines it as the seven Baby B's: birth bonding, breastfeeding, babywearing, bedding close to baby, belief in baby's cries, beware of baby trainers (rigid and extreme parenting styles that teach you to follow a schedule instead of your baby) and balance (don't be overzealous with AP by neglecting the needs of yourself and your marriage).[88] These practices have been commonplace in many parts of the world for centuries but have not been in use by Westerners until fairly recent times. Interestingly, in societies where AP has been practiced for centuries, infant potty training has also been the norm. In this sense, I consider it to be an eighth Baby B (bladder and bowel awareness).

P.S. . . . Animals Toilet Train from Birth

Most mammals, with the exception of man and possibly the great apes, lick their young from birth, not so much to clean them but to stimulate organic and behavioral development, including the function of elimination. In *Touching: The Human Significance of the Skin*, Ashley Montagu found a common factor in observations reported by persons who work with animals (veterinarians, animal breeders, zoo staffers, farmers and ranchers), namely that:

"The newborn animal must be licked if it is to survive, that if for some reason it remains unlicked, particularly in the perineal region (the region between the external genitalia and the anus), it is likely to die of a functional failure of the genitourinary system and/or the gastrointestinal system."[89] In short, most mammals have to first be stimulated then later taught how to eliminate or they will die. Until this essential function of licking was discovered, many orphaned neonate mammals in captivity could not survive. They can now survive if a caregiver simulates maternal stimulation.

N. Blurton-Jones and Ben Shaul found that baby animals that are cached typically do not eliminate or soil the nest unless stimulated by their mothers. This is presumably a way to avoid attracting predators to the nest by scent.[90]

Why even mention the topic of toilet training by other mammals? It is interesting to note that many other mother mammals deal with the elimination of their young from birth. In their case, it is a matter of life and death, whereas humans have the choice and option to delay toilet learning for years by using diapers.

TESTIMONIALS
– USA

chapter 1
a 10-month-old graduate

Lois Baas is a nurse living in Michigan. She has a BSN from Calvin College. Her husband, Craig, has a BA in psychology. Lois gave up her nursing career to be a stay-at-home mom. She made a conscious decision to use cloth diapers instead of disposables, unaware that there was an even better option to consider, until she read a short piece about "potty untraining." It had very little "how-to" advice but enough information to inspire her to give it a try. Her son responded impressively to the devotion of, and close communication with, both of his parents and their attentiveness to his elimination needs. Much to their surprise and delight, Zachary graduated at 10 months of age. At this point, he met the criteria identified by the Asian and African definition of "toilet trained," namely, being basically accident-free combined with good communication skills that allowed him to signal his toilet needs to his parents. Their amazing story, submitted in 2002 when their son was 2½ years old, follows. Bear in mind that finishing this young in the West is exceptional, and you should not expect the same results. Please do not feel discouraged if your baby takes considerably longer.

I recall my mother sharing that my siblings and I were all potty trained by 2 years of age. I thought this was a realistic goal to strive for with our first child and figured I would follow traditional potty training, but start earlier than many of my peers who were waiting until closer to 2–3 years of age to begin.

However, a brief testimonial in a parenting book inspired me toward a whole different approach than planned. The author wrote of observing infants being trained in a third world country and of successfully using this with her next two babies. Four days later, after reading this account and discussing it with my husband, our 4-month-old son peed for the first time in the toilet. A week later he pooped in the toilet and never soiled another diaper!

Starting Out

From his birth, I had our son wearing cloth diapers with vinyl covers during the day and a disposable for nights. When I began this method, I did away with the vinyl cover when at home during the day and began using cloth diapers with a vinyl cover at night. This way I could easily identify when he peed, as the cloth diaper was obviously wet. I replaced the diaper in between toilet visits and changed it diligently when any sign of wetness occurred during the day (nights are addressed later). The first time I tried to pee Zachary, he went! This was very encouraging and gave me the incentive to continue to pursue this approach. Zachary already had good back and neck control, and I positioned him on the adult toilet as per my limited reading indicated, supporting him against myself as I straddled the seat, sitting (or standing at times) behind him as we faced away from the tank. I was not about to get peed on if possible! As he went, I would say "pee pee," and it wasn't long before positioning him and giving him this verbal cue was all he needed. Eventually all I had to do was position him and he knew to eliminate. When he voided in this position, he emitted a stream over the seat or between the seat and bowl. Could he shoot far! But I was just so thrilled that he went and was learning that I did not make much of it except to get a wipeable mat to replace the toilet rug surrounding the base. I learned to help him with aiming down and this worked until he was big enough to straddle the seat further back; this new positioning allowed him to shoot into the bowl more efficiently without my assistance for aiming downward, and it also eliminated the "skid marks" from his BMs.

Bowel Movements

Bowel movements were easy to identify as Zachary's cues were obvious. He would grunt and grimace, and his face would flush. Observing this, I would take him to the toilet and position him as I did with peeing, and as he went, I would give the cue "do do." At home, positioning in response to these overt cues was eventually all that was necessary. On a rare occasion, if he needed redirection or was away from home, the verbal cue came in handy. His movements were not frequent, though he was breastfed exclusively for 6 months and continued breastfeeding until 18 months. I identified a pattern, too, which helped. He would typically go once a day or every other day, after his mid-morning nursing. This pattern shifted to after his morning snack when he was eating finger foods regularly. If Zachary didn't have a BM, the next day he usually had two. Knowing this, I looked for a second one later in the day or before bedtime. It seemed, too, that he could often wait until he was sitting down to pee to have an impending BM at the same time. By 10 months he was signing and giving other cues (mentioned later) for the potty, not differentiating whether it was to pee or poo. At 15 months he was verbally cueing "do do" every time he needed to go and did what I dubbed the "do do dance" as he would prance around and run to the bathroom.

Peeing

"Catching" pees was elusive. It seemed to be a hit-or-miss phenomenon as Zachary didn't have any obvious cues with these for some time. As I look back, I believe I was gradually tuning in to some sort of timing while I also became aware of his anatomical cues of slight scrotum contraction and penis extension—especially with an *impending* pee. Zachary peed very frequently at first—something you become more aware of when you change a diaper upon each sign of wetness rather than wait until it is saturated. It wasn't uncommon to potty him, put on a fresh, dry diaper, only to have him pee again. Many times he would begin peeing before or just as I got his diaper off and before being positioned on the toilet. This improved as he developed control and when he transitioned to training pants, with easier removal versus diaper pins. If I missed a pee or noticed Zachary in the process, I would give the verbal cue "pee pee," remove his diaper and position him on the toilet to reinforce where to "go." As he gained even more control, he would stop and wait for me to sit him on the toilet before finishing. Initially, running a stream of warm water from a peri-bottle (squeeze bottle) between his legs or running the tap would often promote an impending pee, helping him to relax when first learning. Sometimes other types of distraction helped, like a quick visit from his pet dalmatian or Daddy. Often just sitting for a short time was all it took, with Zachary looking up adoringly at me and my returning his gaze with smiles.

I believe he learned to associate his body's response-to-relaxing to my verbal cue of "relax" as we implemented the above. This wasn't intentional training, but did prove beneficial. If Zachary ever became fussy or signaled to get off the toilet by arching or stiffening up, I would take him off and leave the bathroom, keeping him in-arms and diaperless. I figured those times he didn't have to go yet, but with his great frequency, I anticipated he would need to go soon and would return within 5–10 minutes to try again, with success. Keeping him in-arms assured me of preventing accidents, as he demonstrated a desire to not "go" when being held. Having the diaper off meant ease at returning him to the toilet without interruption. Doing this helped me discover his timing intervals and helped him learn some control as he "waited" to try again.

After a month of "winging" it with the limited information I had, I read *Trickle Treat*. I attempted to discover Zachary's cues, but confirmed that he did not have any obvious signals nor a regular timing pattern. I relied on his subtle anatomical cues and obvious timing patterns, such as upon awakening or after nursing, and on my developing intuition. I would think to myself, "Zachary hasn't gone in a while," or, "Maybe he has to go." If I trusted myself, he rewarded me with going and keeping dry, but if I doubted myself or was distracted, I would miss.

Between 5–6 months, much to my delight, he began to communicate with grunting. This worked well until he began to use this new form of communicating to signal for other things (i.e., to nurse, for attention or to practice newfound vocal abilities). It was at this time that I became unsure of myself and took my son more frequently than necessary to the bathroom. It is easy to misconceive that all this becomes a perfect routine, rather than a development of communication. I soon found out that other mothers went through the same thing and that the best thing to do was back off and relax. It was around this time, too, that I discovered what I call a "warning pee." I would check my son's diaper when uncertain if he had cued and find a warm, wet spot. This prompted me to take him to the bathroom where he would commence to pee a large amount, after patiently waiting for me to remove his diaper and position him. This was a fascinating development in communication during this phase of second-guessing myself. It also reconfirmed that he truly was developing control at such a young age!

Between 6–7 months, Zachary was rolling onto his tummy more frequently, and although he'd signal with his grunt, it was often too late, as this position would put pressure on his bladder. I got into the routine of giving him full reign on his tummy after a nap when he had emptied his bladder thoroughly—having voided a couple of times. Then I would rely on timing to try to toilet him before an accident could occur. Though this was not foolproof, he could play longer in that position uninterrupted. At just 7 months he awoke after rolling onto his tummy for the first time in his sleep. I toileted him and found that he was still dry. I suspect that the pressure on his bladder woke him up, and he was able to wait until he was on the toilet to pee. He was sitting up more now and learning to crawl, too, thus keeping him off his tummy. Other cues began to emerge. Zachary was cueing visually with a beckoning or imploring look. Upon seeing "the look" and responding/taking him to the bathroom, he eliminated with success on the toilet. It was so encouraging! After beginning solids at 6 months, I also became aware that when he seemed to lose interest in eating earlier than usual, it often meant he was concentrating on "going" or was about to "go." As I continued with this method, I was becoming more in tune with him and starting to experience subtler forms of communication. It would just "hit" me that he needed to go, and then I began to connect this with what he was or was not doing at the time. I would share these findings with my husband and he, too, would help me focus in on these cues. How connected I felt with my son!

At 6½ months I introduced Zachary to training pants. I first began for short periods when his timing was more predictable, during late afternoon to early evening. After about a week or so, I bit the bullet and went full time with them, as I found these more convenient (easier and quicker to remove) than a standard cloth diaper with pins. At first, while out and about and at night, I used a vinyl covering over the training pants "just in case." By 7 months he seemed to be able to hold it and wait, demonstrating a degree of development of control that he had not shown even a month prior, and by 8 months I was utilizing training pants with him exclusively, without the vinyl covers. As a result, I became even more in tune with Zachary, being "forced" to focus on him and his communication. We would have 0–3 accidents a day and often go several consecutive days without any accidents. I also began to use a timer to help keep aware of when Zachary needed to pee again, based on his timing. This helped me remember when I was caught up doing other things which were distracting and making me lose focus.

At 9 months, he was able to patiently wait to be positioned before "going." In fact, this seemed to happen almost overnight, when the interval between potty sessions increased from 20–45 minutes to up to 2½ hours, just a week into his 9th month.

Outings

I toileted Zachary upon leaving home and upon reaching our destination. In between, if necessary (depending on the duration of the trip), I relied on timing and cues. Sometimes he would release a tiny trickle of pee when pottied and then not want to go more until we got home. Upon arriving home much later, he would pee a large amount. When he held it this long, I wondered if he sometimes didn't like where I was taking him when we were out. Or maybe it was that when he was not "bursting," he preferred to wait until we got home before peeing. But when he really had to go, it didn't matter where I took him, he would go. I became comfortable pottying Zachary in the great outdoors, if necessary, and became "fluent" in the locations of the local restrooms.

When traveling longer distances, we would pull over to the side of the road. I would position him on my lap straddling my spread thighs, facing away from me out the open passenger doorway of our truck. Upon giving him his verbal cue, he responded just as at home. He first did this at 6½ months. The open door and sitting in the cab provided privacy while he shot a stream away from the vehicle. One time when we were parked at the side of the road for a pee, a police officer pulled up alongside us. My husband explained that we were giving our son a potty break. The officer looked in the vehicle and asked our infant son if he felt better now!

When colder months came, I provided a portable receptacle: a bowl or covered bucket used primarily to pee in as he seemed to do all his BMs at home. When traveling distances versus around town, Zachary typically was lulled to sleep. Then, when he awakened, I would pull over to potty him. As he got older, he often was able to wait until the next exit or rest area. Once he was awake, I would rely on timing, but more often he would signal if he needed to go again.

From 8 months on, the combination of using training pants and the lack of distractions found at home improved my focus on his pottying when we were out. He stayed dry with longer and longer intervals between toileting. Around 9 months, he was consistently dry when away from home and at nights, without accidents, unless I missed or ignored a signal. He was holding it much longer and waiting until I took him to a bathroom or suitable place outdoors.

Developing Communication

Around 8 months, he started to come to me while saying "ma, ma, ma," and then would tap my leg to go potty or nurse. Then he started crawling to the bathroom when he had to go. There were times where he would drop his toys or interrupt his play to do this. If I was sitting on the floor, he would crawl to me and tap me on the leg or else crawl up onto my knees and into my lap if he had to go. At 9 months, I observed him lean towards the bathroom with his imploring look as he watched his father go there to shave. Another example of this type of signaling happened shortly after he had just peed in the toilet and left the bathroom. A few minutes later, he came and tapped me on the leg. I questioned it at first since he had just nursed and been toileted. Then it dawned on me that he probably had to poo, so we went back to the bathroom and he pooed in the toilet!

At 8½–9 months, he was staying dry with rarely an accident, both day and night, and wearing only training pants under his clothes. His cues proved to be reliable. When he would indicate that he didn't need to go, he stayed dry. When he cued to go, he consistently had to go. Occasionally, he would use the more subtle cue of dropping everything to concentrate, so I still needed to be in tune to this.

Near the end of 9 months, he began crawling to the bathroom and pulling himself up to stand at the toilet. He would even open the lid and pat the seat at times, while waiting to be positioned. Other times, he would hold my hand and we would walk to the bathroom together. Also at the end of 9 months, we began instructing him on the ASL sign for "toilet" by making the sign every time we asked if he needed to go and every time we took him to the bathroom. When he gave indication of his need to go, we again would use the sign as we took him into the bathroom. He caught onto the meaning of the sign before he tried to use it. Next, he practiced making the sign, at first not consistently using it at the right time. Then, all of a sudden, within a week of introducing him to the sign, we all clicked with it. He would even sign "toilet" when he heard someone else flush or when someone uttered the word "toilet." Signing was decidedly helpful in public settings such as church in that it was a subtle communication and only we were aware of why we stepped out of the service for a moment! Here are a few things I wrote about his signing at 10 months:

Yesterday while nursing, he took himself off and looked at his fist. He appeared to be signaling, so I asked if he needed to go and gave the ASL sign. He looked thoughtful for an instant, then resumed nursing. After a bit, he again unlatched and signaled. I took him to the bathroom where he pooed in the toilet! Also, as we've been teaching the signing, which has only been about a week, he began to look or lean toward, or crawl to, the bathroom. I've been teaching him the whole process, letting him crawl or helping him walk to the toilet where he opens the lid. I help with undressing and positioning him, then he eliminates, I help with dressing, and together we flush (which he loves!), close the lid, turn off the light and leave the room.

A few days later, while he was happily playing, I realized it was quite a while since he'd "gone" so I inquired, "Do you have to go potty?" and gave the ASL sign. He looked at my hand, dropped everything, crawled to the toilet and lifted the lid as he waited for me to get him undressed to go. When he is in-arms and I ask both verbally and with the hand signal, he pats the hand I am using to "sign" when he has to go. Otherwise, I see him either stare at the fist he makes or else position his thumb as he waves the fist around. He can't twist his fist yet so can't quite get the sign right. Also, he tries to get his thumb positioned between the forefinger and middle finger but doesn't always manage this yet. Then, instead of making the sideways twisting motion with his fist/wrist, he waves it! When he cuddles up over my shoulder, I feel the movement of his signing. The "waving motion" with his arm makes his cue pretty obvious when I cannot see his hand. And tonight while nursing him, I was sleepy and may have dozed a bit. I suddenly noticed he was off the breast and that he was "waving" over and over, so I took him to the bathroom for a pee. He signals clearly and most certainly knows what it means!

At some point, he figured out that if I was closer to the bathroom than he was, he could get a free ride to the bathroom in my arms, and resorted to "the look" when crawling towards me or calling out to me. He was a very resourceful little boy!

He began to say "bah, bah" for "potty" around 10½–11 months, in addition to signing. This was his first verbal communication to eliminate. He began to say "potty", "pee pee," and "do do" around 14–15 months and eventually dropped the signing altogether.

Nights

I did not address nights initially when I began this training. From birth, he slept in a bassinet in our room and then transitioned to his own room around 3 months. Any time he awoke, we did not automatically assume it was to nurse and checked his diaper and changed it as necessary. By just over 4 months, almost a week after beginning infant potty training, he was sleeping through the night. Interrupting his nights to potty him had never occurred to me.

When Zachary was about 6½ months old, I had found and read more material on this method and discovered his restlessness at night was a cue for his need to pee. If I ignored his restlessness, he would often go in his sleep. When I responded and toileted him just as I did during the day, he would pee, then return to bed asleep, no longer restless as he had been prior to being toileted. I now felt challenged to pursue nights in addition to my daytime focus, to meet his toileting needs around the clock. An underlying concern I held was long-term bedwetting, especially since I had a boy. This was something that ran in both sides of the family. Having read that this method tends to prevent this also attracted me to address nights. I had already switched to using cloth diapers with a vinyl covering prior to this time as the disposables made it difficult to determine if he was waking up dry or not (such absorbency!). I am sure, too, that wearing cloth diapers helped lead to his awareness of wetting at night.

Sleep Deprivation

He became fully awake for toileting at times, even regularly for a while, and with this, Zachary also resumed nursing in the night to return to sleep. I felt that this pattern had created a perpetual need for him to awaken again at night, since his bladder would fill again. I found that he would awaken to pee 30–60 minutes after having nursed and fallen asleep at bedtime and then would awaken every 2–3 hours thereafter. But I was determined to meet his needs around the clock and do feel that this diligence led to his being dry at night much sooner than expected.

Admittedly this was exhausting in the beginning, for I responded to every little sound. When he was around 7 months, I had him sleep with me, as I was so tired. I had been running into his room, just across the hall from us, at every noise, checking him frequently throughout the night to be sure he didn't wet in his sleep. The temporary family bed arrangement seemed to stop the accidents at first as I was able to sense his restlessness and respond immediately; sometimes he remained asleep as I toileted him, and occasionally he nursed back to sleep. I absolutely loved this closeness at night, but unfortunately I became sleep deprived. Though at first he was restless every time he needed to go, this pattern changed. He began to awaken to be toileted or as soon as we returned to bed. With my availability, he began to nurse constantly throughout the night, not just to return to sleep after toileting. He also began to have an accident every once in a while; this was probably because I was so tired that I was no longer in tune. I believe it also impacted my day progress, too, in that I would have less success and find myself losing patience. This was *never* taken out on my son. But I sure was hard on myself! It warranted evaluating our specific situation to guard my sleep in order to promote a relaxed environment. Sleep deprivation jeopardizes this method! Once I heeded the advice of both husband and friends and relaxed at night, and once Zachary resumed sleeping in his own room around 7½ months, we both slept more at night, and the accidents decreased markedly.

Overview of Nighttime Approach

Step 1 consisted of responding to Zachary's restlessness in his sleep. Whether he awoke fully or not, I took him to pee. He would often pee (or on a rare occasion, poop) on the toilet in his sleep, leaning against me with his eyes closed while he eliminated and afterwards just sigh. At first when he partially awoke while being toileted, he would start to pee, stiffen and not finish going. I would then do as I did during the day and encourage him to relax, whereby he did and would finish. This assured me of returning him to bed with an empty bladder.

For Step 2, I applied timing in addition to watching for restlessness at night. Timing helped me know when to take him to the toilet on occasions when he was in a deep sleep and didn't stir at night. The transition to training pants also eased our nighttime routine. For a while I would remove his training pants before picking him up to take him to the bathroom, to help communicate that this was why I was coming into his room when he was supposed to be going to sleep. If he was already asleep and I knew it was time to pee, it was convenient to remove the pants en route to the bathroom and replace them when finished. He was sleeping in training pants and pajamas with a super absorbent bed pad over his sheet in case of accidents. The pad was easy to remove and replace when necessary, and Zachary would often sleep through all this undisturbed.

Step 3 happened around 8–9 months when he began to wake more and more on his own to be toileted, as opposed to my responding solely to his restlessness or timing. Upon awakening, I would hear him moving and find him up on his knees, waiting to be taken to the toilet. He seemed to connect that Mommy or Daddy would respond if he awakened to pee at night.

Step 4 happened around 9–10 months when he cried out to us, got up in his bed and waited to be toileted. At first, on a few occasions when he was in a deep sleep, he would begin to pee, awaken, stop peeing and cry out to us. Upon being toileted, he would finish peeing, as evidenced by his voiding a *large* amount. He soon gained even more control and would wake up dry. The absorbent pad was now obsolete.

From this point on, we used a combination of all four steps, and accidents soon became a thing of the past. At 9 months, his pattern was to pee before his bedtime routine, nurse, and then pee again before going to bed awake. I found that if he did not fall asleep right away, relying on timing helped avoid a potential accident. Using a timer proved essential in preventing accidents and meeting his elimination needs when not with him, as it helped remind me to toilet him when I could not observe cues or would become distracted doing other things. The timer was also helpful in confirming his *need* to go versus his desire to stay up longer by using toilet visits as a bedtime delay tactic. To accomplish this, he would cry out (or at 10 months sign), and when we got to the bathroom, he would void just a trickle of pee. Once he learned we would be faithful by taking him when he truly needed to go and that we would not fall for any "mischievous miscommunications," his cues resumed reliability.

At 10 months when he awoke on his own, he would call out to us and then upon our arrival, we'd find him standing or on his knees, making the ASL toilet sign by emphatically waving his little fist.

When he nursed at bedtime only (versus in the night once or early mornings at times) at around 15 months, he consistently slept through the night again, though he was doing this on and off prior to 12 months. I assumed his marked decrease in night frequency was likely related to his bigger bladder, being able to hold it longer and not refilling his tummy each time he was toileted.

After he weaned at 18 months, he did not awaken at night unless he had something to drink prior to bed that made him have to go at night. He continued to be reliable in waking up when he needed to go to the bathroom. Imagine having a young toddler who can drink before bedtime or in the night and still stay dry, awakening on his own to be toileted!

Relations with Others

Other than my parents, who had given us the book from which we were introduced to this method, we did not initially discuss this outright with anyone. It was in part because we lacked knowledge about it and were "trying it out" and also because we did not want to put pressure on our son as he was learning this with us. I was discreet when in public or at friends and family. Many assumed we used their bathrooms to change a diaper when in reality we were toileting our son.

Though he wore training pants to his 8-month healthy baby checkup, it wasn't until his 10-month visit that a nurse took notice and inquired if we were starting potty training already. Imagine her shocked expression when I explained that we were essentially done! She was flabbergasted but asked several appropriate questions. As I explained, she responded with interest and understanding. By the time he returned for his 12-month visit, it was common knowledge in the doctor's office that Zachary was potty trained. The nurse on duty was skeptical and said Zachary was "a first" for them and that he would be an "experiment," whatever that meant. The "growth and development brochure" they handed out for 12–18 months states, "Most children are not ready to be toilet trained at this age." When the doctor touched on the subject, he was reminded that we were already done with this, but he never broached for details. At Zachary's 18-month visit, the doctor caught himself as he went through his list of "what to cover" that visit, recalling that we were already done with potty training. It was just "accepted" and never challenged.

We have been fortunate that our inner circle of friends and family were very supportive, especially after they were educated on the method. I was very protective of Zachary, though, maintaining a casual approach and not encouraging an audience, which could create undue pressure to perform. This was affirmed by other moms doing this who reported from experience that it could cause a child to "seize up." With the exception of my spouse, it wasn't until a month or so before Zachary "graduated" that I even had others help with toileting him and only then when visiting in our home.

Reflections

Would I ever do this again if I had the opportunity? You bet! Would I do anything different? Much would remain to be seen. I would definitely relax more, which I imagine would come easier from experience, knowing more of what to expect and having more confidence. I would expect to use my experience as a springboard, adding the nuances of a different personality of another infant. Having a daughter versus a son and starting from birth rather than at 4 months of age would definitely warrant some changes. But I would still be diligent to both day and night training, though starting both from birth.

The pluses far outweigh the challenges. Though early completion of training was a draw to this method, I honestly did not think he would "graduate" before he walked independently, especially as I did not start this with our son until he was already 4 months old. I was hoping to finish between 12–18 months or so, but was prepared for it to take a full 2 years. In the meantime, Zachary was out of diapers and using the potty very early. What a thrill it was to see him respond so well to this! I cannot imagine ever choosing diapers now! I packed away diapers when he was 8 months old, after they had sat around for a month unused, and needless to say, my laundering was cut down significantly. I never hauled the diaper bag with me on short errand trips once he was in training pants, and I packed it away before he was a year old, having only been using it for toys, snacks and a change of clothing which never got used. Zachary never experienced diaper rash nor had a phobia about using an adult toilet or flushing his excrement "down the hole." I was never limited in where I pottied him with this method, so never had to interrupt it. He is not a bedwetter. And the ultimate kudos to this is the incredible endearment to my son! This method compliments the bonding that already is promoted through nursing. I would highly recommend giving this method a try. After all, what have you got to lose . . .? Oh, yeah . . . , all those hundreds of wet, dirty, smelly diapers! Blessings!

chapter 2
two 16-month graduates

Laura Moore first heard about infant pottying when she read a *Trickle Treat* book review in an environmental newspaper. She successfully potty trained both her children in infancy without using disposable diapers. Laura holds a master's degree in advertising from the University of Texas at Austin. Her husband Tom Griggs is a professor of teacher education. Laura provided the following information in 2000 with a short update in 2006.

Sara

Although I had a difficult labor and an unexpected cesarean section with Sara, these didn't deter me from starting IPT in early infancy.

First Week

There are no potties small enough for an infant, so I've improvised her first potty from a set of nesting plastic mixing bowls that each have a smooth edge, a handle and a rubber nonslip rim on the bottom. I figure that as Sara gets bigger, she'll just progress to the next size mixing bowl until she's big enough to sit on an official potty.

The day I tried IPT for the first time, I confidently held my tiny Sara over the smallest mixing bowl and presto! behold—a trickle treat! It was amazing.

It has been a little hard these first few days because Sara is breastfeeding on demand and eliminating frequently. Also, I'm still recovering from the C-section, but all things considered, we're doing okay with the potty training. By the end of the first week, I feel I've had quite a bit of success in figuring out Sara's potty patterns and rhythms, especially her nighttime patterns. I keep her in a cloth diaper when she's not on the potty since I know I won't be getting all her pees in the potty.

Two Weeks

Sara gets up about every two and a half hours at night. Last night, after sleeping for two and a half hours, she was still dry. I woke up, put her to the breast and held the little mixing bowl under her. She immediately pooped and peed in the pot. This has been a consistent pattern for a number of nights now—waking up three or four times dry, nursing and using the potty successfully at the same time.

Everyday it gets easier and easier to get her to go in the pot. In fact, she usually goes right when I hold her over the pot, or soon thereafter. Sometimes we have to wait for a while. If she doesn't go fairly soon, I take her off the pot. But I know that eventually she'll go, so it's a matter of trying again in five or ten minutes.

She is still nursing on many occasions when I hold her over the potty. I just place the potty in my lap under her bottom while she nurses. I think she is very, very aware of the "potty position," whether she is nursing or not. She doesn't like a wet diaper, so I think she appreciates going in the pot.

Her signs to pee are pretty subtle so far. I haven't quite put my finger on them yet, so it's mostly by timing that we go to the potty. It's easy to tell when she needs to poop. She gets squirmy or fussy. When she is in the process of peeing or pooping, she relaxes and makes a certain facial expression.

There are three main cues I use to let her know it's potty time.

1. I hold her in position in my arms, the same way every time.

2. I use the potty in the same place in the house.

3. I ask her if she has to go potty. I use a certain intonation or inflection in my voice and ask in a singsong way, "Shall we go potty?" or "Do you want to go pooter in the pot?" It hasn't been necessary for me to make a specific sound related to the function to get her to go. Sometimes she'll reach down and feel the pot there, and this is another way she knows what's going on.

I put a diaper on her in between feedings because I know I won't be around to take her potty every single time she has to go.

Tom is very supportive. He hasn't had a lot of opportunity to hold Sara over the pot yet because she's just 2 weeks old and mainly goes while she is nursing, but he looks forward to helping when she's a little bigger.

This method is about being diligent. When you know it's time to go to the potty, you shouldn't blow it off and think, "I'll just let the diaper catch it." I've been disciplining myself to take her to the pot, and it's starting to pay off already. It's frustrating when I don't get her to the potty on time, but I'm never angry at her about it.

Five Months

Sara has graduated to the medium-sized mixing bowl now, and she likes sitting on it. I sit cross-legged with the potty in my lap, then hold Sara in my arms and on the pot. It's a relaxing position for both of us. When I put her on the potty, she always tries to make herself go, even if it turns out she doesn't have to.

We put her on the potty several times a day. If she wants to get off, she'll start squirming and let me know, and I let her off. Many times she just plays with her toes or we'll chat, and she'll take her time. She'll just remain sitting on the potty until she has to go. Tom helps when he can. I've also had some help from my mother and grandmother when they are around.

I've learned to figure out more of her patterns such as how much she needs to go. She'll have an initial surge. If I take her off the potty right away, it's usually too soon. If we wait, there is usually a second round of elimination.

I can usually tell by timing when she has to pee. Now that she is a little older, she urinates less frequently. Her bladder is larger and stronger, so she is holding it in longer, and we go to the potty less frequently than the first months. It seems like she pees more when she's active than when she's calm.

I still keep cloth diapers on her when she is not on the potty. If I miss a few pees, it doesn't matter. I don't beat myself up for using diapers in between potty sessions. I'm using far fewer diapers than if I were not doing IPT. She has never had diaper rash since she is rarely wet or soiled. When I don't have the potty with me, I invent potties and she goes for me.

She still squirms or gets fussy when she needs to poop, so we've had great success with poops. Another cue from her happens in the mornings—she will pass gas and I know she'll soon need to go. I get 90 percent of her poops in the potty now. From the standpoint of hygiene alone, it's worth doing this.

She is still nursing all she wants, so the poops are still loose. This is another advantage. If she ever goes in her diaper, it's very messy to clean the diaper and her bottom. The mess ruins the diaper covers, and I have to wash them right away. It's so convenient to have her go in the potty instead. I wipe her bottom with toilet paper, then we fill up the potty with water and rinse it down the toilet—finished, done, I don't have to deal with it anymore. She stays very clean using the potty, even when she has diarrhea.

It feels like I really accomplish something when she does a big poop in the potty in the morning. Now that we have been doing this for five months, I can't imagine *not* using a potty with her. Often when I lay her down to take off her diaper, if I don't put her on the potty, she'll end up peeing anyway. She associates my taking off her diaper with potty time. So I just pick her up, put the potty under her, and she goes in the potty instead of on the diaper.

She is sleeping more through the night, from 11 p.m. until 5 a.m. She'll wake up dry, and as soon as she wakes up, I put her on the potty and she pees a lot. She signals me when she is through or if she wants to get off the potty.

It often seems like she purposefully waits until she is on the potty before she goes. I think it's the positioning. Once I get her in this position, she knows to go. Maybe she wouldn't have gone in her pants at that very moment, but as soon as she is on the potty, she goes.

We like this method of toilet training. I have a closer relationship with my daughter because of it. We communicate and are close throughout the day. I'm more aware of her rhythms. We're doing something together that we wouldn't otherwise be doing together if we were using diapers all the time. It helps the environment. I don't feel like I'm wasting a lot of water or trees.

Six Months

All I have to do is hold her a certain way without her diaper and if she needs to go, she goes right away. She doesn't need verbal cues anymore. Once she gets in the position, even if she wasn't going to go right then, she goes unless there is absolutely nothing to eliminate. I don't keep her very long on the potty now that she is more active. She is good at letting me know if she doesn't need to go or when she wants to get off the potty.

We're doing very well, getting almost every poop and many pees in the pot. Doing this helps keep us bonded. Since I'm spending time breastfeeding her and not going to work, IPT is just a logical extension of my lifestyle. It makes sense to teach her now. I'll be finished when most parents are just starting.

I still need to pay attention to her timing and body language, which helps my awareness of her rhythms remain strong. Her pattern of a big surge followed in a few moments by going a little bit more continues, so I just keep her on the potty a little longer after she initially goes. Her other clues, such as passing gas before she poops, are the same. She poops four or five times a day, mostly in the pot.

She has the routine down really well. Sometimes I encourage her, remind her exactly what we're doing. If I'm late getting her to the potty, I try not to let it upset me. I used to get frustrated because I feel so responsible, but now I'm more relaxed about it. At first I thought it might confuse her or make it more difficult to potty train her if I don't get her to the potty all the time, but this is not the case.

There are times where she doesn't appreciate going on the potty, like when she is playing. I'm sensitive to situations where I know it's time for her to go on the potty but she is busy playing. I don't force the issue. I don't interrupt her play a lot, because I respect her as a person. I respect her boundaries.

Eight Months

Since she sits so well now, I decided to stop holding her over the potty. She has graduated from using the mixing bowls in my lap to sitting on a regular freestanding portable potty. When I sat her down on her new potty for the first time, she pooped right away for me. No problem with the transition to a regular potty. I carry the potty with me everywhere, even room to room. We take it in the car and on trips.

If I am ever without the potty, I find a makeshift substitute. One time I held her over a plastic bag in a park when she had to poop. Other times she'd poop in the grass, and I'd scoop it up with a plastic bag like I do for my dog.

Nine Months

From a health-and-hygiene standpoint, IPT can't be beat! She hasn't had a bowel movement in her pants for months. We're up to about a 99 percent success rate with the poops. She has still never had diaper rash.

When we travel, if I don't have a potty handy, I hold her over a diaper and she goes for me. Even though there is no potty under her, she knows it's time to go when I hold her in the potty position.

I still keep a diaper on her. When she's active, she pees every 30–45 minutes. If I get involved in something and don't take her to the potty on time, she'll pee in her diaper. In other words, I'm pretty diligent but not fanatical.

If she's in the vicinity of having to go and I place her over the potty, she'll go. She can make herself go. I don't have to hold her and wait for a certain moment. This tells me she has pretty good control over her potty muscles.

When friends ask me to tell them about this method and I tell them my daughter hasn't had a poop in her pants for months, they don't believe it.

IPT gives my daughter a sense of self-respect. After my experience with infant potty training, I would never consider delaying the start of potty training until she is 1 or 2 or older.

I now work in my home and have help with Sara. She won't let the caregivers potty her, so I just told them not to even try. They still help though. They know when Sara has to go and let me know, "Sara looks like she needs to go to the bathroom. Do you want to come in and hold her over the potty?" Then I hold her over the potty and sure enough, she goes.

It's true this method takes time, but in most cases potty training takes time regardless of when you start it.

Twelve Months

She does most of her business in the potty. She has excellent control of the elimination functions.

We've been in some unstable situations, moving, house-sitting in unfamiliar environments, but it doesn't disrupt her potty training. She's relaxed about it wherever we are.

Sixteen Months

She can now verbally communicate her need to eliminate, so I have stopped putting diapers on her altogether. As soon as I stopped with the diapers, she was able to go to the potty on her own. I don't have to be very diligent anymore. She has had a few "accidents" (pee) during the day, but never fails to poop in the potty. I'm so glad to have her completely out of diapers.

Since she is still sleeping with us at night, I was a little nervous that she might have some nighttime "accidents," but my fears were unfounded. To this day, Sara has *never* wet the bed.

Looking Back . . .

Looking back, it's obvious that all my diligence has paid off. Sara was completely out of diapers before 18 months and potty trained way before any of her friends. Most people who saw me taking her potty as an infant were curious but skeptical. They would say, "Nice for her, but never for me," or make comments like, "It's easier with girls." But every once in a while I'd meet someone who was more open-minded, and some of these moms have successfully potty trained their own babies.

Sara is 7 years old now. An amusing leftover from her early potty training is that she still always announces when she has to go to the bathroom. She still has some memories of her infant potty training, partly because we sometimes talk about it and have videos and photos of her first few years, including some potty scenes, and partly because her baby brother is using the method. Beausoleil was born a year ago, and Sara has been helping me potty train him since he was born. Needless to say, she's an expert on the topic. She is mature for her age, and we're still very close.

Beausoleil

After the success she had using infant potty training with her daughter Sara, there was no doubt in Laura's mind that she would potty train her second child from birth too. At the time of publication, Beau was 17 months old.

First Week

I started potty training Beau when he was 4 days old. The very next day I was reminded (after several years' break between babies) of how important it is for me to be available on time for his elimination. Timing is everything with this method. As with Sara, I nurse Beau while holding him over the baking-bowl potty since he eats and "goes" at the same time a lot. Beau pees more often than Sara did, so it's pretty hectic and intense at the moment.

I'm using the same small plastic mixing bowl that I used with Sara. As with Sara, I'm keeping a diaper on him in between potty visits. Since he pees so much more than Sara, I'm using a diaper service to get through this phase. Another reason to keep the diaper service is that we plan to move soon, and I don't have as much time as I need to devote to Beau's pottying.

One Month

Beau is 4 weeks old, and we have moved into our new home. Because he was born 3 weeks "early" (before the due date) I hadn't finished all the packing before giving birth. As a result, I had to do a lot of packing and other things to get ready for the move during the first 4 weeks of his life. Therefore, I haven't been totally focused on doing the method. Now that we have moved and are settled, I have started using the method in earnest.

Three Months

He's starting to settle down to a more predictable routine. I am able to catch more and more poops, although still using the diaper service and going through 140 diapers a week. Since he sleeps in the bed with us, I keep a diaper on him at night, just in case. He's a great nighttime sleeper and often wakes us with a dry diaper. I hold him over the potty bowl when he wakes up in the morning, and he makes a BIG pee and sometimes a poop.

Four Months

I'm having continued success with the method. One day he went 12 hours using the same dry diaper since I was able to respond to his needs to eliminate in time. I'm having much more success now that he is holding his head up better and having more predictable bowel movements.

He's sleeping 6½ hours straight at night. Until now, I was getting up at night and putting him on the potty when he squirmed at night. I've decided we both need more sleep, so I'm letting him fall back to sleep instead of putting him on the potty. He has been dry in the morning, and I get a BIG pee in the pot, sometimes even a poop, when he wakes up.

Five – Six Months

We're down to 90 diapers a week. He's sleeping longer at night (8 hours) and still waking up dry. He really has the hang of using the potty bowl and is quite content with it. If he doesn't need to pee and I set him on the potty bowl, he will arch and stand himself up. If his penis is at all stiff, I know he'll need to pee soon, so I wait a moment, then put him back on the potty and he cooperates—stays on the potty and pees. As with Sara, pees are trickier to get 100% since babies pee so often.

His first tooth appeared, and I've introduced solid food (mostly banana). These two things have combined to impact his digestion. His poops are more solid and predictable. I now realize he signals his need to eliminate using body posturing and distinct breathing.

I canceled the diaper service. We own 30 diapers and three diaper covers. I wash a load of diapers only once every three days.

Seven Months

Since he can sit up well on his own now, I bought him a BabyBjörn® potty. He has adapted to it well.

Eight Months

I get quite a few pees a day. Since his top teeth came in and he gets more solids in addition to nursing, the consistency and timing of his bowels varies. There has been a transition period with his bowels since starting the solids. I missed his poops for a few days—what a drag! He now goes a day or sometimes two between poops, but not always, so I'm doing better with the poops.

I have begun to use sign language for simple, everyday communications with Beau since he cannot speak yet. The sign for "poop" is a clenched fist. I have signs to use when I ask him things like: Finished? More? Food? Pee? My theory is that he will be able to communicate with sign sooner than words, and this might enable me to finish with diapers even sooner.

Ten Months

He has a bad case of diarrhea but is willing to let me hold him over the potty. Fortunately, he is doing all his diarrhea poops in the potty. Needless to say, I feel very committed to this method since it has kept him so clean and eliminated so many messes for me to clean.

Eleven Months

He has diarrhea again, and even though his signals sometimes get out of sync, it's still well worth using the potty. It takes me 10–15 minutes to do the whole procedure—undress him, potty him, wipe him off and dress him. When I consider the amount of time it takes to clean all aspects of a diarrhea mess (diapers, clothing, baby, my hands, etc.), I much prefer spending time cuddling him on the potty and getting him to poop there instead of in a diaper. I also feel it's a matter of dignity for him not to poop in a diaper.

Twelve Months

We no longer use nighttime diapers since he always wakes up dry. Beau now gives the sign for poop while he's pooping. I'm using his BabyBjörn® potty less and less since he doesn't like it. He protests if I put him on it, so I either hold him over the original mixing bowl or, if he needs to pee only, the sink. If he has to poop, I hold him over the toilet. He lets me know if he doesn't need to go or if he doesn't feel like being held. Sometimes I give him a toy or something to distract him and then he'll calm right down and pee. There's some intuitive analysis going on when he protests at the exact time when I sense he really needs to pee. Sometimes I let him go back to what he was doing, then I'll try again a few minutes later and he'll happily pee. I respect his communication and don't force the issue at all.

Thirteen Months

Beau is walking more and more, and my goal is to have him out of diapers by the time he's walking full time. The success goes back and forth. If I keep him out of diapers, I really have to keep him in sight. He will sometimes give me the sign for poop before he goes, but just by seconds, and I have to immediately respond or he poops on the floor. More and more often, he comes to me and I intuitively know he's telling me he needs to go. There's no overt sign, just his being there and my instinct. It's quite an effort, this training, but one great thing is that he is absolutely clear about what the potty is for, and he can make himself pee. Once, he has actually walked up to his little potty (when his diaper was off), sat down and peed. I was so excited! I'm ready for more successes like that!

Fourteen Months

He was doing well, then went on potty strike. He has had several accidents with his diapers off, so I've had to resort to diapers again. He has been wearing them off and on for a few weeks. He hates being held down while I put on his diaper. I haven't figured out why he is on strike, but we'll weather the storm.

Fifteen Months

His potty strike lasted about one month in total and has now ended. It was frustrating for him to be held down while I put a diaper on him during that time.

One day I just looked at him and said, "You're ready." I put him on the potty, and he was happy to start using it again.

The other day he sat on the potty by himself and pooped. Then he moved the potty over to his toys, sat on the potty again and pooped more. He signals me with body language and gestures. If I ask him, "Do you need to poop?" and the answer is yes, he grabs his crotch to let me know. If he has an accident, he comes to me and grabs his crotch to let me know.

Sixteen Months

Beau is now toilet trained day and night! He wears pants without a diaper or underpants. This makes it easy to pull down his pants in a hurry when he has to go. Although preverbal, he has no problem letting me know when he has to go. He will often come and find me, take my hand and lead me to the throne.

A recent bout of diarrhea caused me to be on extra alert for subtle signals and timing. I continued with my resolve to not diaper him. We made it through the illness without an accident, thanks to both our efforts. We are triumphant! No more diaper wars! All at the tender age of 16 months!

In 2006, when Sara was 14 and Beau was nearly 8 years old, Laura reported that her children had never experienced any regression or bedwetting since they graduated. A video case history of both children and a reunion 14 years later can be seen on the *Potty Whispering* DVD.

chapter 3

kamala's 9 successes

Vivian Kumjian ("Kamala") has toilet trained nine children from infancy—the first baby starting at 5 months of age, and all the rest starting with the meconium at birth. Seven of these are her own children, two girls and five boys. All the babies she worked with were toilet trained by the time they walked, anywhere from 10–14 months of age, depending on the child. Kamala didn't notice any difference in the degree of difficulty in toilet training boys and girls. Her story, from 2000, is mainly one of communication on various levels.

My first baby, Naya, was born in 1974 in Virginia. We spent much of his infancy in Mexico. When he was 5 months old, I made an interesting discovery. He was lying on a blanket when he seemed to be trying to tell me something. He made a slightly distressful vocal sound while looking me in the eye and waving his arms and legs around. For some reason, I picked up on the idea that he might have to pee. I squatted down and took him in my arms, leaning him against my chest while holding him by his legs. This seemed a natural and comfortable position for us both. As soon as I held him in position, he peed. Of course, I was thrilled that my son had responded to my cue. I had never heard about infant toilet training before, although I had a sense that a mother has the ability to be in tune with her baby's elimination.

From that day on, the toilet scenario with Naya became like a game of responding to sound and body language. It was touch and go for a while in that he wouldn't pee every time I thought he had to. I had to try different solutions.

When I say it's like a game, I don't mean that you are training your baby. It's more a matter of training yourself than training your baby. It's a question of training yourself to listen, pay attention, be aware and respond. It is just as natural to respond to toilet needs as it is to respond to a baby being hungry or tired. Your baby tells you when he wants to eat, sleep or play and when he is angry. He also tells you when he has to pee or poop. You have to really want to participate in the play, in the game. You have to bond with your baby and learn each other's sounds, timing and body language. For me, responding to Naya's cues to pee or poop was part of a whole, not a separate thing or task that had to be done.

I worked on getting us into a symbiotic relationship, in tune with each other's timing and communication. The fact that I carried Naya around in a rebozo (sling) everywhere I went made it easier to constantly be aware of all his needs, including his elimination timing. He would make a sound or cry when he wanted something, and I gradually learned to figure out exactly what he needed. If I felt it was time for him to eliminate, I'd hold him out.

I was very interested in learning to communicate with Naya on a psychic level. I believe in telepathy and that most of us haven't learned how to use it. I had to untrain myself in some ways in order to be able to listen to Naya. I had to learn to listen to the voices inside me and respond to my son. It's like hearing a thought in your head and someone remarks, "I was just thinking the same thing." This happens a lot, but we don't always pay attention to it. The same sort of thing happened with elimination communication with Naya (and later my other babies). I heard the thought and had the feeling that he had to go, acknowledged that thought/feeling, and he responded by peeing for me.

Since Naya signaled to me vocally, I listened carefully to his vocalizations and took the time to learn their meaning. The sounds he used were not the same every time. He'd make a noise to call to me, like someone trying to grab my attention. Of course, he couldn't yet say anything like "hey," but he created his own sounds to get my attention. I responded to his elimination cues by picking him up and holding him in position to go. I made a "shh-shh" sound or else just said "pee" when I was holding him in position. Using the sound reinforced the communication between us. From the moment I understood that he always yelled or cried when he had to go, I never again needed to depend on timing to tell me when to take him to eliminate. Once I learned his language of vocalizations, he was always the initiator of the communication.

Of course there were times when I wasn't available for him. It's not possible for any mother to be present for every single pee! If I wasn't around when he signaled and it got to the point where he couldn't hold it any longer, he'd just pee in my absence. I'd say, "You had to pee, and I didn't catch it." I never made a fuss or a big deal about it, and I certainly never felt or expressed anger.

When he was 10 months old, we moved to the wilderness, among the sequoias in Southern California. Living in a natural environment made it easy to continue since not putting diapers on a baby makes toilet training much easier. By the time a baby can walk, it's just a matter of his knowing where he has to walk to pee. Another advantage of living in the country is that it involves a different sort of timing. You're more relaxed, and it's easier to be in tune with your kids. You're not worried about your house, carpets and belongings. I'm not saying that it's necessary to live in the wilderness to do this, but for those who have the opportunity to live in a more natural environment, it can make it easier.

The experience with my second baby, Ituri, was different. I held him out right after birth to empty out his meconium. We were in a very lucid time and space immediately after the birth, and holding him out established a unique form of communication between us from the very beginning of his life. I learned from Ituri that babies are aware of elimination at and from birth. This proved to be the case with the rest of my kids too. In the minutes, hours and days after you give birth, you are very lucid. This is when communication is the most open between you. Things happen at a very slow pace and seem very clear. You are in a different dimension. After the first week or two, the communication starts getting more difficult because that "clear space" starts getting more cloudy. You have a lot of things you have to do. There are distractions and activities around you so it's more difficult to tune into your baby. It becomes more of a challenge to stay in close communication, but it is possible.

In addition to the close bond established at birth, the same pattern of communication and attention-getting that I had experienced with Naya happened with Ituri—and in fact, with all seven of my kids and two other babies I worked with. At 6 months, Ituri got to the point where he would hold his pee and yell until I got the message. I'd hold him out, he'd pee and then he'd sigh with relief.

I was living a communal lifestyle when I was in my twenties. We spent three years in the wilderness. I gave birth to Ituri and my third child, a daughter named Sodasi, there. There were two other babies from different families born there too. We adults were all training ourselves to open up to be in communication with the babies. This was our focus. All the babies in the commune were toilet trained from birth. All the adults came together to help each other with this. Sometimes I had to be the interpreter of babies' signals since some adults couldn't figure out why a baby was crying. We strove to change our conditioning in order to identify, bond and communicate with all the babies. It was like living in an extended family where all family members spend time raising the children.

I have read books stating that babies can't control their bowels or bladders, but this hasn't been my experience at all—not with my own seven infants and not with other babies I have worked with. All my babies learned to control their bowels and wait for me to pick them up and hold them out. They would get really mad at me if I wasn't paying enough attention to hear their calls. It was like they said, "Come on! Wake up! I have to pee!" Ituri was the first of my kids to use such clear communication. Naya was more mellow about it, probably because I had started later in life (5 months) with him. It was less important for Naya in that he didn't mind as much if I didn't make it on time for him. But Ituri demanded it—and he demanded it loud and clear!

The sound and quality of communication shapes a baby's mind from birth. The best part of toilet training for me was the quality of communication. It was a real thrill. It wasn't a matter of me training my baby. It was more like changing or enhancing a relationship through natural communication. It opens you up to a whole new quality of communication with your baby. Communication about elimination is not a separate thing, just part of the whole repertoire of communication and caring. All my kids communicated vocally with me most of the time, but there were also times where I picked up on their need before they communicated. It was a give-and-take communication, a symbiotic relationship. I was pleased but didn't reward or praise my kids when they peed for me. I considered it a natural thing, just like eating, something that didn't need praise or special recognition.

We are all born with natural instincts, and mothers have a natural ability or instinct to be in tune with baby's body language, timing, communication, play, feedings, etc. In the industrialized world, many mothers don't follow or identify with their instincts. They have adapted to civilization and industrialization and try to make their children adapt quickly. Everyone wants to train their kids to fit in society, and they miss a lot this way. Everyone is always busy, in a hurry and operates with a linear mind, which is not how a child's mind works.

Following our natural instincts is similar to the way an animal is in tune with her babies. Animal maternal instinct overrides (nearly) every other instinct. And speaking of animals, one of our dogs had nine puppies. She died, and we had to raise the pups. We put them in our tent at night. In the morning, they would all file out together, waddle out into the woods and take care of business there. Everyone knows that it's harder and messier if you delay house training a puppy. If you were to wait for a puppy to self-house-train, it would never happen. Why do we expect puppies to be toilet trained when they are babies, yet think our own babies aren't capable of what puppies can do?

My babies were never alone. When they were tiny, I carried them around with me in a rebozo. Once they could sit up, they didn't like the rebozo anymore so I carried them on top of my shoulders or with their legs wrapped around me like a monkey. At night, they slept with us. I'd use a pad or a towel with a diaper on top to protect the bed. I didn't put a diaper on my babies at night. I tried to get up based on timing, but this was difficult, so I wasn't very diligent about this aspect.

When a baby starts crawling, the situation changes a lot. They get involved with their surroundings, forget to signal and go on the floor. You need to pick them up, tell them it's the wrong place to go, carry them to the right place and tell them that's the right place. They eventually catch on. By the time my kids walked, there was no problem at all. They graduated from (a) crawling to (b) knowing where to eliminate to (c) walking and being finished with toilet training. All my kids were finished with toilet training when they started walking, anywhere from 10–14 months. This included nighttime too.

We moved to the countryside in New York in 1990. My youngest girl, Roshi, was 13 months old. Living in New York was the first time I experienced any reservations from people about infant potty training, but most people ended up reacting positively after seeing how well adjusted my kids were. They have always been very social, communicative and centered, and they aren't whiners. Their behavior makes people stop, think and realize that the scare tactics about infant potty training are false.

I find it sad that American doctors and pediatricians don't recognize infant toilet training as a positive and wonderful method. It's awful seeing 2-year-olds and 3-year-olds in Pampers. Doctors and other professionals learn what they know from books and not from experience. Look at all the children wearing diapers in daycare these days. I had a friend visit me with her 3-year-old boy in diapers. He totally refuses to communicate with her about going to the bathroom. Her doctor had told her it's okay to wait, "Let the child lead," and all that, but it wasn't getting any better as he got older. It was getting worse. Doctors and teachers claim a baby is not capable of understanding going to the potty. They say it takes time and that a child should be the one to initiate potty training. Nowadays they say a 3-year-old doesn't have the intelligence to go to the potty if he isn't "ready."

This brings us back to intelligence. I think a lot of parents have trouble potty training their kids because they cannot acknowledge the intelligence of their babies. Parents use baby talk and treat their babies like cute objects or pets. When there is respect for a child and acknowledgment that he knows what he's doing, it makes a difference. If you talk to 3-year-olds more as adults than as babies, they will acknowledge it. At age 3, all my kids and all the 3-year-olds in our group communicated well. They could understand and articulate their thoughts and desires. I have found that 3-year-olds in diapers refuse to learn to communicate. This is, in part at least, because of the way they are (or aren't) communicated with.

I think the fact that my kids vocally called to me when they needed to pee or poop is due to my acknowledging their communication on all levels— vocal sounds, body language and psychic communications. Responding to a baby's communications without putting up barriers in the form of questions and doubts is crucial. For example, if a baby could verbalize his request to pee, my response should be to take him to pee, rather than responding by repeating his question or request. If a baby could say, "I have to pee," I should not respond by repeating his question and double checking, "Do you have to pee?" or showing doubt, "Are you sure you have to pee?" I should just hold him out to pee and give a direct response that way. It's a spontaneous response.

I was 42 and still living in New York when I had my last baby, Osel. He's 5 now. I hadn't had a baby for a while and was more mature. From the beginning, I had total communication with Osel. The moment he was born, we were in sync. He would hold his elimination until I or one of his brothers or sisters could take him and hold him over a pot. He was never alone since I carried him almost everywhere and also because he had four brothers and two sisters to hold him and take him to pee if I couldn't. There is a communication of love among brothers and sisters, and a baby senses that. A baby knows when he is being cared for with love rather than someone just doing a babysitting job.

Osel would make sounds or grunt until we'd pick him up and hold him to pee. My experience has been that babies will wait for a reasonable amount of time to be taken to the bathroom. In this sense, they have some control from birth. Osel confirmed that what I had to do was let him initiate the communication, let him tell me if he had to go. I didn't have to anticipate it or wait very long while holding him to pee.

I went on a trip to Europe with Osel when he was 18 months old. Even though he had been potty trained since he started walking at 10 months, I was apprehensive of dealing with the airplane lavatory on such a long flight, so I put a diaper on him. That was a real mistake. I kept telling him, "Just pee in your diaper," but he wouldn't. There was no way he was going to pee in a diaper! He cried in protest until I took him to the lavatory, removed the diaper and held him out to pee. I never tried putting a diaper on him again!

chapter 4
elimination timing teacher

Linda Penn ("Natec") has authored her own book on the topic of infant potty training and has taught the technique to many infants, mothers and caregivers. She calls the process "elimination timing." She began with her son at birth, weathered a two-month communication strike with him at age 14 months and gave away any remaining diapers at 20 months. Her report is dated 2000.

Elimination timing is oriented towards getting parents to realize that they need to learn and work with baby's natural timing, rather than forcing baby to comply to the timing of adults. Elimination timing involves looking for baby's elimination patterns and timing.

I learned the term "elimination timing" from my teacher, who realized it through travels in Asia and Latin America. When he returned to the States in 1976, he told a friend of mine about it, and she immediately began elimination timing with her infant son. She showed me the technique.

I advise parents to start with the meconium. To catch the meconium, cradle the newborn in your arms while holding his rear end over a disposable pad or a receptacle. A "chuckie" (blue waterproof pad used in home births) is ideal for this. To avoid using diapers, use a waterproof pad with a diaper or towel on top. The reason I recommend beginning elimination timing as early as possible is that it's easy to see elimination signals in infants.

The first week, continue having the baby go on something disposable. After that, use a pot, bucket, sink or other receptacle. Some mothers hold a receptacle under their infant's bottom while nursing so they don't have to interrupt a feeding. In warmer climates, peeing baby outdoors is another option.

New mothers are flooded with information about all sorts of things. Once you settle down, you'll see that, in general, a baby makes some kind of movement before pooping. Then you'll see patterns. When babies wake from a nap, they usually pee. There will also be a pattern related to feedings. Some babies pee or poop during a feeding while others go after they eat. Each baby is different, but a pattern is there. Some patterns are regular while others are not so regular. The combination of the pattern and noticing any particular movements or other signals tells you when to take the baby to pee or poop. Hold the baby in position, make the "pssss" sound and talk to him. You can ask questions like, "Do you have to pee?" If baby has already peed, confirm this by saying, "All right, you peed." It's not so much a process of the caregiver doing it to the child as much as it is the child and the caregiver working together. What starts getting this established is the communication back and forth between baby and caregiver. If you carry your baby, he will usually wiggle, squirm or fuss right before it's time to pee. When baby squirms, you can cue him with sound and hold him out to pee. If he has to pee, he will. If he doesn't have to pee, he won't, and that's that.

On one level, babies are aware of elimination from the start. If an adult caregiver gives a symbol to this, the concept becomes concrete, and this is how a child keeps that awareness. My experience is that babies communicate consciously about elimination with a caregiver by the age of 3 months. At 3 months, babies can also hold their bladders. Doctors in industrialized countries say that children can't do this until 18 months or older. This has never been my experience since my introduction to elimination timing in 1976.

Babies respond well to your verbal cues. Be careful not to cue a baby before you have him in position or he'll go in the wrong place. There have been times where I said to babies who are 5–6 months old, "Oh, you have to pee," then I'd have to immediately say, "Wait, wait, wait, not here, wait!" They hold it until I get them in position and tell them, "Okay, now." Then they pee.

Some babies I've worked with give vocal signals before they need to go. Of course it's easier to know when to take baby to go if he gives a vocal signal. Some babies chirp before they have to go. I remember a 5-month-old who would scream in bed at night until someone took him to pee. He refused to pee in the bed. A 13-month-old girl made a unique sound, a creaking inhalation sound, when she had to eliminate.

Perhaps the hardest signals to pick up are the psychic signals. Those are tricky. You have to pick them up by feeling and intuition. It's like the feeling we all get from time to time, "The phone is going to ring and it's going to be Susie." It's a symbiotic, intuitive, telepathic hookup between mother and child. There are generations of people in tune like that. They get a feeling, an intuitive flash that tells them what is going to happen. We tend to test these intuitive flashes by ignoring them. Then when they come true, we say, "I knew that was going to happen. I knew he had to pee. Why didn't I listen to myself?" This is a typical reaction after you get peed on. It's a matter of getting in tune with your baby and in sync with his elimination patterns.

New mothers get really excited about communicating with their baby in such a productive way. They praise the baby. This is fine. I did it with my son. If you have another baby or work with other kids, it's not as exciting and you don't tend to be as exuberant. If you have more than one child and do this with them, like everything else you do with them, it gets easier, you get more confident and it's not such a big deal. The important thing is to let the child know that you know he has responded and done the right thing. Your reaction can vary from matter-of-factly stating "you peed" to being very excited, clapping, jumping up and down. It doesn't matter which way you behave, the baby will understand. When a baby feels the caregiver feeling happy, that's a reward.

There are significant psychological benefits for all concerned. Fathers who might feel left out in the beginning stages of child rearing can now have another essential role. My experience has been that all parents feel empowered and thankful to learn a compassionate communication skill with their children.

People often ask if girls learn elimination timing faster than boys. I don't think there is any difference. I think girls are more work because you have to wipe between the folds to clean and dry them.

After you've done this for a while, it becomes second nature. It's totally natural, in the flow and no big deal anymore. It takes a commitment to do this. There are some mothers who give up and go back to diapers for one reason or another, and that is okay. This is not an achievement test for parents, so there are no failures. For everyone who does try, remember that the key to this whole thing is to just relax.

When my son Kawa (now 12) was born, we caught the meconium and continued elimination timing with good results for the next 14 months. I had a lot of help from his father and a group of friends we were living with. My friends called me "Natec," which means "heart of the date palm," and some friends still call me by that name.

It was easy to tell when Kawa had to poop. He would get a red face and grunt. His pooping pattern was very regular, so it was easy to have him poop for me. Peeing was fairly regular in some ways but not in others. Five minutes after he began nursing, he'd pee. Sometimes I'd interrupt the nursing to take him to pee after the first five minutes, but if I felt he didn't want to stop nursing, I'd hold a receptacle under him. It was a flexible arrangement between us. After that very predictable pee, there was no regular pattern to his peeing, and he did not give any obviously consistent signals.

He was nearly done with my supervision at 14 months. Then his life and environment changed drastically. His father and I separated, and at the same time, I moved away from the group of friends we had been living with—the caregivers who had also raised Kawa. I moved to Hawaii alone with my son, and he stopped signaling me. This was a big problem. I had to put him in diapers for the first time at age 14 months! Two months later, he remained dry at night but still did not signal me. He was out of diapers, though, because he would go outside to pee. Since we were living in a rural area and a warm climate, this was no problem. When he was 20 months old, he spent the night at the home of his uncle. When Kawa went outside to poop, the uncle told him in no uncertain terms that pooping outdoors was not allowed at his place. After that night, Kawa started using the toilet.

Most kids don't go through problems like this. They go straight to the potty as soon as they can sit and don't go on strike, but occasionally you get a child who will test you or have emotional upsets and use elimination as a means of protest. Looking back, I realize Kawa went on strike because his environment and social surroundings had changed so drastically.

Hawaii is a great place to work with elimination timing since the climate is so mild, and babies can be minimally dressed most of the time. There are lots of people with alternative lifestyles living in Pahoa. People learn about me by word of mouth. There have been so many elimination timing babies in this area that in 1999, the local health food shop posted a sign that requested: "Please no babies without diapers in shop."

You can read more about Linda Penn ("Natec"), her philosophy and teachings, in her booklet *Infant Communication: Raising Babies without Diapers, and More*. The book is 28 pages, $6.00 including shipping, and can be ordered by writing to: natec@interpac.net or Natec, HCR2 Box 6838, Kea'au, HI 96749.

chapter 5

dentist mom

Liz Reiter is a dentist in the San Francisco Bay Area. Her husband Holger has a Ph.D. in neuroscience and is a businessman and a researcher who works from home. They have a son Nicholas who is 4 and a daughter Erika who is 2½. Liz did not learn about infant potty training in time to try it with her first child. Her testimonial is dated 2000.

I was introduced to this kind of potty training by another mother. She gave me the book *Trickle Treat* and told me how she had used it with her daughter. It sounded interesting to me. I thought it was a good idea. It made sense to me, with my background in science, to potty train my daughter from birth. It reminded me of Pavlov's dogs and similar behavioral theories. My husband read the book and was positive about the idea. I had a nanny working for me at the time since I was working three days a week. My nanny read the book, found the idea interesting and said she'd be happy to help me with the potty training. We started with Erika when she was 7 weeks old.

I was very diligent with the potty training and so was my nanny. My husband helped out when he could and was thrilled with the results. I hired a second woman to help around the house a few hours a morning for a while. She read the book, was positive about it and helped us with potty training too. Erika had no problem when people other than myself took her to the potty.

I did not find it overly time consuming to use infant potty training. I didn't have any real problems other than it seemed to go a little slow during the first month or two, meaning we didn't succeed in getting Erika to pee for us on a regular basis at first. I would hold her over the potty for about 30 seconds, and if she didn't have to go, I'd stop and try later. We decided that if we could get her to pee twice in the potty in the morning and twice in the afternoon, that we were having a great day. We called them "catches," and if we got four catches in an entire day we were very happy. Even if we only got a few pees or poops a day at first, it was apparent that she knew why I was holding her over the potty. The interval between when I started to hold her and when she would pee got shorter and shorter, so I knew the association with my signals was working. After about two months, it seemed to just start clicking: I knew her cycle better, and we didn't have to hold her as long to get her to go.

As for pooping, she used to wake up around 4:30 in the morning when she was tiny. I'd hold her over the potty and she'd immediately poop. It was really easy to know when Erika had to poop. She would make faces and grunt and then I'd quickly take her diaper off, hold her over the potty and catch it. When she got a little bigger, I'd take her into the bathroom and she'd poop for me there. I hardly ever had to clean a poopy diaper after she got the hang of it. That was great, especially after changing dirty diapers for almost three years with my son.

The potty I used for Erika was a little white potty bowl insert from a blue older-style potty chair that my neighbor had used with her kids. The potty insert was just the right size to hold under Erika's little bottom. I just held her over it, like the pictures in this book show. In the beginning, I always took her to the potty in the bathroom, in front of a mirror, and I always made a "sssshh" sound to cue her to pee.

When Erika was about 6 or 8 months, I started using the potty in other places besides the bathroom. I took the potty with me everywhere I went. I would also often stand or walk around the house with Erika on the potty (See Chapter 3, "The In-Arms Phase," in Part 1 for a photo of this). My nanny put Erika on the potty in many different places at home, sitting or standing. We did this more as Erika got older.

I continued my dentistry work until Erika was 10 months old then sold my practice in order to stay home with the kids full time. My nanny continued to work part time with me after I stopped working. She worked mornings almost every day until just recently. My mother, grandmother and everyone in my family have been supportive of Erika's infant potty training, but most of my friends (except the one who introduced me to the idea) think it is strange. They couldn't understand what I was doing, even when I gave them the book to read.

When Erika was nearly 13 months old and walking, we put the potty insert bowl back into the blue potty chair, and by 14 months she'd walk to the potty chair on her own. I would say, "Let's go potty," and she would just run in there and sit down. Occasionally she used the potty with no prompting at all. But she wouldn't use the bigger regular toilet until she was almost 2 years old. When I went out, I'd have to hold her over a diaper to go since she wouldn't sit on a regular adult toilet until 20 months. I didn't push the "big potty" issue, then one day she told me she wanted to use the bigger potty. After that, she'd sit on any potty.

I haven't done much about night training since Erika only occasionally wets at night. I have always put a cloth diaper on her at night. When she was smaller and used to wake up for feedings at night, I would hold her over the potty and keep her clean and dry this way. Ever since she started sleeping all night, I have just let her sleep through the night and put her on the potty before bedtime and when she wakes up in the morning.

When Nicholas was about 2½, we started potty training him the traditional way. Erika was already being put on the potty all the time when Nicholas started, so he knew what the potty was and this helped him. It was one of the benefits of having the children close together and of learning about infant potty training in time for Erika. Since I was doing it with her already, Nicholas just naturally knew what was going on and tried to do it as well. He was interested but not as easy to convince to use the potty. We tried various things and eventually got him to pee on it and then poop. He was harder to get to use it to poop. We knew when he was pooping, but he refused to use the potty chair until we tried giving a reward when he used it (a small gift from Santa—it was Christmas time).

It got to the point where I had to have two potties in the bathroom. When Erika had to go, Nicholas wanted to go. And when Nicholas had to go, Erika wanted to go too. The encouragement was great for both of them.

I found it frustrating to introduce traditional potty training to Nicholas when he was 2½. At that age, kids want to be independent and play. They aren't interested in sitting on a potty if they never have before, whereas my daughter was used to using the potty from a very young age, so there was no transition at all for her. It was just gradual learning until she could go on her own, and by the time she reached that stage of independence, she could be truly independent since she had already finished with potty training.

At 2½, she knows when to go. I don't have to prompt her at all. She doesn't have accidents anymore either, whereas my son who is 4 still has some accidents. It took me over a year to get to the point where I didn't have to prompt him anymore by asking, "Do you have to go?" He quickly mastered pooping but took over a year to really learn to not have peeing accidents. Erika is already completely out of diapers. I hadn't even started with my son when he was Erika's age, yet I'm completely finished with her. I think it's much better for a child. It's great not to have to wear diapers all the time.

It does take diligence, but the reward is that your child will be out of diapers early and completely independent around 2, whereas nowadays most parents don't even start until 2 or later. It's much messier to wait. And Erika never had diaper rash because she was always dry.

I would certainly use infant potty training again if I had another child. When anyone asks me about it, I tell them it's the greatest potty training I ever learned. I thought it was fantastic. I don't have anything negative to say except it would be nice if people were more supportive of it. I think one reason people are negative is that they are thinking of the old way early toilet training was done in this country in the past. It's not the same method at all.

When I told my grandmother I was using infant potty training, she said, "Oh, I did that with your mom. I sat her on a potty with a little tray and left her there until she went." I told her what I'm doing is different, that you don't make the child sit there until she goes. When my grandmother used to tell me that my mom would poop in the potty at age one, I didn't believe her. This was when my son was a little older than one, and I thought there was no way he could have pooped on the potty at age one. But when I did it with Erika, I could see what my grandmother was talking about. It's a totally different mindset when you've never done it.

Every mainstream parenting book I have read, like books by Penelope Leach and Dr. Brazelton, all say to delay potty training until your child is "ready," and they sternly warn parents not to use early toilet training. I read in many books that you should wait until your child gives you signs that he is ready to be potty trained, and this was very confusing to me. They tell you to wait until your baby goes two or three hours between pees, wait until your baby wakes up dry from naps and all that, but with my son, these things never happened! When he was 2½, I thought, "This is getting ridiculous." I started potty training him and it was fine. Another problem with the mainstream books is that they all made me very fearful of starting potty training "too young." They teach that if you start young, you will scar your baby, your baby will be emotionally disturbed if you potty train him too young or that it won't work. What I don't like about those books is that they don't even recognize that there are other possibilities available.

Jeanne Reiter

The Reiters with their children at the beach.
(left, Nicholas age 4; right, Erica age 2½)

When infant potty training is done in a totally positive, loving, nurturing way, when it's never forced on a child, it works. You just hold the child over the potty, and if they don't go, you take them off, and there is no negative connotation involved. I didn't have any trouble with Erika. I was happy to use this method. Everyone who helped me was excited too.

If I mention my success with Erika to a pediatrician or people with a background in science, they say, "Well, you just trained yourself. You didn't train your daughter." That was true in the beginning. I was training myself to recognize the signals Erika was giving to tell me when she needed to go, and I was timing things to see how long until she would "go" after a feeding. But at the same time, she was learning to associate my cues (holding her a certain way in a certain place, making the ssshh sound, etc.) with going in the potty instead of in a diaper. One thing I always noticed was if I put a diaper on my son or daughter, they would use it. If I took them out of diapers and told them to try to stay dry, they would make more of an effort not to go in their pants. It's so simple and logical.

Erika was out of daytime diapers when she was 18 months. People still are surprised and impressed at her and ask me how she can be out of diapers so young, at 2½. But I have also started hearing comments like, "My friend had a 2½-year-old, and he was trained in just two weeks. So why did you go through all that work when you could have waited until Erika was 2 and then done it fast?" Well, there is no guarantee that a child is going to be one of the few who learn potty training so easily. I have met many other children who are 3 and sometimes 4 years old and still use pull-ups or diapers. Why take the chance? Why use so many diapers? Why put up with messy diapers for years? If you use infant potty training, you know your child will be out of diapers at a young age. It makes kids happy about being in control of their bodily functions so young. They like to be in control of everything, and this is one more thing for them to feel good about doing themselves.

chapter 6
twins!

Lucia and Randall Wright are the proud parents of twin girls. They live on a farm with livestock, and the girls roam freely in a natural environment. At the time of this 2007 testimonial, the twins were 28 months old and potty independent, meaning they used a potty on their own, without prompting, and removed their own clothing, but asked for help with wiping, setting up the toilet insert, or with difficult clothing.

Settling In (1-3 months)

For the first three months, I focused on nursing (not easy with twins!) and did not worry much about pottying. On day 12, I sensed that Tsameret needed to go and held her over a bowl while saying "poopy."

We did a combination of cloth diapers with pins, disposable diapers, and "nakey" time with a prefold underneath them or between their legs. Both girls cried when wet, and we changed them day and night. At night, Randy and I took turns changing them when they fussed. For a while, we went through about 50 cloth diapers a day between the two of them, but it was no big deal since we had a washing machine.

At the end of a six-week bonding leave, Randy returned to work and stayed in the city Monday through Thursday. I felt unsure of myself, overwhelmed by nursing difficulties and alone a lot of the time. I knew I wanted to do this, but wasn't sure how, or even if it was possible with two babies. I had help three times a week during the day, but for three nights a week I was alone. That's when I started to tune in to my girls. They were very different in their styles. Moriah was very impatient while nursing, and she wiggled and popped on and off the breast a lot. Other times, she was almost placid and had a very long and piercing gaze. Tsameret made less eye contact but was more vocal. When she needed to pee, she let out an urgent cry that became a clear elimination signal over time.

In the third month, Randy and I did a "day in the life" with the girls to focus on them more. We recorded everything that happened for a day, with pictures, notes and video. It became clear to me that Moriah's squirming and fussing were usually elimination cues. We caught some poops but missed most pees. Many times when Tsameret made one of her piercing "Oh my god I'm gonna pee!" cries, Moriah would look at me with a "Mommy, do something!" look. She was very concerned and aware, and I was getting better at picking up and responding to their cues.

Tuning In (4-6 months)

During the summer, we spent a lot of time on the deck with the girls on absorbent mats and diapers in our laps. We did another "day in the life" in the middle of the 4th month, and I learned that when Moriah fidgeted during a feeding, I should keep her latched on while holding her over the bowl and then she would pee and burp more easily. I didn't worry about catching everything. I was happy to catch one or two pees or poops per day. At 6 months, Moriah started to scoot her way to the edge of the bed at night and cried out in her sleep. It took me a while to understand that this was a nighttime pee cue.

Success at Night (7-9 months)

If not for Moriah's diaper rash, I might have given up on nighttime pot-tying. I had started using paper diapers at night in order to give myself a break from nighttime diapering. When they were in cloth at night, they fussed when wet, and I was up changing diapers while half asleep. I eventually realized that they would wake and stir only if they were hungry or needed to go. When they started sitting up and scooting off the bed, I figured out that this was a pee signal. The days were stressful keeping track of two babies, and I was lucky if I caught anything. At night however, they lay quietly next to me and I could pick up immediately when they stirred and needed something. In short, our success rate became much better at night.

Sometimes the girls were in sync, fussing and peeing at the same time every night. Tsameret became especially clear in her communications. Moriah seemed less in tune with her urges, or maybe it was just that she was less vocal. A first at 9 months: When Tsameret fussed in her sleep, I held her over the pot and she went without having to nurse. She never even woke up! During the day, when Moriah needed changing, she started to come to me with a special look, as if to ask me to change her.

At naptime, I observed that they would whimper and wake up after about half an hour and that if I pottied and nursed them, they would go back to sleep. This was important information because my girls had never napped for more than half an hour during the day, and rarely at the same time.

At 9 months they started to hate diapers. Moriah began to walk and Tsameret followed at 10 months. The minute I took their diapers off, they peed on the floor. We went through a period of many misses, and I thought our pottying adventure had hit a dead end.

Then I found a wonderful online community of mothers that provided incredible support and inspiration. This helped me persevere and put things in perspective. I got in touch with another mother of twins who assured me that yes, it is possible! She stressed the importance of using timing with twins, the need for two potties, and warned me against having expectations and wondering who will "graduate" first. I started to take detailed notes on our pottying and posted monthly updates online, a simple ritual that helped me tune into myself and my girls. When Laurie Boucke put out a call requesting video footage of multiples for her *Potty Whispering* DVD, I started taping the girls extensively and was amazed at how the videotaping helped me learn more about their elimination signals. I felt encouraged and that we were on the right track.

Potty Time! (10-12 months)

I finally bought potties, diapers with Velcro closures, training pants and woolen longies for the winter. When the potties arrived I distributed them throughout the house: two in the bedroom next to the bed, two in the bathroom, two near their toys in the living room, and two in the kitchen near their highchairs. It was tiring enough to move from room to room with two babies. I did not want to drag potties around the house, and of course we always needed two at any given point in time because when one went, the other one would be triggered.

To get them accustomed to a potty, I held them over their potties until they started going and then lowered them onto the potty seat. I also started to use the "pssss" sound to prompt them, which worked much better than using words. And I introduced crotchless pants. Tsameret soon took the initiative to sit on the potty and peed in it all by herself.

The more I let the girls toddle around bare-bottomed, the more their awareness increased. They climbed off my lap, the couch or the bed when they needed to go. One morning Randy woke to see Tsameret pulling on the pee bowl and crying. He undressed her and held her over it and she peed. He was amazed and inspired. Then Moriah walked towards me with "the look" in her eye, and I just knew she had to go so held her over the bowl, and she went.

I sometimes feared that because I had never been able to catch a lot of pees, IPT might not work. But it seems that even an imperfect program can succeed. As they became mobile I sensed them taking charge and communicating more than before. And their styles were still so different! Moriah often peed while standing then just kept on walking, whereas Tsameret would cry out loudly in an urgent plea for help and would more willingly sit on the potty or pee in the bowl. I also came to realize that they were often in sync with each other, and so instead of cleaning up misses if one had an accident, I learned to go catch a pee from the second one instead.

At 11 months, my girls came to me with wet or poopy diapers and knew what to do with a potty. I introduced the ASL potty sign at this point. By the end of the first year, most of our success continued to be at night, and communication during the day improved dramatically. Both girls woke up at night when they needed to go. I started to use more consistent timing and offered them the potty upon waking, after eating, and before and after rides in the car. When I heard grunting, this enabled me to get there in time to catch their poops. When I wore them in a sling, they wiggled to let me know they needed to go. When traveling in the car, Tsameret would yelp and I would pull over and hold her in the classic position by the side of the road. When they started fussing while shopping, I took them to the ladies room and they used the toilet. It really worked quite well when I made the effort. I was getting better at acting on my intuition and random pee thoughts. I started sensing small pauses and silences in their play, or how much time had passed since the last pee and when it was time to offer the potty.

Communications Improve (13-15 months)

The girls spent their second summer "nakey-butt" or in open pants, with two potties on the deck where they played. During this period I had the sense that they were beginning to "get it" and to communicate with me very clearly. At 13 months they started to use the potty sign. At 14 months, they both started saying "pee pee." Moriah would sing "pee pee" in the car seat when she needed a pit stop. Tsameret would yelp when she needed me to stop driving. Often in the morning, when Moriah crawled off the bed after nursing and I knew she had to pee, I would point at the potty and say "pee pee in the potty." I was usually nursing her sister and could not jump up to help. She learned to set herself on the potty and pee as I watched from the bed.

At night they were diaperless and only wore T-shirts in bed. The mattress was covered with a wool blanket and flannel sheet. Cotton hospital bed pads covered the upper half of the bed in a layered fashion. If one of the girls wet, I changed the pad under her. After a 9 o'clock bedtime pee, they usually needed to be peed again around midnight. If they resisted the potty, I carried them to the sink and peed them as they were cradled in my arms half asleep, nursing at the breast. If I was not in the bed when they needed to go, they started getting up and looking for me while half asleep.

The girls invariably peed at my feet when I sat at the computer. They soon started to tell me when they pooped on the floor by coming to me while crying. I noticed they usually pooped mid morning. On the other hand, every once in a while I discovered a poop or a pee sitting in a potty all by itself, so I knew they understood and could even take themselves. Then, at 14 months, Moriah came to me, holding potty in hand with pee in it, smiling proudly. Potty play took off as the girls took charge. "Cleaning up" with diapers and wipes was a real favorite, as well as throwing the potty down the stairs. Squatting and grinning at me to get a reaction and then running off laughing was another favorite game. Moriah often resisted being put on the potty, while Tsameret would sit there happily for a long time.

The Turnaround (16-18 months)

It used to be I could lie in bed in the mornings and tell them "pee pee in the potty" but then that changed. Tsameret went in the potty if I took her hand and guided her there, but Moriah would just laugh and run away, thinking it was a game. Around 16 months there was a turnaround. I looked up one morning and there was Tsameret, proudly peeing without prompting. Moriah started asking to sit on the big toilet with an insert in the mornings, and learned to close the lid and flush. One day when Tsameret had an accident, I said, "Go get a diaper and clean it up." To my amazement, she went over to get a prefold from the diaper pile and wiped up her own pee!

At 17 months I felt the girls start to "graduate." They were progressing fairly quickly because they watched and learned from each other all day long. Tsameret stayed dry most of the time with my help. I would come across potties with pee in them all over the house and was cleaning up fewer misses. Moriah still had accidents, but when away from home, she was very attentive and careful. When sitting on a neighbor's couch one day, she got very agitated and worried. When I asked her if she needed to pee, she hesitated, stared at me, and then blurted out in distress "yeah!" They rarely peed on the floor at my feet anymore while I was at the computer. I remember the day when suddenly one girl, and then the other, went to get a potty, set it down near me, and the two of them sat there watching me and peed while I worked at the computer.

I felt proud of my girls and grateful for the bond I had been able to form with them. Randy felt the same way. We had good communication with them. They were open and responsive, listened and paid attention to us. I believe that EC'ing played an important role in this because it helped us both tune in to them in ways we never would have if we hadn't been doing IPT.

Wright

At 18 months, the twins used their potties independently during the day and stayed dry all night.

Randy felt a close bond with the girls as a result of helping with their potty learning. He got to know them better by tuning in to their pottying needs, and their relationship blossomed: "I remember holding them by their legs and aiming them so they could pee over the edge of the sundeck. I felt capable and important as a result of being able to participate. Sometimes I could sense or just knew it was time. When they were little, wiggling prompted me to check and see if they needed to go. Very often Lucia knew better. Now they tell me clearly of their own accord."

Staying Dry (19-24 months)

By now, both girls were staying dry most of the time with my help. Tsameret was very reliable about using the potty and at 19 months she started to pull her pants down, even when wearing split crotch pants. One day I saw Moriah race to the potty in time to catch a pee. Both girls clearly understood what a potty was for and knew how to use it. When we were away from home, they were still much better at staying dry.

At 21 months the girls were saying "pee pee" or "poo" every time they needed to go or else right after a miss. It was winter and they wore underpants with pants all the time. One day, I noticed they had gone the whole day without an accident until evening when they got tired. That was a first for us. Usually, we had at least 2 or 3 pee accidents each per day. And poops started landing in the potty instead of next to it!

At 24 months, Moriah started saying "ow pee pee" before going. I prompted them in the morning, before and after naps, before and after car rides, and in the evening. In between, they were on their own. When I did prompt them, they often shook their heads and said "no." If they had an accident, they asked for help getting wet clothes off, selected dry clothes, and dressed themselves with just a bit of help. And there were no more poops on the floor! Both girls were dry at night, usually with a midnight pee. I rearranged the bedding so only one strip of chucks went across the bed at hip level.

Independence (25 months)

At 25 months, the girls entered their third summer and were excited to be outdoors again and not have to wear so many clothes. They took themselves to the potty and pulled down their pants on their own. The only thing they needed help with was wiping and dumping the potties or setting up the child's toilet seat.

At 27 months, they provided a running commentary ("pee pee") on their way to the potty, while on the potty, or after they had finished. After their 9 p.m. pee, I still helped with their midnight pee when they got restless and sighed a lot. In the morning, if I asked, "Who needs to pee?" and made the cueing sound, they got very agitated, shook their heads and shrieked, "No!" They would pee on their own after rising. If they asked to nurse during the day and started squirming, I would suggest they use the potty, but mostly they took the initiative on their own. There was a lot of commotion and activity before poops. At the dinner table, they would ask to "get down" in what seemed like the middle of the meal and would sometimes say "pee pee," but often they simply asked to get down in a very urgent tone of voice. We still have potties distributed around the house for easy access. They started choosing unusual receptacles and placing their potties in unusual places, like on top of the trampoline. The cutest memory I have is of them "tandem peeing" at the river's edge, both squatting, Tsameret behind Moriah, embracing her.

The other day, I heard Tsameret say to her baby doll, "I hear you, honey" and was very touched. I have said that to my girls whenever I can't respond to them right away. I acknowledge them and let them know their needs will be met whenever possible. That has been my goal from the start with the pottying—that they should always know that I hear them, even if I cannot always respond, which is a constant source of frustration and anxiety for mothers of twins.

I am very impressed with how well this has worked with twins! There were many times when I couldn't attend to one or the other, and yet they have both done so well. It goes to show what a strong instinct it is in them, and how a little can go a long way. It has truly been a wonderful journey.

Update at Age 6 ½ Years

For anyone wondering about the long-term effects of infant potty training it is the beginning of a long and rewarding journey of parent-child communication. With twins there is also the bond that develops between them around pottying. In our case, there was tandem use of potties as a social activity long past potty independence. The kind of observation, attention and listening that infant pottying requires of a parent models communication skills that were absorbed by our twins in relation to each other. And as pottying receded in importance, we applied the same kind of listening to their emotional and intellectual needs. Infant pottying formed a foundation of communication and trust that still continues to serve us well.

chapter 7

elimination communication

Rosie Wilde (pseudonym) lives in Seattle. She discovered EC
when her first son Dakota was 3 months old. He finished at
22 months. Rosie started at birth with her second son Ian,
who was 14 months old at the time of this interview (2002).

First Son

My first son was 3 months old when I stumbled upon this method. I was
surfing around on the Internet and found an article on elimination training in
infancy. I read part of it but was so upset by it that I turned off the computer.
My upset was due to skepticism about being able to do this within the confines
of our culture. My curiosity got the better of me, and I switched the computer
back on and continued reading. Before reaching the end of the article, I stood
up, went to Dakota's changing table, took his diaper off and said, "We're going
to try something different. If you need to pee or poop, try and let me know.
I'll try to understand you. If I don't seem to get it, try telling me another way.
We're both going to make mistakes. We'll do this for one hour and see how it
feels." I returned to the computer to read the rest of the article. Before I had
finished, he wiggled, squirmed and grunted a bit. I took him to the bathroom,
and he pooped for me. We continued doing it from that first day until he was
finished with toilet training at 22 months.

In that first hour of trying, he pooped once and peed a few times. Then
it was time for us to go to bed. I thought to myself that I had been lucky for
that first hour but that I'd need to find out more about it the next day. That

night I didn't put a diaper on him when we went to bed. When I woke up in the morning, I said to myself, "This is silly. It worked so I'm not going to *not* do it, now that we can do it."

For about the first month, I carried him around with a flannel under his bottom, until I learned his signals. Up to 4 months of age, I kept a little bucket in the room with us, but then he started letting me know far enough in advance that I could take him to the bathroom. He preferred going in the bathroom where he saw us use the toilet and soon refused to use the bucket anymore.

We had varying degrees of success over the months, depending on his mood. He was a pretty high-needs child. At times he was involved in teething or learning a skill and didn't pay attention. There were a few difficult days where we missed nearly every pee or poop. No matter what happened, it was always a cooperative effort between us, and I learned not to fear making mistakes. Some days we "hit the pot" 90% of the time; on other days just 75%. Either way, we were connecting all the time, and I loved it.

With my son, the communication was often by psychic means. This meant I had to be tuned in to him. It might sound strange, but I often heard the word "pee" in my mind when he had to go. It was very clear. Whenever I received that communication, I took him to the bathroom and he'd go. I don't communicate telepathically in other ways, so it was very hard for me to trust it.

My husband had the same experience with hearing "pee" in his mind. When Dakota got older, a very good friend of mine named Alice started coparenting with us, and she had the same experience too. She would suddenly hear the word "pee" in her head, take him to pee and he'd go for her. For people who wonder whether or not babies are telepathic, we have anecdotal evidence that they are!

The communication with my son was not only psychic in terms of hearing a word, but I eventually realized that I was also *feeling* it in my body. I actually felt what his body was telling me I needed to do. It took a while to figure out what was happening because this feeling was not a feeling in my bladder. The level where his bladder was in relation to my body is where I felt it. For example, I felt a full bladder at my sternum when he was small. It took me a while to realize that he was communicating the impression of "This is what my body feels like, Mom. Can you help me do something about this?" As he got taller, the feeling moved down in my body. That's when I started to understand the feeling. When it got low enough to be felt in my abdomen, it felt like I needed to pee, but I knew I didn't need to. Then I'd hear him say "pee" in my head, and I understood that he was letting me know what his body felt like. I once read about an anthropologist who asked an African mother how she knew when her baby needed to go. The mother replied, "How do you know when you need to go?" I think this may be the origin of that quote, from the mother actually feeling her baby's full bladder.

Dakota signaled me in a number of other ways. I had the best results reading his signals when he was in the sling and when I was relaxed about the whole thing. I made the "pss pss" noise in an attempt to get him to vocally signal to me ahead of time. He started making this noise around 7 months, but only when we were out in public. He would also holler ("Mama, Mama!"), cry (usually only when waking up with a full bladder), crawl to the bathroom door or crawl to me and look at me. The times I missed getting him to the bathroom were when I was not focused—talking to someone, reading or otherwise not tuned in to Dakota. I know many other mothers whose babies vocalize in some way to get their mothers' attention before they can speak.

Sometimes Dakota signaled and I took him to the sink where he would try to go but nothing happened. If I turned on the water, the sound usually helped him pee. If that didn't work, I kept his pants off, walked around for a minute or two, then returned to the sink and asked if he wanted to try again. I think this is a more relaxed approach than spending a lot of time waiting at the sink, which could create performance anxiety.

My husband helped with toilet training. When he wanted to focus on tuning in to Dakota, he was 75–80% able to know when Dakota needed to go. My husband doesn't like the type of deep, intimate communication needed for this, so the first few months he had a lot of wet T-shirts and sometimes used diapers. It challenged his emotional intimacy issues. It is much more emotionally intimate to be in communication with a baby than to just stick a diaper on him. I think that is another reason why people resist this so intensely. Diapering is a lot of work, yet most people prefer to do that than be in tune with their children. It makes me think that we have an entire culture that is invested in being dissociated.

Once my husband got over that, he was glad to help. He griped about it occasionally, but what let me know that he liked it was that he told his friends about it and was proud that we weren't diapering our baby. When I say "proud," I mean proud that we were listening to and meeting our son's needs.

When Dakota started scooting and crawling, things got a little confusing. He peed on the floor a lot without giving any cues. We figured out that the pressure on his tummy and bladder made it difficult to control his bladder. We placed him on a mat during this phase. In the same vein, sometimes he would be playing on his belly, ask to pee but when we got to the bathroom, nothing happened. I think that when we picked him up, the pressure on his belly was reduced, and he no longer felt the urge to pee.

In general, the only time I diapered him was to take him shopping. I always asked him to let me know if he had to pee and assured him that I'd take him to a nearby place, remove the diaper and let him go. When we got home half an hour later, his diaper would be dry. This was a baby who normally peed every 10 minutes. This told me right away that he had an ability to hold it if he wanted, at least up to a certain point. Once we saw that he was holding his pee in an effort to avoid going in an unfamiliar setting, we constantly encouraged him, "Don't hold it if you really have to go."

As for travel, we cloth-diapered him and gave him the option of letting us know when he needed to go. He always stayed dry when he napped, so we scheduled traveling around his naps. Whenever we got to a rest stop, we took him to pee. Very rarely would we arrive somewhere and find he had a wet diaper. This concerned us, and I kept telling him that if he needed to go in the diaper, he should go.

By the age of 7 months, he had reasonable control. We didn't have to diaper him anymore to take him on a 30-minute trip to the grocery store. By 9½ months, he always told me if he had to go, unless he was teething, preoccupied or in a resistant phase of saying no to everything. At 11 months, he only peed about once an hour, and if we were outside or driving in the car, he was great about signaling me verbally. By 14 months, he took care of all his own pooping. Of course, I had to wipe his bottom, but he walked to the potty and sat down on his own. Sometimes he said "poop" to call me to come and sit next to him.

We took a casual approach to nighttime. If I didn't care about him wetting the bed, I didn't wake up. Until he was 6½ months, I kept a little bucket by the bed. After that, I took him to the bathroom sink. Sometimes he didn't wake up fully, and I didn't disturb his slumber. He just peed for me and fell right back to sleep. I hardly woke up either and certainly never felt sleep deprived. By 12 months, he was capable of communicating his nighttime needs to me and holding it until I woke up and got him to the bathroom. He did well at this most of the time before he was a year old, but by 12 months, we didn't have a wet bed unless I was sleeping really heavily. I have found that babies don't go in their sleep unless they are extremely relaxed or in a very deep sleep. I discovered early on that when Dakota woke up, it was because he needed to pee, not because he wanted to nurse or was ready to wake up. I've cross-checked this with many mothers and they all agree that what seems to wake a baby up at night is a full bladder.

Around the age of 11 months, Dakota went through a really intense potty strike for 6 weeks. He stopped signaling, and when we took him to pee, he arched his back and yelled. During that time, we diapered him. That was the only time he wore diapers throughout the day. He didn't like it at all. He preferred going bare-bottomed or wearing pants because they were less restrictive than a cloth diaper.

I found that babies only go on strike if there is an emotional issue involved. It is your job to figure out what is bothering your baby. Since babies cannot speak or physically do much, they sometimes communicate by *not* doing something—like a nursing strike to let you know that erupting teeth are painful.

When he started his potty strike, I tried using positive reinforcement, but soon found that it caused an intensification of any resistance he was having. I'm sure I prolonged his strike by 3 weeks by praising and rewarding him. On the rare occasions, about once a day, where he communicated and we got to the sink on time, I got excited and told him it was great that he had communicated and that I really appreciated it. That was followed by a day of running away from me and peeing on the rug or in his diaper. I posted this dilemma online and got a reply that said that maybe he was perceiving my praise as pressure. We soon learned that Dakota felt manipulated by praise unless he initiated it. This applied to all aspects of his life. If he wanted to celebrate the accomplishment of something, he ran to us clapping and we clapped with him.

I finally found the cause of his strike. He wanted to use the big toilet instead of a potty. Once I figured it out, he started signaling again. He liked the adult toilet so much that at first he often signed when he hardly had any pee in his bladder.

My good friend Alice was living with us when Dakota was born. She didn't have a chance to help with toileting until he was about 14 months old. This was when they were bonded and close enough that I could go out for an hour and leave Dakota with her. It clicked for them immediately, and Alice never got peed on. When we were both in a room together, we both heard "pee" in our heads when Dakota needed to go!

He didn't start taking over his own peeing until about 20 months. I think it irritated him that he had to pee so frequently. He was very busy and didn't like stopping what he was doing. At 22 months we gave him free reign of the bathroom where he used the adult toilet, and he has been potty trained ever since.

Second Son

I started at birth with my second son Ian and was much more relaxed. It's the same with other things you experience with your first and second child. You are more relaxed with everything, like nursing or when they fall down. I literally had never held a baby before I had Dakota.

Starting with a newborn gave my second son more confidence in me than my first. Dakota went through 3 months of me not having a clue. One day, when Ian was 3 or 4 days old and nursing, I looked down at him and said, "You need to pee, don't you?" He unlatched and looked at me. It felt like a cooperative arrangement with Ian right from the beginning, instead of me saying at 3 months, "I'm sorry. I completely missed the boat. Can you help me figure out how to do this?" This is why Dakota had to "yell in my head" to get my attention. With Ian, if one of us needed a break, we'd both take a break.

It took him two months to learn to crawl, and during that time, his message was, "Do not bug me about elimination communication!" And it didn't bother me. "Okay, fine. I know we'll just pick this up again in a month." And right now, he's learning to walk and we're doing the same thing again. If he's in-arms, he never pees on me unless he is sick or if I just consumed dairy products. If I pick him up and he doesn't want to go, he just stretches his legs out to tell me "no" and I put him down. I know that in another few months, we'll be 99 percent potty trained.

With Ian, the sensation of having a bladder in my chest is gone and none of us hear the word "pee" when he needs to go. Instead, we've all just had a sense that "it's time for Ian to go." I think the fact that the communication is different is due to me. Dakota had to work really hard to train me, and any communication I got from him was strong. The second baby knew the receptors were already working, "Mom has already got this figured out. I don't need to work as hard."

Elimination Communication

I found this method very easy, far superior to any of the alternatives. It was easier than the mechanical work of diapering and washing diapers. I much preferred spending time focusing on my sons and reading their cues to dealing with diapers and laundry. In addition, it was good for the environment, cost free and perfectly compatible with our lifestyle. It promoted all the positive aspects of attached child rearing that I wanted to include. It went along with breastfeeding, meeting my children's needs, carrying them in a sling and not leaving them alone with another caregiver in infancy.

I believe a child is born with a set of instincts based on where we were thousands of years ago before we started developing culture. The instincts have not had a chance to catch up. Infant toilet training is one of those instinctual behaviors. It's not a matter of survival, but this doesn't mean it's not important. A child communicates elimination needs from birth. The fact that a child communicates this from birth tells me it is important, that the communication happens for a reason. If you leave a need unmet or unacknowledged, you cause a person to shut down in that area. This can happen at any age, but especially with a very emotionally defenseless infant. It's no wonder that children conventionally diapered and potty trained have a terrible time toilet training because they have had to literally shut down the part of their brain that communicates their need to eliminate.

Even after you tell people this is baby-led, many still think it is something artificial you are forcing on the baby. They can't understand that it is part of an infant's needs set, along with being warm. They say, "This isn't really learning. This is the infant training the parent," which is not such a bad thing. Babies train us when to feed them and train us when to hold them. What's wrong with letting them train us when to take them to pee?

People striving for potty perfection might want to rethink things and relax. I have a slogan that might help: *Even EC done imperfectly works.*

Of course, when you think it would be fun to show it off, you get peed on. It's useless to try and have babies do potty tricks because they will pee in your lap if you do. It must be an unwritten rule to always pee in mom's lap when she is trying to impress her mother-in-law.

If anyone comes to me with an EC problem that can't be resolved by taking their baby to a different location or using a different position, especially if the problem started right around the time the baby started eating solid foods, I recommend they try eliminating dairy and wheat from their diet for a month to see if it helps. For example, a mother was doing well for 7 months and then suddenly her baby was no longer responsive, so she went back to full-time diapers for 6 months. If she tried to pee him holding him under the thighs, which flexes the pelvis, he would scream. It was very painful for him. Having had irritable bowel and irritable bladder from dairy allergies, I can totally relate to this. When he was 13 months old, I convinced her to change her diet. Within 48 hours, her son was peeing and pooping exactly as he had been at age 7 months. It was astonishing. There are a lot of kids who are allergic to wheat and dairy, but it goes mostly undiagnosed

We discuss elimination communication topics online and share our joys and insight. It's helpful to learn things such as fresh baby pee is basically sterile.

With strictly breastfed babies, pee has no bacteria as it comes out of the body, unless you're sick. It's full of discarded nutrients. The moment it hits the air, it starts growing bacteria, which is why it starts to stink and is also why wool is such a lovely substance to waterproof your bed with. It's also helpful to use wool pants over a diaper with no cover. It won't allow bacteria or fungus to grow, so it doesn't smell once the urine is dry.

I've inspired hundreds of mothers to use elimination communication, if not full time, at least part time. They have all found it easy. Many found out about it after their babies were born. Some started relatively late, one at 9 months and another at 11 months, and they did fine. I think it's okay to start this late if you are gentle, neutral and relaxed. I think the chances of success for late-starters depend a lot on how much their babies' communication has already been respected, as well as how the babies have handled not having that need met earlier. One little boy who started at 9 months had days where he would take a diaper to his mother and want to be diapered. The other days, he did not want to be diapered at all. His mother paid attention to his cues and followed his lead. He's 2 now and toilet trained.

chapter **8**

a mom & two nannies

Sherri Tomlin is a chiropractor living in San Jose, California. Her husband Robert Martines is also a chiropractor. They have their own practices. Sherri first heard about infant potty training when their son Lucas was 7 months old. Here's what Sherri had to say in 2000.

I was in an attachment parenting playgroup and one day one of the mothers started talking about infant potty training. The first thing I thought was that the woman was crazy. She demonstrated how the method worked with her little boy, and I found it interesting. I went home and thought of all the reasons why it wouldn't work for me: because I work, because I use babysitters, because my husband might object, etc. I had lots of doubts, but this is the way I always process things, by working through my doubts.

Several days later, I woke up, went into the kitchen and got a bowl to see how it would fit Lucas. I wondered if he would accept or reject it. He was seven and a half months old. I had been told that six months was the maximum age that I should start this, but I also had understood that it needs to be done before babies disconnect from their sense of elimination. Being a chiropractor, I understand how the nerves and the nervous system work and that it's extremely different from individual to individual, no matter what the books say or what other people's experiences are. There are always exceptions or unusual circumstances. The way I started potty training Lucas was to just test a bowl to see how it would work. The bowl was from a set of nesting plastic bowls from the kitchen. I sat him on the middle-sized bowl in my lap since that was the way my friend had held her baby and also because the bowl wasn't stable on its own. Lucas didn't object, and we just went from there.

At first, I tried to get all his pees and poos in the bowl, even at night. I wasn't sure if he was "too old" to start infant potty training and wanted to communicate by my actions that I was doing everything I could to help him stay connected with this natural ability.

Before we had started the potty training, Lucas used to cry frequently during the night. When I started getting up and putting him on the potty, it quieted him down. I realized his crying was his way of letting me know he didn't like to be wet, and in this way, I knew for sure that he was still connected with the sensation that he needed to go potty even though he was over the recommended threshold to begin infant potty training. He confirmed that I wasn't too late to use this method with him.

I got up at night with him for a month or two, then decided I didn't want him to wake up crying, so I started using a disposable diaper at night since it suppresses the feeling of wetness and could last through his wettest nights.

I still tried to get the pees and poos during the day for a while and even now I still get quite a few. I know if I put more time into it that we'd get more pees in the potty, but lately we're mainly concentrating on the poos. He's 12½ months old now and usually goes when he gets up in the morning, once in mid-morning and then again in the afternoon.

Lucas has two caregivers or babysitters. The caregivers happened to already be good friends of each other when I first met them. They even live on the same street. One of them is a nanny and the other is a school teacher, so they are both very experienced in working with children. One of them takes Lucas three mornings and the other takes him two afternoons, for a total of five half days a week. When I first met them, I told them about infant potty training, but they were reluctant to try it.

I knew I could do infant toilet training with or without the help of the caregivers. I understand that even tiny babies know the difference between individuals and will test different individuals in different ways. They'll do one thing with Grandma that they won't do with Mom. If the babysitters wouldn't use the method, I planned to tell Lucas, "When you're not with Mommy, just go in the diaper." Then when he was with me again, I'd say, "Tell Mommy when you need to go." I verbalize with him because that's how I communicate best, even if he's picking it up on a different level—from my tone of voice or body language.

I got the book *Trickle Treat* and immediately gave it to the caregivers—I hadn't even read the book yet! At first, they didn't want to commit to it. After some days, one of them came to me and confessed that they had been doing it for three days. They talk to each other every evening. They had been discussing it with each other and had decided to give it a try.

Lucas works well with the caregivers. In fact, sometimes he is easier with them than with me. I found out that their original hesitation was that they feared they wouldn't do it right. They wanted to do it perfectly. They feared they would make a mistake or somehow harm the child. They discussed it with each other and decided that either they would both do it or neither of them would do it. They thought it would be wrong for one of them to do it and not the other. They thought it would be okay if I did it and they didn't, but they saw each other as a unit. I advised them to do their best, have fun with it and above all to have no "judgment" about it.

They are very proud of their success. They keep a notebook for me. Everyday I get a page of detailed notes of what went on the during the day, and this includes the potty progress. They write if he peed or pooed in the potty or if they missed getting him to the potty on time.

We used the little plastic bowl until one day someone dropped it and cracked it. Then I bought a potty. Since it had a stable base, I could let Lucas sit on the potty on the floor instead of in my lap. He had no trouble sitting on it. I kept my arms around him at first. It was like I was the one who needed to go through the infant process instead of him.

I've noticed that sometimes he'll pee three times within five minutes. He doesn't always release everything the first time he pees. Sometimes he shivers when he's peeing on the potty. When he shivers while he's nursing, I realize he just peed. I've talked with other mothers who have noticed that their babies shiver when they pee too, but it's too late to get them on the potty at that point.

I have had troubles here and there, as do most parents using any type of toilet training. At each new stage, there is something for me and Lucas to work out, or for my caregivers to work out. Above all, I listen to Lucas, and not other people, about what's going to work with him. I figure things out and go with the process without any judgment about it. We live day to day and don't use percentages or anything like that. Sometimes we have several perfect days in a row, and some days it is difficult. On difficult days I try to focus on not getting frustrated. I strive to just accept the frustration and feel it fully so I can let it go and move on.

Some say that this method is too inconvenient for Americans. My response is that I didn't have a child for my convenience. I'm not potty training Lucas for my convenience. When I started doing this and telling people about it, there seemed to be more doubt from other people. The more I gained certainty about it, the less I would hear negative things from other people. I explain that it's something that third world countries do and that we used to do a long time ago. They drop their jaw, open their eyes and say, "Yeah, I see."

I was raised with a lot of wilderness camping, so I've used some of that with taking care of Lucas in that I'll take the potty anywhere. I wish I had trained him earlier to go over a toilet in a public bathroom because he won't, so I take his potty with me and use it in the back of our sport utility vehicle. I open up the back and say, "Okay, Lucas, we're going camping now." And I put him on the potty in the back of the car. At first it bothered me when people looked but now it doesn't.

One time we were at a restaurant and Lucas was grunting so I took him out to the car in the middle of the dinner and left my husband at the table. Lucas pooed in the potty, then I took him back and was feeding him in the restaurant when he started to grunt again. I took him back out to the potty in the car again. I started wondering if I should be interrupting my dinner and leaving my husband alone in the restaurant for long stretches. I wondered what others were thinking. Out in the car, we had success with the potty. Later I heard my husband talking to other people and telling them that we were doing this method and that he didn't care if he was in a traffic jam in the middle of the San Francisco Bay Area, he would pull over on the side of the road where everyone could see what he was doing, but he was going to take care of his son and do what was right for him. I understood then that he didn't feel inconvenienced by me leaving the dinner table at the restaurant. Interruptions like this don't happen very often but when they do, I don't mind.

Lucas started to crawl relatively late, around 10½ months. Since then, he has been more interested in everything in his environment, in exploring things, and it has become more difficult to keep him on the pot. Sometimes I put him in a diaper, then set a timer for five minutes and put him back on.

Sometimes when he won't sit on the potty I take him outside and let him wander around naked. That seems to give him a little space, time to deal with things and then he goes back to the potty. It's really a dance—a pushing and pulling. Sometimes it's a struggle. Sometimes when we're dancing we step on each other's feet, but most of the time we're having fun with it.

One thing that helps him stay on the potty recently is lots of snuggles and hugs. I kneel down and play with him, do pat-a-cake and hug him a lot.

His cues for pooing are (1) he grunts, (2) he cries, (3) he's quiet and trance-like or (4) he crawls behind furniture. Rather than going to someone, he goes away from us and gets very quiet, which is unusual for him since he's usually very vocal. The babysitter says he's hiding from her. I think he just wants to be alone for a minute while he poos.

I think Lucas has fairly good control over his muscles at this point because sometimes he'll sit on the potty and wait for me to put his diaper on, then immediately go in the diaper. He only does it for one elimination, then we're fine for a while. When he does this, I don't feel like it's something he is doing to me. He is experimenting. When I hear the term "testing," some people think the child is doing something in order to see what you'll do in response to it. Well yes, that happens because I'm part of the environment, but he's testing loads of things besides me. He is testing his nerves, his muscles, his sensations of what it's like to not go in the potty and to go in the diaper. Then he makes a decision and frankly if he decides to go in the diaper for the next month, that's his decision. If it's because I'm not paying attention, then I'll work harder but if it's because of something he's choosing, then I'm fine with it.

I don't praise him a lot when he goes potty. I try not to praise him about much. My husband praises him, but I don't. I just simply state fact. When he started crawling, I didn't clap and say, "Yay, good boy! You're so wonderful." I just stated, "You're crawling," and he gets from my tone of voice that I'm excited about it. I'm not a robot about it. When he falls, I don't make a big thing out of it. I look at him and say, "Oh, you fell down." He hardly cries when he falls down, compared to other kids I've seen. When he goes in the potty, I state fact, "You went pee pee in the potty," or "You went poo in the potty," or if he does a big poo, I'll say so, "Oh, you did a big poo."

My mother-in-law is a pediatric RN and thinks this is wonderful. She is very open-minded in many ways. My mother also thinks infant potty training is interesting. She says that my grandmother would be proud of me. When I started doing this, my mother said, "Oh, my goodness, this is what my mother tried to do with my children." So I found out that my grandmother, whose mother was German, had put me on the potty whenever I visited her when I was an infant, but it only happened occasionally because she lived in another town. My grandmother didn't see it as a special method, so she couldn't explain it to my mother. Even though my mother likes the method, she is hesitant to put Lucas on the potty. If he has to go, she brings him to me and I put him on. This is helpful. The only time she'll put him on the potty is when I am not around.

We travel to a lot of seminars with Lucas, and of course I take the potty with us. Our flights are usually short, just an hour. The seminars are in the hotel, so he's with me there. I find potty training easy in the hotel.

Unfortunately, people have been told you get Freudian results if you potty train a baby too early. My reply is that it's me who is being trained, and I'm doing something that is still being used in the majority of the world. In this country, even the most conservative people have an understanding of going back to what we used to do before technology took over.

I feel wonderful about this method. I'm really happy we're doing it. It fits in with the lifestyle we chose before we even knew about Attachment Parenting or infant potty training. We were already doing the family bed and carrying him a lot instead of putting him in a stroller. Since he spends about four hours a day with a babysitter, I feel it's important for me to hold him a lot when I'm with him. I know from my chiropractic training about the nervous system that brain development is enhanced when babies are held and moved about. I think the most important aspect of the potty training is the spiritual side.

There are three main ways that I know he needs to go potty. First, timing. A lot of it is based on timing, putting him on the potty just after a meal or when we get up in the morning. Second, communication. He signals me in different ways like grunting, crying or crawling over to get me, although sometimes he crawls to me right after he has peed in his pants; I take this to mean he is un-comfortable and wants to be changed. The third element I use is my intuition. For example, one day I was leaving the office. It was late in the day and I was just pulling out when I had a thought, "I wonder if Lucas needs to go poo? When was the last time I pooed him?" I almost did something that is typical of me, which is to say to myself, "Oh, he's fine. I'll do it when I get home." I almost drove out the driveway. That was the moment I realized, "Wait a minute. That's the little voice in me, talking to me." The more I listen to that little voice, the clearer it becomes. I backed up into the parking lot, nursed Lucas, then put him on the potty in the back of the truck, and he went. I had a successful outcome from listening to that little voice.

I think listening to that voice is important. The times that I have missed getting him to the potty on time and I feel frustrated with myself are times when I'm on the telephone, doing the laundry or driving somewhere. In other words, something is distracting me, and I'm not listening to that little voice. I have to listen to that little voice about many things, not just elimination. That voice really connects you with what you need to do in life. This is what I love about this method and from being with my playgroup. They have helped me be more certain about what I'm doing, and I don't need to defend myself when

Robert Martines

Lucas takes a pee . . . in the family SUV.

I'm with the group. It's like an island of peace. It's not that society attacks us for doing unusual things, but people are curious and question me, and I always have to explain things. In the playgroup, I don't have to explain myself, so I feel a lot of support in that way.

When a new idea comes along, people go through four phases. Christopher Columbus went through this. First he said the world was round and that he could travel around the world. People said he was crazy. After a while, they looked at his information and said, "That's interesting. I wonder if it will work for him?" They funded Columbus and said, "Go ahead." They saw him sail around the world and thought, "I wonder if that will work for me?" Then some of them got on a ship and tried it. Eventually society said, "I'm glad we thought of this." This is how a new idea becomes accepted. It goes from "You're nuts" to "I see it works for you" to "I wonder if it will work for me?" to being accepted as normal.

I understand this firsthand as a chiropractor. Society and individuals are going through those phases now in regards to what I do every day for people in my office. I went through that process in a matter of days with this elimination method. I thought my friend was nuts when she first told me about infant potty training. Now I think of her as a genius.

This method isn't for everyone, but people should at least know it's a viable option. If it sounds right for them, they will try it. In trying, they will succeed or fail. If they succeed, great! If they fail . . . no harm done, but it's certainly worth a try!

chapter 9

a physician speaks out

Dr. Lauri Nandyal graduated from medical school in Cincinnati in 1989 and completed her family practice residency in 1992. She worked in rural Ohio for 4 years until 1996, doing full-scope family practice including obstetrics and, consequently, a lot of pediatrics. Lauri has three girls of her own, ages 8 years, 5 years and 1 year old. Since her third child was born, she has reduced her clinical work in order to stay home with her family. Here is what the doctor had to report in 2000.

I didn't learn about this method of toilet training in time to use with my first two girls. It was merely by chance that I learned about it when my third child was about 2 weeks old. I was chatting with my neighbor, who happens to be from India, and she told me that she had toilet trained her children from early infancy. I was completely flabbergasted to hear this. As a physician, I had never even given this type of thing a moment's consideration. Even in my many travels before motherhood, I was oblivious to the practice of infant toileting. It's just one of those things that doesn't enter your consciousness until you're a parent. Plus, in medical school we're taught that it's physically impossible to toilet train an infant, and this is what we tell our patients. So the concept really took me by surprise. Needless to say, I set to work right away and was thrilled to learn that my baby could hold her bowel movements and later her urine.

My neighbor told me how she had toilet trained her children. Her first two were born and raised in India where she was under the wing of her mother, sisters and sisters-in-law and had their help and guidance. Her third child was born in the United States where she was on her own with toilet training. Her method involved holding her baby on her feet. After a feeding, she would sit on the floor or the bed and prop her baby on her feet over a newspaper or a diaper, and in response, he would "perform." She further mentioned that in India, at least in more traditional families, mothers carry or hold their babies much of the time, and babies don't wear diapers. One way mothers stay dry is to take their babies to the toilet every 45–60 minutes and prompt them to go. They may squat the babies in a corner in the bathroom or outside and make a "sssss" noise to cue them to go.

My neighbor in Ohio used the same sound with her children. I haven't had a great deal of success with my baby responding to any particular sound for urination. Also, I don't have the energy to undress my baby from several layers of clothes, socks, etc., and put her on the toilet that often. I feel good if I manage to take her every hour and a half. Aside from the initial explanation by my neighbor, my learning process consisted mainly of on-the-job training. I didn't find any books about this until my baby was about 9 months old. At that time, I read a chapter in a book on toilet training which mentioned "other methods" and gave some credence to early toilet training but did not really encourage it. That was the extent of the literature I found until Laurie Boucke's *Trickle Treat.*

Since I really didn't feel comfortable with the actual method my neighbor described and since I figured that the procedure would eventually lead to using a toilet anyway, I decided to start there—that is, using the toilet—from the beginning. The position I use with my daughter involves me squatting in front of the toilet or else sitting on a small stool placed at the front of it. I prop my elbows on my knees and hold her securely with a hand under each armpit. In this way I was able to support her head until she had good head control. She is in a squatting position over the toilet, facing me, with her bottom hanging over the toilet bowl. This position is all she has ever known, and she has never seemed frightened, as some might expect. I always have two hands on her and have always provided adequate, comfortable and secure support. One word of warning: Little girls can "shoot" when they urinate. If my baby is not aimed downward, she'll pee on me and the toilet seat. I have to lean her a little forward to pee straight down. If she doesn't really need to go, she may resist me positioning her. I've come to trust her knowing when she's done too. She'll straighten out her legs and stand upright. Occasionally, I've hurried her off before this signal, only to be sorry later. Also, in this way, I don't have additional dirty diapers, apart from the ones she wears between toilet visits. We use diapers between potty sessions, mainly because I can't find any training pants that are small enough to fit her. (The smallest are size two. I guess they figure no one here buys size one, but they must be selling them somewhere!) At night we use a diaper, to spare the bed from accidents. She may awaken during the night indicating she needs to go, but I can't arouse her enough for her to happily use the potty, so the diaper is there just in case. When she goes in the toilet, I usually say "good girl" or give her a kiss. I don't jump up and down with excitement. I did at first because I was so surprised, but now I'm a bit more matter of fact, just smile and say "good job" or something like that.

I started by concentrating on bowel movements rather than urination. I don't recall her ever soiling a diaper at night. Early on it was a part of her routine to stay clean at night, perhaps because we started this practice so early. This encouraged me to take her to the toilet for her daytime bowel movements. I waited a while after a feeding, anywhere from 10 to 30 minutes, then held her over the toilet. I was amazed the first time it worked. In fact, I didn't even realize she had gone because BM is so liquidy at that age. I suppose I was expecting more straining to accompany it. Her timing at first was pretty unpredictable since I breastfeed her. I take her to the toilet at least five or six times a day, usually after a feeding. At first, we had success about one out of three times. We eventually got her BM routine down really well. Since about 6 weeks of age, she has rarely soiled a diaper even while awake.

When she was about 6 months old, I realized I could also TIAN (toilet in advance of need) to try and get her to urinate in the toilet. She had started being dry upon awakening from naps. So Mommy became trained to take baby to the potty after naps and by keeping an eye on the clock. I rely on a sense of how long it has been since her last elimination, and sometimes I have the presence of mind to pay attention to her signals. Her signals aren't terribly blatant yet. She doesn't make a specific sound or noise that I've been able to discern as a signal to me about her need to pee. With bowel movements, she "toots" or passes a little gas, and this lets me know she has to go. About 90% of the time, a BM is preceded by a toot of some kind, but not all toots are followed by a bowel movement so it gets a little tricky. If she toots and hasn't had a bowel movement, I try to get her to the toilet. If she has more than one a day, I may neglect to act on that signal. Fussiness may be another one of the ways she signals, but fussiness can mean a number of things, so again it can be tricky.

The point is that even though her signals aren't always obvious, I do feel she tries to signal me. I suspect that some of the cries and discomfort expressed by my older two girls were ways they were trying to let me know they needed to go. I was in another world with regard to toilet training then and didn't pay attention to their cues. We think that when a baby cries it is because she is already wet or dirty. But maybe it's because she doesn't want to wet herself and she is trying to signal us to do something about it.

As for our prompting the baby to go, we grunt or make a bearing-down noise to cue bowel movements. We also have been trying some baby sign language. We may hold, pinch or wrinkle our nose, as a sort of "stinky" or smelly sign, to ask her if she has to go. For urinating, we make a water-flowing sound. Lately, she sounds like she's trying to say "go" and sometimes pats her diaper to let me know.

Parents who define toileting readiness by verbal cues or signs from their babies announcing that they need to go may be disappointed at first. The way my baby communicates is too rudimentary for this. There are times where we miss—I'm too distracted and don't listen to her signals, or we are out and can't get her to the toilet. Other times I misread her, take her to the toilet but she doesn't have to go. It also depends on whether I have the time to take her first thing in the morning and what solids she has eaten previously. They change her pattern somewhat. If she drinks apple juice, she has more frequent bowel movements. To do this, you just have to learn your child's biological time-clock and practice patience.

When our daughter was 9 months old, we spent 3 weeks in India. My husband is from Andhra Pradesh, India. While there, I interviewed my sisters-in-law about infant toilet training. My husband was unaware of how he had been toilet trained in infancy. He was the last of 10 children and since this isn't something that most fathers do with their babies anyway, he was not familiar with this method. Early one morning, my baby seemed to be very uncomfortable. Her diaper was totally dry, so I figured she might be signaling to let me know she needed to go to the toilet. I raced her to the bathroom and just barely got her there on time. She really let loose as soon as I held her in position. Up until that point, I hadn't given her credit for being consciously continent. She had been dry during the day for several days, and I now realized she was indeed aware and trying to communicate. I don't know if there was a consciousness that awoke in her sooner than that or if it was my projecting on her what I was hoping she could consciously do. The pattern of displaying discomfort before needing to go has happened more frequently since our trip abroad, and as soon as I get her on the toilet, she usually goes. I definitely feel that my daughter has some control, or else she would just go in her diaper without first signaling her discomfort.

Here in America we have certain societal norms that are more restrictive than in many other societies. For example, regarding breastfeeding in public, only lately can American women feel relatively at ease about nursing in public. If we were as liberal about public toileting as they are in many parts of the world, we'd really get ourselves in trouble. However, I think that public sanitation is a very good thing and is to be thanked for most of our public health advances in the West. A downside of the Western lifestyle with respect to practicing infant toileting is that we raise our children pretty much in isolation. In India and many other places, at least before industrialization, they raised their babies in a community setting, and mothers had help. It makes a big difference. It gets lonely here, and it isn't easy to toilet train an infant, and run a house, cook, chauffeur and supervise older siblings and do all the other things we'd like to do, but if you believe in it, it's a great thing to do for baby, parent and mother earth.

Sure, this method seems inconvenient. Some days I dedicate an hour to the potty if you add it all up. It's just another thing to think about, and our society is too busy, too distracted with so many things to do. My reasoning is that we have to deal with our babies' bottoms one way or another, and we can do it right from the beginning or postpone the process and have to reeducate the child later when it may be a bigger hassle. We can't change this pattern unless we really have the will to change. It's a mother's individual decision. I don't feel badly if someone honestly admits she is too busy to do this. I think, though, if more people really understood the impact on the environment and the potential harm it can do to children sitting around in wet diapers or by exposing children to chemicals like dioxin for so long, parents might be more motivated to try this. As a physician, if I see a mother whose baby has diaper rash, I'm able to prod her a little and recommend the child be in cloth or "flapping in the breeze" or that something "new and different" be done like infant pottying. There has to be a motivation to change behavior. Our society doesn't make it easy. Paper diapers are just too darn convenient . . . at quite a price.

I pooh-pooh the stories about psychological damage resulting from infant toileting. I have read the comments of Freudian psychologists and think the concern about trauma has only to do with the coercive way early toilet training was practiced in the early 1900s. Back then, folks were encouraged to tie their kids to potty chairs and got angry at them if they didn't perform. Of course, that was a warped approach. Spending time with your child and playing with her cannot be harmful even if it's on a potty. Obviously, I never leave my baby alone on the potty at this age. If my daughter is tired of sitting on the toilet, I quit. I never force it on her. My baby enjoys spending time with me wherever we are. I strongly feel that this method cannot harm my baby any more, and likely much less, than the customary Western way that I used with my older two whom I began retraining around the age of 2 years. I'm sure they sensed the frustration I tried so hard to hide when they had toileting accidents or wet the bed. Now I realize that I was asking them to follow a new set of rules after I had miseducated them from infancy about where bodily waste belongs. I dared to blame them when I was the one who decided to change the rules, as one must do when using conventional toilet training. I regret missing the opportunity to educate them properly from the beginning.

Western medicine teaches that it is not possible neurologically for babies to be toilet trained in infancy. I don't know where that idea came from. It appears to be "medlore," simply something that somebody passed on from their own experience. It's not coming from an in-depth study on the topic that I've ever found. What the layperson doesn't realize is how much of medicine is just hearsay. We don't have "randomized, double-blind, placebo-controlled" studies backing up more than about 30% of what we do. Much of medicine is an art or approach that has been passed along. Our present advice on postponing toilet training until 15 months or later due to "neurologic immaturity" is obviously ignorant, given the wealth of evidence to the contrary in cross-cultural reports. Who should you believe, millions of babies dry by age 6–9 months or the so-called experts?

The medical community may play a word game with you and say that an infant isn't consciously continent, or isn't holding it, but just letting go in a timely fashion or due to conditioned reflexes. You can rename it whatever you want, but the fact is, my child can stay dry longer than it takes for her bladder to fill up. She can hold it. There is no question, if you wait until 1 or 1½ years to start introducing babies to the toilet, it will take them a while to unlearn what you taught them and accept the new rules. But if they start with a continence program at birth, they will know that there is more to life than just sitting in a diaper. Although my personal experience with infant toilet training is limited to one child, I know that the rest of the world doesn't toilet train the Western way. My sisters-in-law have children who stayed dry day and night at the age of 6 months, so I know our babies have more control than we think they do.

Other "experts" may say that mom is the one who is trained. Whomever! The point is, waste goes where waste belongs, and a baby can learn from the beginning that sitting in a wet diaper is not necessary or welcome. Yes, the mothers are integral in initiating the process, but their babies can sleep through the night, wake up dry and wait to go to the toilet after sleeping 8-10 hours. Babies abroad aren't any smarter than ours, but maybe their parents are!

There's a relatively new field of ethnopediatrics—the study of child-care practices around the world. *Our Babies, Ourselves*, a book by anthropologist Meredith Small, is wonderful and clarifies how relative our child-rearing practices are. It also underscores the point that our babies are capable of much more than we realize. We even underestimate their abilities regarding something as basic as communication. For example, they have the ability to learn expressive sign language before one year of age, yet few parents attempt to communicate with their preverbal babies in this way. (There are some good books on this topic.) We probably haven't tapped the surface of what they can do.

Another factor in suppressing this technique of infant toileting education in the United States is commercialism. Too often, doctors are unwittingly fronts for a particular marketeer—whether it be a pharmaceutical, baby formula or diaper company. I am very aware of how much of my education about prescription drugs came from pharmaceutical representatives who had a product to sell. Manufacturers of disposable diapers have everything to lose from doctors encouraging the infant toileting method or the use of cloth diapers. From the start, hospitals provide paper diapers, which they say are more sanitary than cloth diapers, but all doctors know it is the caregiver's hands that are the real culprits in the spread of germs and that the type of diaper has little to do with it. It's very difficult to get into the ivory towers of medicine. It is a real challenge to change the way doctors get their information. Now that about one third of doctors in the USA are women and many of them are mothers, these issues may be more open to dialogue and reeducation.

I think Western medicine will slowly accept the principles of infant toilet training. Minds are opening because patients are demanding more alternative approaches. Given a little more time and publicity about this issue, I think it will become more welcome in the West. It's a slow process until we "die off" some of the older ways of doing things. I hope we don't have to wait until we suffer more consequences from the environmental impact of our "conveniences." As cultures rub against other cultures and patients begin to pressure their doctors for new information, doctors will become more receptive. It's a revolution that needs to happen.

chapter **10**

my diaper-free babies

Christine Gross-Loh is the mother of four and a freelance writer with a Ph.D. in East Asian history from Harvard University. She has lived in both Japan and Korea on multiple occasions and submitted this testimonial in 2010. She has been a key player in the activities of Diaper Free Baby and has written her own book on the topic of diaper-free babies.

As a mom to four EC'ed children, I'm an enthusiastic proponent of infant pottying, but I wasn't always this way. Before having kids, I spent time living with a family in a small village in Japan. I would watch my host mother helping to care for her newborn twin granddaughters. I was very surprised when I would see her help them to eliminate by periodically holding them over a bowl while making a *shii shii* sound. I thought it was fascinating, but the whole concept was so unfamiliar to me that I could barely imagine any one I knew—let alone myself—really doing it.

Years later, I remembered what I'd seen when I read about a practice called elimination communication, or infant potty training, while researching cloth diapers online for my first child. I didn't think it was for me though—by then I'd absorbed the Western concept that potty training shouldn't begin until children hit a whole slew of so-called "readiness" checkpoints around age 2 or older. Soon after my son's first birthday, however, my mother, who was raised in Korea, came for a visit bringing a cute little potty. I was surprised and even asked her to take it back home—thinking that I, a modern parent, knew better than her. However, my son seemed very interested in the potty so I sat him on it to humor him. To my astonishment, he actually peed in it right away then and several times later that day whenever I sat him on it.

EC quickly became a way of life for us. The full-time use of cloth diapers during my son's first year turned out to be beneficial—he had never really lost his awareness of the sensation of elimination (which disposable diapers can muffle), and I had also developed an unconscious awareness of his patterns. This head start in being in tune with him helped us both with the potty-learning process, and within two weeks he was completely out of diapers.

It was so interesting having a young toddler who could barely speak yet was completely potty independent. The whole experience was so positive for us that I started EC with my next child right after he was born. We found our own path with him—he was ill as a newborn, so we used cloth diapers liberally and EC'ed just occasionally at the beginning, then more regularly as he was able to sit up. For both children, seeing each other use the toilet regularly helped make pottying as unremarkable as eating or sleeping. Like my first son, my second child was also out of diapers and completely potty-independent at a very young age.

It was certainly helpful that I had spent so much time abroad and had observed that there are many different ways to parent, and that what we tend to hold as gospel in this country is only a societal norm. It can be hard to go against the cultural mainstream when you have no support, so another thing that helped when my second son was a baby was having a community of other local parents who were practicing EC. We'd meet monthly and share support. It was nice for our children, too, to meet other babies who used the potty. Two moms from our group eventually went on to found the wonderful nonprofit organization, Diaper Free Baby, which provides information and support for parents practicing EC.

Elimination communication and Diaper Free Baby increasingly got a lot of press, and I hosted meetings to help spread the word to interested parents and the media. The media attention helped many more people to recognize that EC was possible. There were also a lot of misconceptions, though, and it's been interesting to observe how perceptions of EC have evolved over time. At first, people doubted that infants were even physically capable of pottying; then, there was worry that this was coercive or would put pressure on modern mothers or that you had to do it in an all-or-nothing way and that this would be too time-consuming. A last misconception was that EC was really messy. This last one was particularly amusing to me as I'd always found diapering to be messier. Having your baby go in a toilet or potty is much neater!

Because I'd done EC in various ways—late-start, part-time, and so forth— I had a lot of thoughts about these misconceptions and wanted to let people know that there were many ways that they could incorporate EC into their modern-day lives and still reap its emotional, health, environmental, and financial benefits. Many of these thoughts eventually found their way into my book, *The Diaper-Free Baby*. I finished the book while pregnant with my third child; she was born just before the book was released.

I'm just about done with the EC journey now for the last time with my fourth child, my second daughter, who walks, talks, and takes me by the hand to take her to go potty. My experience with her astounded me all over again. My first daughter had a strong mind of her own and was always quite obvious about her pottying preferences. I experienced more "potty pauses" with her than I had with my first two children, and it was a great learning experience. It compelled me to be creative and relaxed and also taught me so much about who she is. My second daughter has been EC'ed since the day she was born, and it has really helped me to tune into all her subtle ways of communicating and to see her as her own unique little person.

When I think about how gratifying EC has been, I feel astonished that even though infant pottying was the norm in our country just decades ago, people have so lost touch with our babies' awareness of their own bodies and what they are capable of. At its core, all that EC requires of us is a simple and pure willingness to listen to our children. It really is that easy. My hope is that within a generation, if not sooner, EC will be widely recognized as a completely viable, and in fact, optimal, alternative to full-time diapering and conventional potty training.

You can read more about Christine Gross-Loh in her book *The Diaper-free Baby*, HarperCollins, 2007 and on her website: www.christinegrossloh.com.

chapter 11

author's narrative

When my first child was born, I knew almost nothing about babies. And so, as happens with many new mothers, I was trained to train my first son to use diapers. I dutifully followed suit with my second son. Both experienced conventional European potty training. They started at ages 18 months and 15 months, and they stayed dry during the day at ages 3¼ and 3½ years, respectively. Both wet their beds at night for several years.

When my third son was born, I dreaded the thought of another bout of conventional toilet training which would entail additional years of diapers, and began seeking a better solution. I learned the basis for an alternative technique through a mother named Bibiji visiting us from India. She was horrified when I told her the way Westerners handle the "waste disposal issue" and explained to me the way things are done "back home" in her culture. I was skeptical when she told me that there is no need to use "the cloths" on an infant unless it is "ill of the stomach," feverish or wets the bed most nights.

Bibiji had successfully potty trained her two children from infancy. I asked her to teach me, and she was delighted to help. I expected it to take several hours, but she just smiled and said, "It is very simple. It will only take a few moments." I looked at her in disbelief and said, "Can you really get my baby to pee for you?" Another smile lit her face. I asked, "How will you know when he has to pee?" She took him gently and confidently in her arms and said *karega*, which is Punjabi for, "He will go." And he did.

I was amazed . . . and proud at the way this woman, basically a stranger to my son, had somehow communicated with him. I was still a little skeptical, thinking her success might have been a fluke, and asked her if she could get him to go again. She said, "When it is time." Then about 15 minutes later, she picked him up again and made a "sssss" sound. He immediately peed for her again.

She then explained that part of the trick was a matter of timing. "When you know the baby needs to go to the toilet, take him in your arms and give him your signal."

It seemed far too simple, natural and logical. She showed me positions commonly used in India. A few were geared towards outdoor or village living and involved seating the baby on the mother's feet. Two other positions seemed more suitable for life in the West, and I adopted these for Rob. They both involved holding him in a squatting position in my arms. I made a comfy cradle of my arms which supported his back, neck and head while I held his thighs with his legs slightly spread apart. He was held in this position over a potty place. A variation on this position is to hold baby in the same fashion but for the caregiver to squat down over a potty place.

Then Bibiji told me it was my turn to pee Rob. This was about 15 minutes after she had peed him. I carefully held him over the plastic basin we were using, signaled to him and was amazed to see him respond so quickly. When I asked Bibiji if there was a word or name for her method, she laughed and said, "No, it's just the way we do it."

On that very first day, I gained confidence in both Rob's ability to respond and my ability to carry out the whole procedure. Bibiji showed me that it was simply a matter of responding to his timing and/or body language and transporting him to the toilet on time. Each time I did this, I signaled for him to go, using the watery sound "sssss" for urination and a grunting "hmmm" sound for defecation.

The body language I first noticed as a signal from Rob was something I had often observed in the past few months but had not comprehended and had thus ignored. About midway through his early morning feeding, Rob would begin to twist and grunt a little, with a slightly contorted facial expression. I had assumed it was just gas but now realized that this was also his body language telling me he needed to go. I soon noticed that there was a pattern to this and was able to put this elimination pattern to good use. These two things formed a feedback loop between us.

Rob did not demonstrate any clear warning signs for urination, but by following the intervals of his natural timing, I managed to be effective in that department too. Within a few days, he understood what my signals meant. I soon found that I was able to use just one sound ("sssss") for both functions.

I kept a journal of development, medical records, significant events, experiences and my thoughts on being a mother for all three of my sons. At the time I learned and used infant pottying with Rob, I had no idea I would one day write a book on the topic, so I did not keep detailed notes about our experiences. There are entries on his potty progression from time to time, and some of them are included here.

Since I didn't know of any official term for "infant potty training," I referred to it as "Indian-style toilet training" in my journal. Back then, the term "toilet training" was used more often than "potty training." The first journal entry on this topic reads, "I started toilet training him Indian style, and it works well. He responds well to it."

His pee pattern consisted of (a) peeing when he first woke up in the morning, (b) peeing every 20 minutes after a feeding, on three or four occasions and then (c) peeing about once every 45–60 minutes up until his next feeding. This seemed intensive at first, but I soon learned that it was not essential to get him to the sink or basin for every pee. That would have worn me out. I took him to the potty place several times a day and this worked fine for both of us. His pattern was fairly consistent, which helped a lot.

About three weeks into it, we went on holiday in France. I didn't let travel deter me and took advantage of our host country's special plumbing fixture called a bidet. A bidet is an excellent toilet place to use with infant pottying because the size, shape and plumbing are perfect. This little discovery inspired me to be creative, to seek and improvise unique potty places and receptacles whenever necessary and wherever we went.

Intervals between pees gradually increased over time, making it less intense for me. Within a few months, I no longer needed to give the audible signal at all. Whenever I held him over a receptacle in a certain position, he understood why he was there and responded. Each time he went, he was praised. It was a natural, spontaneous and sincere form of praise, a sort of celebration since I was thrilled. We continued to grow closer and improve our communication on a regular basis. I never picked up on any clear pee signals from him, but this didn't matter.

Rob started crawling at 6 months and sitting around 8 months. When he was 9 months old, my journal reads, "He doesn't let me hold him in my arms very long anymore for toileting. I started putting him on the potty instead." We bought him a very small, transparent potty. I highly recommend a transparent potty since it allows you to see exactly when your baby goes. The instant I saw Rob "go," I would celebrate and as soon as he finished, would let him off the potty. A few weeks later, my notes read, "He does very well on the pot. It is a joy to see him consciously go in the pot at such a young age. He pees less often now."

At 9 months, there were occasions where he refused to pee in the potty and instead went as soon as I put his training pants back on. My notes read, "He is quite good at the toilet training, but sometimes he won't pee when I try to have him pee, and then when I put on his diaper or underwear, he pees in it." I knew this was just a phase and fairly common behavior, so I didn't let it bother me. Besides, there were days where I was less diligent than others, where I was tired or busy, occasions where I didn't get him to the potty on time and caused him to wet his pants, so how could I complain if there were days when I had to change him?

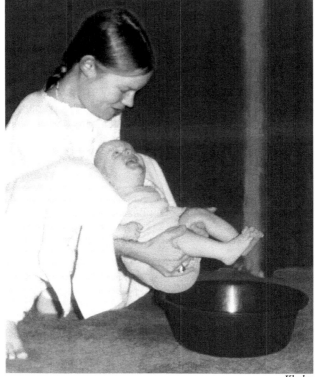

Khalsa

Rob at 9 months, just prior to graduating to the potty.

Sometimes I would feel like I had let him down. I'd feel guilty or frustrated if I didn't get him to the potty on time. I felt very responsible and knew he was dependent on me to make things work. After a while, I learned not to be too hard on myself. It took a while to realize and accept that being uptight and angry at myself was a disservice to Rob. Once I understood the consequences, I modified my behavior and remained positive and relaxed.

At 14 months, my notes read, "He touches his penis and makes himself pee when I put him on the pot." This was further evidence that he knew exactly what the potty was for and that he could consciously make himself go. He'd pee and then either look at a book, play with a toy or leave the potty for some other activity.

The communication between us coupled with his ability to stay clean and dry at the age of 14 months was so effective and inspiring that I wrote an article on the topic. This was in 1980, and the article was entitled "Conscious Toilet Training," with an emphasis on the intelligence, consciousness (awareness) and sensitivity of babies. The information in this article formed the basis of *Trickle Treat* (published 11 years later).

I was fairly consistent with infant pottying and did not relent when we traveled or visited friends and relatives. Since we were living in Holland, we traveled home to California at least once a year. We also frequently traveled through various European countries and made some visits to India. Wherever we went, I took the potty and used it. This included airplane trips, airports, airport shuttles, rest areas along the roads, camping, hiking, restaurants, just about any place you can imagine. Whenever necessary, I would improvise a potty place.

I remember visiting Lisa, my former roommate and surfing buddy from our university days. When Rob and I visited her, she was staying on her parents' ranch. Her parents employed a woman named Ceska as nanny and house-keeper. Lisa, Ceska, Rob and I were walking along a ranch road when I sensed it was time for Rob to pee. I whipped down his pants and held him in my arms, whereupon he immediately peed along the roadside. Lisa didn't have a clue what was going on, but Ceska grew excited and exclaimed, "This is what we do back in my country of Czechoslovakia!"

I found that wherever we went and had the occasion to improvise a toilet place—whether traveling or doing errands—we encountered curious and puzzled onlookers. Sometimes we even met people (mainly immigrants) who were familiar with IPT.

There were occasions from the very start when I traveled without Rob and left him with caregivers. Some of the caregivers were willing to potty him while others didn't take the time and put him in diapers. In short, there were times where I was away for a few days or weeks when no one pottied him. Upon my return, we had no problem picking up where we had left off. It did not jeopardize his progress to stop for a few days or weeks. While I would not recommend anyone purposefully stopping for no particular reason, it is good to know that a break does not automatically spell doom.

At 15 months, Rob started to walk and had developed a small vocabulary. A few of my journal entries around this time read, "Sometimes he cries or whines when he needs to pee," and, "He refuses to sit on the potty when he doesn't need to go." We didn't know about potty sign language since it wasn't used in India, but we did fine without it.

At 17 months, I wrote, "He sings and talks to himself while walking. His walking improved so much that we have to be careful he doesn't slip away from us. The toilet training is going well. He sometimes walks to the potty on his own."

When he was 25 months old, my notes happily announce, "He's 100% toilet trained, including nighttime! He tells me every time he has to go."

Looking back on the toilet teaching of all three of my sons, it took both my first son and Rob 21 months to complete daytime potty training, while my second son took 27 months. Since my first two didn't begin until they were over a year old, they didn't finish until they were over 3 years old, which meant a lot of dirty diapers. By contrast, Rob started at 3 months and finished around 2 years, which meant that neither Rob nor I had to deal with poopy diapers for more than a few months (the months before we started IPT). If including all the months of diapering before we started toilet learning, my first two were in diapers for 39 months and 42 months, respectively, compared to 25 months for Rob. In addition, my first two wet their beds at night for many more years after staying dry during the day, whereas Rob never wet his bed at night (except for one time when he was ill) from the day we started.

Some people ask if different means of toilet learning make a difference in other things later in life; in other words, is an EC baby superior? My reply is no. Having said that, there is no doubt in my mind that infant potty training is well worth the effort for parents, babies and the environment for all the reasons presented in this book.

part **3**

TESTIMONIALS
– AROUND THE WORLD

chapter 1
vietnam

Randy Mont-Reynaud raised three children using infant potty training from birth. She holds a Ph.D. in Developmental Psychology from Harvard University. She studied with Jerome Kagan and conducted research for her dissertation on emotional and cognitive development among Vietnamese infants in the second year of life. She is currently at Stanford University.

Dr. Mont-Reynaud went to Vietnam in 1967 to study child development. She lived in Saigon for six months, attained a modest level of competence in speaking Vietnamese, then returned to the United States and obtained her master's degree in anthropology. In 1972 she returned to Vietnam and spent two years studying child development and religious beliefs in a village setting. She took up residence in the village of My Duc where she adopted her first child. Her son was rarely in diapers in Vietnam and comfortably (i.e., without stress) made the transition to toilet behavior by the age of 18 months when the family moved back to the USA. Dr. Mont-Reynaud raised two more children, a son and a daughter. Like their older brother, they were kept out of diapers as much as possible. Her report was written in 2000.

In Vietnam, where I learned about infant care and toileting, infants and toddlers are held off the porch or at arm's distance of a lap or taken outside to "go." I call the process "mother training" or "caregiver training" because what it really relies on is the mother or caregiver being responsive to the infant's cues and getting the child to the proper place. Adult "toilets" in Vietnam may be shanty structures over a fishpond or river—not an appropriate place for babies! "Misses," in the form of caregivers failing to carry babies to the proper place at the right time, are occasions for laughter . . . and that's all.

The process starts with a newborn. First, you observe when your infant pees or poos and make a little whispering noise at that instant—or soon after. Infants quickly recognize that when they relieve themselves this way, they also hear the whispering noise. Second, make the whispering noise when you know your baby is about to pee or poop. The baby will respond to your cue and "go" for you. It's Skinnerian, basic behaviorist psychology. It is undergirded by the simple fact that newborns pee and poop all the time. It all boils down to training children to respond to stimuli. It's hard to miss, especially if babies are not diapered and you are holding them. Then soon whenever they hear the noise, they will respond if they need to eliminate. The important thing to remember is that it works if they need to go—"if" being the operative word here. Obviously, if you don't have to go, you don't have to go.

It doesn't take long before an infant (around 1 month old) understands what you are doing. I say "understand," because you're not sitting down and explaining to the baby, "Whenever I do this, this is what you'll do." It's an association of feeling states. The baby is first feeling a sensation, feeling that he is peeing or pooing, then hearing your cue. Within a week, when you make the little whispering noise, the baby will go on demand (providing s/he needs to eliminate at that time).

If you don't have any help, the process is fairly intensive in the beginning. After labor and delivery, you may not feel like paying attention to this all the time. Sometimes you'll be too tired, busy or breastfeeding. At times it is hit or miss. If you make a good effort, it won't harm a child if you aren't there for every pee or poo. Babies still get it. You can't do it round the clock every single day. If you sometimes don't get to do it or forget, it's not crucial. The important thing to note here is that in the village, folks are not establishing correct toilet behavior as a goal at this stage (or later). This is just how they handle the situation until the child understands and is physically able to walk to the proper place.

Underlying all of this is the expectation that all children will "catch on," sooner or later. Villagers count on the child's natural growing awareness to take over. The early "mother training" seems designed to "coach" the right behavior. The villagers do not see themselves as "teaching potty training," anymore than they would be "teaching breastfeeding" to their babies.

Don't fasten a diaper around a tiny infant. It's better to place the infant on a diaper, but don't enclose the baby in the diaper in the traditional fashion.

When you're nursing your baby, if the child is wrapped loosely in a towel or diaper, you'll know instantly when your child goes.

How do you know when your baby needs to go? I asked this question in the village. The women looked at me and said, "Well, how do you know when you need to go?" This tipped me off to understanding the connection between toilet learning and the mother-child bond or the caregiver-infant bond. They are a very close unit. You come to know when your baby has to pee/relieve himself (same as we "know"—or think we know—when a child is hungry or tired. You just "know"!). Most mothers/caregivers (this could be a grandmother, sister or aunt) who are involved, in tune and bonded with a baby know when the baby is hungry or tired. Parents attribute some feeling state to a crying baby. The attribution may or may not be correct at first, but eventually over a short period of time it becomes correct as you get to know your baby.

It helps if you can keep your child bare-bottomed. Of course this is easier in warm climates, but you can do it anywhere. This method eliminates the diaper rash problem, and it's about keeping a baby clean. The bottom line is this: If you do not want your child to poop in a diaper, take the diaper off!

You have to spend time with your baby or have a reliable caregiver in order for this to work. Siblings do this in Vietnamese villages for younger siblings. The caregiver needs to be responsive and know your child's needs.

When babies start crawling or walking, keep a little potty where they can see it. It's amazing, they just go there and do it. By the time babies can walk, they get where they need to go if they have observed that behavior. Around 15 months or so, kids begin to understand there is a standard. They understand they are supposed to be somewhere to go potty, that there is a place (i.e., potty) to pee and the rest of the world is not where you pee.

The Vietnamese regard mother training as a natural process. They don't expect children to have difficulties with it—and babies don't. The Vietnamese don't expect it to be problematic for the mother, and it isn't, although there are occasional "slipups." Mother training is something everyone accepts and expects, like breathing. No one teaches us to breathe, but we all do it. Mother training is not something that is learned. It is just something babies do from the moment they are born. They conform to a behavior. By comparison, people in Western cultures have made potty training into an unnatural act and an ordeal.

It is the mother who is primarily responsible for what Westerners call potty training. You might think that the mother never gets a break, but in Vietnam, the baby may be passed around to a whole cadre of siblings and extended relatives or other folks.

In the villages, mothers don't use a potty, and traditionally there are no diapers. They sometimes wrap a towel around the baby on their lap. If the baby needs to pee, the women just hold the infant facing away from them, either on their lap or at the edge of the porch. The baby quickly comprehends, "I move through space to do this elsewhere."

There are usually no toilets in Vietnamese villages. In the rare situations where there is a toilet, it's a Turkish squat-toilet. Obviously an infant can't squat. The mother goes to the area, squats down, holds the baby with legs spread apart and the baby goes. So you bring the child to a part of the house, or a place outside the house, where it is to go.

Of course this is not a perfect system, and accidents do happen. The Vietnamese attitude towards accidents is very casual—elimination is just a normal thing, this is what babies do and when necessary, you clean it up. If a baby is starting to pee and he's on your lap, you just hold him over the porch to go, or you mop up the spill from the tile floor. If it's a dirt floor, you don't have to worry about it. In our culture there are other things to worry about like carpets and expensive clothing.

In Vietnam, it is a significant rite of passage to become a mother. We only pay lip service to this in our culture. Motherhood is not a rite of passage in America. It's a brief interlude on the way to something else, like waitressing your way through college.

When I lived in Vietnam, disposable diapers were fairly new, and some U.S. agencies were airlifting them into the villages. Laundering was one of the few paid occupations that poor uneducated village women could get, and the USA was airlifting in disposable diapers. People had no means of disposing of them—you can imagine the pollution problem. They were regarded as unsanitary anyway, which of course they are. The Vietnamese found a lot of creative uses for things we airlifted to them. Disposable diapers could be used as bandages, for example. We used to send them baby food in jars, and they thought that it was absolutely disgusting. They were living in a nation of banana trees, and we were sending Gerber's bananas in a jar! When they saw banana in a jar, they wondered how old it was and thought it was rotten. They'd throw out the baby food, rinse out the jars and use them as containers, candleholders, jars for fish sauces or incense burners.

I adopted my first child in Vietnam when he was 4 months old and began mother training immediately. The Vietnamese taught me a simple form of body language that baby boys exhibit when they have to pee. You know a boy needs to pee when you see his penis wiggle. This of course assumes someone is watching a baby boy's penis, which in our culture is a no-no. We don't look at genitals here, but in Vietnam, they do so without impunity. They know that a penis wiggles just before a baby boy has to pee. I'll bet mothers in this country don't know this because we have been bundling babies and toddlers up all these years.

By the time my baby was able to sit up, I could place him on a pot if I had one nearby. When he started walking at 10 months, he had a regular, once-a-day routine for poop. By age 1 year, he was regular like a clock. By around 10 months to a year, many babies are getting regular, and not peeing and pooing constantly, maybe just pooing once a day and hopefully in the morning. You put them on the pot, they do their business and that's it. The rest of the time it's just a matter of getting them to the pot to pee, which is trivial compared to pooing; that is, if you miss, it's less of a problem to clean. This is certainly accomplished during the first year of life. By the time children walk, they know what the elimination standard is and where they are supposed to be with it.

I took my son to an American hotel with a swimming pool when he was 10 months. In true Vietnamese fashion, he was bare-bottomed and wearing a T-shirt to protect him from the sun. Some American women came along and said it was too hot for him to wear a T-shirt and that he should be in a diaper. I put him in a diaper and took off the shirt. Then some Vietnamese women came along and were appalled that he was in a hot, plastic diaper that retained fluids and filth. They asked me how I could have him in the sun without a shirt. I took off the diaper and put the T-shirt back on. This is a clear-cut example of different cultural values and interpretations.

Since potty training is seen as a natural part of life, there is no official term for it in Vietnamese. If you ask them about it, they'll just giggle. They call it *di dai* which means "go pee-pee." The French say *fais pipi* and use a similar method. The French are notorious for early experiences in this domain. Traditionally, they used to try to have their kids potty trained by 6–8 months of age when they could sit up. When a baby sits up around 6 months, French mothers place their babies on a little disposable plastic potty with a handle. If you think about it, what did we do here 100 years ago? We didn't have washing machines or disposable diapers. I think women just subtly communicated with their babies at a lot earlier age, "This is how you do it. This is where you do it." We have forgotten that. There is no literature on it. Nobody considered writing it down! Women were too busy doing it to write about it, and men were not involved.

After spending a year in the village, we moved to Israel where we spent six months, then we moved to Vermont. I later had two birth children, a boy and a girl. It was a lot of fun trying to implement mother training with them from birth. I was 35 and living in California when my son was born. It might have been easier if I was younger. Between nursing and caring for an older child, an 18-hour labor and experiencing my first birth, it was a lot to handle. It seemed to me that newborns pee or poo at least every 20 minutes. I persevered. During the day when I was nursing him, I'd place him on top of a diaper on my lap. I'd make the "sssss" noise when I thought he had to pee and he'd go, or else I'd observe it after the fact and make the noise as soon as I noticed. After three days of this, I took him to the sink, held him over the sink, made the noise and he would pee or poo for me when he had to go.

There was a huge wall-to-wall mirror over the bathroom sink in our home. When I held him over the sink, he could see himself in the mirror and could see me holding him. When he peed or pooed, of course I was happy and would smile. (In Vietnam they don't smile and don't praise a child for peeing. Why should they?) I was thrilled to see him respond to my cue. He could see in the mirror that I was happy with his behavior. Then he would smile and see his reflection in the mirror, and that would reward him even more. I realized there is a cognitive aspect to this, but no one has put this in the context of toilet training. It is cognitively stimulating, making the association between external stimuli and a physical response; then on top of this, the baby is rewarded. In this context, it's by the reflection in the mirror, the smile on the mother's face.

I coupled mother training with some other customs and practices I brought back from Vietnam and thought were useful, namely using a low-lying hammock. I had a huge hammock and placed a beach mat under it, so if he peed it went on the beach mat. The hammock was low so if he fell, he would fall on the floor, which was carpeted. I added some padding in the form of pillows at either end. I would rock him to sleep during the day for a nap.

The noontime siesta is another useful custom I copied from the Vietnamese villagers. Years after my research, back in California, my son would nap in the hammock for two or three hours at noon and would take a second nap later in the day. He kept on taking his noontime nap until he was in first grade. Later on, when he was playing in chess tournaments at the age of 6 and 7 and we were traveling, he could rest in between rounds. There would typically be two rounds a day, and he would sleep between rounds.

The notion in Vietnam is that people and children *will* sleep and *like* to sleep at noon. You don't have to be tired to sleep. In this culture, we feel you have to knock yourself out before you can sleep or that children have to run around until they are exhausted before they will sleep and that in general they don't want to go to sleep. The Vietnamese do not make this attribution. They put a child down next to them, and the child goes to sleep. In our culture, we want to be out doing. We think children need stimulation, and our children fulfill our expectation.

In this country, we use strollers and infant carriers extensively, and babies are dressed or wrapped and bundled. Parents distance their children in this way. In Vietnam, babies and small children are always held. I continued the practice of holding my baby as much as possible, and he slept with us at night. He eventually slept in his older brother's room. His brother and father also helped with potty access when they were around.

When my son was 3 months old, it was time for his checkup. I took him to the local medical clinic. The doctor was about to examine him and asked me not to take the diaper off in case my son might pee. I told the doctor I'd deal with it, took my son to the sink, held him over the sink and made the noise. He peed in the sink. The physician said, "My goodness! That's the first time I've ever seen a 3-month-old potty trained." Of course he wasn't totally potty trained. I was the one who was "trained." I knew he had to go and knew what to do to make him go. The doctor was totally flabbergasted.

The way I proceeded with my children was to take them to go whenever practicable. They easily acquired the sense that these functions were to be espoused in specially defined places and not indiscriminately all over the house.

The second child I gave birth to was a daughter. I started mother training her at birth. I was living in California and used a hammock with her.

Her little brother was 26 months when she was born. She observed him using a potty and seemed to want to imitate him. This is another thing I had studied at Harvard—imitation and modeling. Children want to be like the model. If they see a model doing something, they want to do it too. Monkey see, monkey do. In our culture, children don't commonly see adults on the toilet. We close the bathroom door. A lot of mothers won't even let their children in the bathroom with them, and this is one reason why traditional toilet training takes so long.

My daughter was able to sit on a pot by 6 months. When children need to go, they see the potty and take care of business. Both these children could do this sometime between 6 and 8 months. They would crawl towards the potty on the carpeted floor in the living room. I would see them making their way across the room and sit them on the potty. If you expose children to the stimulus-response behavior in infancy and let them know what the expectation is, it's amazing how fast they catch on. By 6 months, babies understand that a potty is where they have to go. At 18 months, all my children were able to get to a potty by themselves and could therefore be without diapers. They were actually able to be without diapers much younger than 18 months, but there were no mistakes or accidents after 18 months. Needless to say, you have to be pretty attentive, as a parent, to facilitate this in a Western non-village setting—with carpets, no less!

In this country, potty training typically doesn't start until a child is 18 months or older, and by that age, it's something you have to teach. The child has been taught to poop in a diaper and now must unlearn this. By the time some children are 3 or 4, they are afraid to take off their diapers! Training involves a new apparatus, the potty, or a toilet two feet high off the floor, which may be scary for some children. It also involves getting the child's clothes off. In addition, a mother usually doesn't know when her child needs to go because he has been in a diaper all day. It gets to be a pretty high-pressure situation, and if the child fails to meet expectations, it becomes even a more high-pressured situation. In fact, it becomes such a pressured situation that many families don't begin until the child is 3 or 4 years old. This has been made possible by using disposable diapers. The disposable diaper industry encourages this behavior and capitalizes on the reluctance of parents—particularly new and/or young parents—to deal with potty training.

If a child is in a daycare context with one adult per six children, it is difficult to do mother training. It would be a lot easier if the children didn't have to wear diapers, but in our culture this would be hard. In a daycare situation, the owners would probably lose their license for sanitation reasons. Even worse, tongues would wag about child nudity, pedophilia and molestation.

We hold certain beliefs most dear to us in the United States, and in our belief system, children belong in diapers. If you challenge this notion, you run the risk of being ridiculed. To parents and so-called experts who object to raising babies without diapers: If you don't want to do it, don't do it. Save your carpets!

In Vietnam and other village cultures, toddlers see the consequences of their actions in regard to toilet behavior. It's time to look at what we left behind when we left village life, look at what other cultures have to offer and, without preconceived notions, glean the gems from other cultures. We can't adopt all their customs or import them like soy sauce or tofu, but many customs are worthy of reflection.

china

China is fairly well-known for its use of infant elimination training. The first two testimonials are especially interesting in that they contain reports concerning three generations of the same family—the parents in China and their daughter and grandson who live in a Western society. The first report is by Sun Mengjia and Li Minqian, retired physics professors from Shanxi University in Taiyuan, Shanxi. The second report comes from their daughter Min Sun who holds a Ph.D. in Nutrition Sciences from the University of Alabama, resides in Italy and is married to an Italian pediatrician. Both reports were filed in 2002 and Min Sun's was updated in 2007.

Sun Mengjia and Li Minqian

In China, parents usually begin toilet training around the age of 1 month or as late as 4 months. Sometimes they base it on starting after the first 100 days of life since the first 100 days are important in Chinese culture. Babies are considered to be very fragile for the first 100 days. But many diligent mothers and grandmothers start training within the first month with the expectation that, according to a Chinese proverb, they "get twice the result with half the effort."

The reason for starting toilet training in infancy is to help infants build good habits. Many Chinese books on infant rearing advocate early training and include summaries of thousands of cases. There are now also some authors who follow Western beliefs and advise to begin training at age 18 months. But most parents feel that if training starts at this late time, it is very difficult because you have to correct bad habits which have already been formed.

We raised two children and helped take care of (and toilet train) the babies of some relatives on a short-term basis. We toilet trained our two children according to Chinese tradition. A fundamental principle is: Eating and elimination are two coexisting aspects that should be considered equally important.

We learned the timing and regularity of our babies' eliminations, based on their feeding schedule. At the most likely time for the babies to eliminate, we held them in a specific position and guided them with sounds. For the infant elimination position, the baby rests his back against the mother's chest and the mother holds the baby's legs in her hands. In Chinese, to *ba* a baby means to help a baby eliminate (*ba* is a verb in the third tone). A typical sound for voiding is *xu* and for defecation *eng* is often used. These are used to help the infant develop the ability to control elimination, by building a healthy conditioned reflex.

Infants should not be looked down upon—most of them are very smart. Chinese books on child rearing state that babies can recognize the *ba* position with sounds as early as 20–30 days old; this combination can help them accomplish early training. In China, we are proud when our children are trained early. Toilet training is usually completed between 4–12 months.

Receptacles are used, for example a potty or a bottle. But some parents take the baby to the bathroom instead. In villages, an infant sometimes goes on the floor or in the yard, and then the mess is cleaned.

Parents have help with toilet training. Usually the grandparents assist, but if not, a full-time babysitter or helper (who sometimes stays with the family) is hired to follow the mother's instructions.

In China, infants sleep next to their parents, so babies feel safe. In this way, an attentive mother can feel or observe the movements of her baby. During the night, if a baby moves or wakes up for elimination needs, the mother will *ba* her baby to urinate. If the baby does not stir at night, he should generally not be awakened.

Diapers (both cloth and disposable) and open pants are used. In the past, parents used soft pieces of cloth as diapers. Cloth diapers are affixed by using wide elastic bands around the baby's waist and on top of the diapers. If not too tight, the elastic bands won't cause discomfort. When the babies are about 10 to 12 months old, many no longer require diapers. They are mainly used as tools before babies develop language skills. In more recent times, many families are using disposable diapers made from highly absorbent materials, but these are generally used only as a supplementary tool for easier cleaning and to avoid accidents. Open pants are used for convenience and timeliness of elimination, before good control is gained.

Infant toilet training is the main method of both the past and the present in China. It is used nationwide, in villages and cities, and in all levels of society. Income is not a determining factor. Attitude and tradition are what lead a family to use this method. But because there are now books that provide different outlooks and onset times—many of these books include Western opinions and approaches—there is now some confusion among some parents in cities.

The limit on having just one child has not affected toilet training. Having only one child does not necessarily mean a mother spends time toilet training. It is not a matter of time or income, but a matter of concept, personal attitude, and understanding the importance of toilet training.

We have seen some mothers avoid toilet training by using disposable diapers, in order to save themselves the effort. It is believed that this causes weak functional sphincter muscles and a lack of control. Only lazy mothers rely solely on disposable diapers. Their children aren't toilet trained before two or three years of age, which is late in China.

Although we reside in the north of China, this information is applicable to much of the republic. We are constantly in touch with friends at the university. Many are from different provinces in China. We also have relatives who live in other cities and who share their experiences with us.

Min Sun

I think that infant toilet training was a learning process for me as a mother as opposed to a training process for my children because I learned the timing and communications for their elimination needs rather than actually training them. I helped them build healthy habits from early infancy.

When our son was born, my parents sent information from China on the importance and how-tos of infant toilet training. My first reaction was one of rejection. I thought, if everybody here (in the USA and in Italy) uses diapers, I should do what they do here. In China, babies wear open pants, but I thought my children would be considered uncivilized if I used open pants in Italy.

But I continued to think about it and talked with my husband frequently, sometimes even at the dinner table where this topic may not be suitable! He, as an Italian pediatrician and neonatologist, had never heard about this. Initially he was surprised, but eventually he told me that I could try anything with our baby. So I started toilet training in a way that suited our lifestyle in Italy—I started early, did not use Chinese open pants but used disposable diapers for a while.

When our son was 1 month old, I thought, if I know he is going to defecate, why don't I take him to the bathroom instead of watching him do it in a diaper—it's better to bring him to the bathroom, let him go there and then wash him in the same position. The process began with a thought as easy as this.

I actually learned about the in-arms washing position from an Italian friend who is a nurse in newborn care. It was the exact position I used to help my son eliminate before he could sit. I learned that he gave signals for his elimination needs and also that it was possible to learn his natural elimination schedule.

By 4 months of age, I was able to help him do all his BMs in the bathroom. When he went for me in the bathroom, I praised him and gave him a little kiss. By 7 months, he stayed dry during day naps. When accidents occurred, I blamed myself for not being able to pay enough attention to catch his signals.

At 9 months, I didn't need to observe him so closely anymore. I simply took him to the bathroom when I felt it was the right time. I do think he learned to cooperate with me in that he would sometimes wait by holding it before I took him to the bathroom. He always wore a diaper until 9 months. Occasionally I used cloth diapers but later I gave them up. Sometimes when I was sure he wouldn't void, I let him wear little underpants.

When my daughter was born, my son was 22 months. I was lucky that he was almost through (he finished around 25 months). I started with my daughter at 2 months old but did not separate both processes as I had done with my son.

During the first year, I was often alone with both of them, and it often happened that when I was busy with my son, my daughter went in her diaper. Her patterns were completely different from her brother's. She was never regular with BMs, and she almost never signed—or else I was not able to detect her signals when I was occupied with her brother. I tried to take her as regularly as possible to the toilet, but often didn't have the time, which was frustrating for me. She finished around 25 months, except for the battle with BMs which continued until 30 months. I think her irregularity is due to her being a fussy eater, with a lack of fruits and vegetables in her diet.

Regarding night dryness, there is a strong family history of nocturnal urinary incontinence. When my son was little, I sometimes took him to the toilet at night until his sister was born. Then out of exhaustion, I gave up. At 4 years, he was still not dry overnight, so after observing the approximate times he peed, I figured out when to take him to the toilet. In the beginning it was twice a night and a year later once per night. When he was nearly 6, he suddenly began to remain dry all night. When my daughter was about 4, I started to take her once per night and within a month, she stayed dry at night.

Most of the leading books on child rearing in China state that toilet training starts at 1 month of age, according to tradition. Today some young parents use diapers until 3 years of age before toilet training, like is done in the USA or other Western countries.

Here in Italy, some Chinese mothers bring infant open pants to the hospital when they go in for delivery. The Italian nurses don't understand the function of the pants, so they first put a disposable diaper on the newborn, then put the Chinese open pants over the diaper!

Many Chinese mothers who live in Italy also use diapers, maybe because their grandparents are not here to teach them. But we have continued to chat with friends on this topic. Many are interested in it, but not pediatricians. I have heard that some Italian mothers take their babies to the bathroom as early as 5 months of age. When they tell others about this, the reaction they receive is usually: "Are you crazy? It is dangerous for your baby." When we told some pediatricians about our experience with our son, the first response was that it would damage his neurological development.

A lot of people, whether they are mothers or not, can tell when a baby needs to go, but they have never considered taking the baby to the bathroom for this. Perhaps this is because they have been warned by doctors not to do so, or maybe they just haven't been informed of the whole story.

My philosophy is that everything has to be moderate, and we should not abuse our resources. Diapers can be used before babies gain full control, but learning how our babies communicate their needs is also important and particularly interesting. If they cry due to hunger, feeling ignored or being sleepy or tired, it makes sense that they also cry for other reasons, which include their elimination needs. Babies communicate with us before they can speak. If we don't understand, it is because we don't listen with attentive hearts. If we help our babies eat, dress and wash before they can do these things by themselves, why can't we bring them to the bathroom before they can do this by themselves? Parents should be educated to help children build healthy elimination habits starting at birth, then teach them independent toileting later. This is a civilized and educated way to bring up our babies. All parents should know about this possibility so they can choose whether to start early or after 2 years of age.

Open pants are used
throughout much
of China.

Ivy Makelin

With smaller infants, a cotton
cloth or towel is sometimes
used. The cloth is slipped
under the waistband or else
held in place by a cotton tie.

This style of pants has a
very small opening.

Ivy Makelin

Valdin/Photononstop

An Ouighour baby in split pants.
Grandfather and grandson "hanging out" together.
(Xinjiang, China)

Carol Niravong

Carol Niravong was born in China and left the country when she was two years old. Growing up in Canada, she spoke Mandarin with her family and learned to EC her baby brother. At the time of this testimonial given in 2007, Carol was spending two months in Yichang, Hubei (a mid-sized city) during the last stretch of her maternity leave. She travelled there with her two sons, aged 3.5 years and 11 months, in the hopes of immersing them in the culture and the language while visiting extended family:

EC'ing in China is a lot more about the "E" than the "C." No one seems to think of pottying baby as "communication." It's simply something that needs to be done if you don't want the baby that you're holding—whether yours or someone else's—to pee on you.

Infant potty training in China is also about health: baby's bum must be allowed to breathe. Air flow is important in that area of the body. One afternoon, I had my son in a cloth diaper because all of his crotchless shorts needed washing. We met another mom in the park who insisted I remove the cloth diaper because it was so hot (95°F) and his bum needed to breathe. Given this perspective, I am actually self-conscious about putting my son in a disposable diaper for fear of being reprimanded by mothers and grandmothers everywhere I go.

Whereas it's convenient to use disposables in the West, it's actually more convenient to EC in China. Though cloth diapers are used, especially in winter, these are to be avoided if possible since laundering them is inconvenient. No one owns a dryer and there's limited space for hang-drying in urban areas. Western-produced disposables are extremely expensive here while Chinese-produced disposables easily cause diaper rash (no diaper rash cream on the market yet). Thus, pottying baby is the most natural choice.

In the summer, you can see every baby wearing crotchless shorts or a crotchless outfit. As such, everyone who holds a baby becomes aware of his elimination needs. If someone is carrying my young son and they don't want to risk being peed on, they just hold him facing forward. If he pees on the floor at home, the mop just comes out. If he pees on someone, they just deal with the wetness for a while and wait for it to dry. One day, he peed on our middle-aged guest—twice. His adult daughter said, "Hey Dad, maybe this will give you some good luck."

Compared to my two aunts, I have been lackadaisical about pottying. Whenever I pass my son to one of them, they try to pee him. They've either got their own rhythm or sense, or they are simply offering him many more opportunities than I ever have. One day, I saw my older aunt sitting outside in the front courtyard, holding my son in position to eliminate. There were the usual people walking by, kids running around, cars and taxis on the street. My son had diarrhea and pooped right in the middle of all this activity, and needless to say, no one blinked an eye. After he finished, my aunt just went to get a block of burnt-out charcoal, crushed it over the diarrhea, mixing it up to absorb it, and swept it up.

While the vast majority of people in the West are not familiar with infant potty training, the Chinese have no clue about our own diapering practices in North America. One day, I visited the daycare that my older son was attending and there you could see the two-year-olds in crotchless shorts while the three-year-olds were in regular shorts. Whenever a boy needed to pee, a teacher would bring over a bucket and place it just under his penis as he remained standing. Little girls would sit down on Chinese-style potties which looked like small vessels. Every child also pooped in the potties.

I mentioned to the teachers that in the West, kids are often in disposable diapers until they're around three years old. The reactions I got were no more incredulous than the reactions you would get from mentioning EC to a Westerner. They bombarded me with questions: "You mean they're wrapped up all day? Don't you have to change them all the time then? Isn't that a lot of work? But their bums can't breathe! How do they get toilet-trained?" They simply had no idea about our "traditional" diapering ways.

Babies in China are carried much of the time. They don't use cribs or playpens or highchairs. The Chinese seem to have the impression that Western babies are often left alone—and how sad that must be. Many of the babies here are not allowed to crawl since they believe that their floors are too dirty. Because babies here are carried so much, they are given ample opportunity to eliminate since it would be a hassle to be peed on or have to clean up.

You can read all you want about Chinese culture, values, beliefs and perspectives but coming here to live, you really "feel" it. And with EC'ing, the most obvious thing is how this is simply a part of life.

chapter 3

india

Neelam and Raj Mehta raised two children in Gujarat, India, using infant potty training. Their daughter Sheil started at four months and completed potty training at 13 months while their son Yash took about two months longer to train than his sister. Here is what Neelam had to say in 2000 on the topic of toilet training her children in the state of Gujarat.

My husband Raj helped me quite a bit with toilet training. We lived with our extended family so I also had a lot of help from my relatives in the home. In India, we nurse our babies, then get a feel for how long after a feeding baby needs to go to the bathroom. Mothers intuitively know when it is time to take baby to the bathroom. It doesn't take long to learn this. The feeling is based in part on timing but not on watching a clock. It is a matter of realizing it is time. Poor people, lower class people in my country don't wear watches. These mothers feel and know when their babies need to eliminate.

The closest thing to a diaper that we use is a little cotton garment called a *balotu*. It resembles a G-string or skimpy underwear. This infant underwear is more comfortable and functional than a bulky towel between the legs, which is how Western diapers appear to us. Our infant underwear is made of cotton and ties onto the baby at the top of the thighs. You can buy these little garments ready-made in shops. We wash them and use them over and over. We use these on infants before we start toilet training and also in the beginning stages of training, in between visits to the bathroom. Once our babies head to the bathroom on their own, we let them wear regular children's underpants.

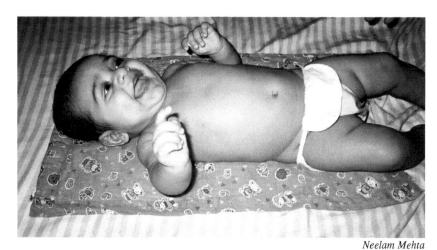

Neelam Mehta

A 3-month-old boy wearing comfy cotton Indian infant underwear.

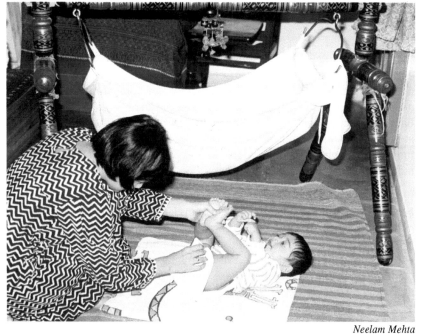

Neelam Mehta

Gujarati mother lifting her baby by the ankles for a poo.

Bathrooms in India are simple and small. Ours was smaller than four feet by four feet. Indian bathrooms typically consist of a tile or cement floor. We don't have plumbing fixtures like a tub, sink or toilet. Instead, we just squat down and go on the floor. There is always a bucket full of water and a bar of soap in the bathroom. We rinse the floor and clean ourselves. This may sound unhygienic to people in the West, but our bathrooms are very clean.

When we want an infant to pee, we start by making the sound "sssss," which sounds like water. After a while, we just tell them to "go pee pee." We don't make a special noise for them to poop.

We do not have a term for "toilet training" or "potty training." In fact, we do not use a potty when we train our children. When babies are really small, there are two things we do to keep them clean. One is to have them lying on a blanket or soft cloth on a cot (bed) or the floor. When it's time to poop, we gently grasp and raise the baby's ankles in order to lift his buttocks off the blanket while he is pooping. This way he doesn't get soiled. We replace the cloth under him with a clean one, then lay him down again. Another way we take small babies to poop is by cradling or holding them in our arms while they eliminate. When our children are old enough to stand and squat, we show them how to squat in the bathroom.

I started toilet training my daughter Sheil when she was 4 months old. There were times where Sheil peed in her underwear at first, but I paid attention to the timing between her pees and learned when to take her to the toilet on time. I would nurse Sheil, then take her to pee about an hour later and then take her at regular intervals after that. I would take her to the bathroom, remove her underwear, make the "sssss" sound and remain in the bathroom with her until she went. I held her in my arms, supported her head and squatted or sat while I waited for her to go. Within a few weeks, the time between pees increased, so I would take her every hour and a half. Then it increased to every two hours. When she went for me, I would praise her, smile and hug her so she would understand she did something good.

At 4 months, I noticed that Sheil would poop three times a day. I wrote down the times she would poop in the morning, afternoon and evening and take her to the bathroom when I knew she needed to poop.

At 6 months, Sheil stopped pooping three times a day and only pooped once a day, in the morning. She was almost finished with bowel training at 6 months. She understood that when I took her to the bathroom and removed her infant underwear, it meant she should poop or pee. Around 6 months, I believe Sheil really understood toilet training. She sensed why I took her to the bathroom and what she should do there. I stopped using infant underwear with her at this stage and used panties instead.

Sheil also started crawling around 6 months. She would crawl to the bathroom door, remain there, look at me and make sounds to get my attention. I think she was trying to say "Ma" or "Mommy." I understood that she was calling me and letting me know she had to go to the bathroom. She would remain by the bathroom door until I arrived to take her to the toilet. As soon as I took her in the bathroom and removed her panties, she would pee.

Sheil took her first steps at 7½ months. At 9 months she walked well on her own and would say "Mommy bathroom, Mommy bathroom" when she had to go. I considered her toilet trained at 9 months, even though she still needed my help to get into the bathroom and pull down her panties. I taught her to squat in the bathroom and showed her how to go without getting herself wet. She was completely toilet trained, able to do everything independently, at age 13 months.

I started toilet training my son Yash when he was 3 months old. From the age of 3 months, he never wet the bed at night, whereas his sister sometimes wet the bed until the age of 4½ months. But for the rest of the potty process, it took my son longer than his sister to learn.

He started to crawl around 4 months but didn't head for the bathroom door on his own until a few months later. I used Indian infant underwear on my son until he was 6½ months. It was harder for me to know when he had to pee than it was with his sister. He would pee more often, so it took more time than I spent working with his sister to keep him dry. He pooped once or twice a day, always in the morning and sometimes in the afternoon.

Around 8 months, he understood what the bathroom was for. At 8 months, he started crawling to the bathroom door when he had to go. At this point, he started wearing underpants. He walked and had good control over elimination at 12 months. In fact, he would always hold it until I arrived to take him in the bathroom. He didn't start talking for another half year, so instead he would use his own sign language to tell me things. He had ways to sign to me if he wanted to pee or poop. I considered him toilet trained at 12 months of age, but he still needed help with his clothing at that age.

Yash was 1½ years old when we left India for the United States. He was almost finished with toilet training at that time so I never used a diaper on him in this country.

Children learn things at an early age in India. This is partly due to living with an extended family where there are always at least eight people living in a house. Children are never alone. There are always two or more people with them. They hear people talking all the time. We talk to our children a lot, and they learn very quickly this way. In my home, if I was not around, my sister, grandmother, mother-in-law or husband would be there for my children. I had a lot of help. I was the coordinator of the potty training. I would be sure someone was always available to take the babies to the bathroom on time.

We sleep with our children in India. In most situations, they sleep in the same bed with the parents for as long as they want. In cases where a baby cannot sleep well in the same bed with someone else, the baby sleeps in its own little bed in the same room as the parents.

In the past, this method of toilet training from birth was used throughout India. Nowadays, I'd say it is used in about 85% of the country. This is because many women now have jobs. In cities, up to 50% of women work and don't have time to raise their kids like we traditionally raise them. The women in cities like to be modern and use the Western-style toilet training with diapers. Families in our cities are living more like Western families. They don't live with the extended family anymore. This is partly because a wife often cannot get along with her mother-in-law. Married couples don't want to have to deal with the rest of the extended family. This means mothers in cities don't have help from the extended family and are using diapers to delay potty training. In villages, families still live together and use the traditional and natural means of toilet training.

In my culture, until recently we didn't think about diapers much. It's becoming fashionable now to use diapers, but when I raised my kids, they weren't used much. Toilet training is just one of many things or routines a mother and family does for a baby, such as feed the baby, dress the baby or walk the baby. We aren't embarrassed about breastfeeding or toilet training. When we visit friends, we use their bathroom to pee our babies on time. Our friends do not mind at all. Toilet training doesn't stress or frustrate people in India. We don't view it as time consuming or a chore like Westerners do. It's just a natural thing, something you do for your baby, part of your duties to raise a child. As a nation, we love children very much and enjoy raising them.

If I had another child while living in the United States, I would still start toilet training in infancy, the same as I did for my other two children. I could not do it on my own since my husband and I own and operate a shop. I would send for my extended family and bring them over from India to be with me and the baby.

Raghu Rai

Sikhs improvising a toilet place in India.

chapter 4

germany

Friederike ("Freddy") Bradfisch lives in Southern Germany. She was a practicing lawyer for about five years and then became a full-time mom. She discovered IPT when her first child was 2 months old. Since that time, she has had exciting results with all three of her children. Freddy was so inspired by her experiences that she created a German website and e-mail list where members discuss IPT. Her report is from 2007.

Before our son Wolfgang was born, I didn't even consider cloth diapers. I thought they would be too much of a hassle. Little did I expect to be doing something far more unusual in our Western world. After using disposables for two months, I came across a German book on child rearing, *Ihr Baby kann's* by Rita Messmer. In the chapter on toilet training, the author refers to the many women around the world carrying their diaperless babies and "just knowing" when they have to eliminate. This inspired her to give it a try with her own son. She held him over the toilet, and it worked. Although there was not much information to go by, it sounded logical to me, so I placed a little bucket by our changing table. The next time I was changing Wolfgang, I held him over the bucket in a squat and said *Pinkelpause!* (pee-pee break), and he peed and pooed!

From then on, I offered the bucket every time I changed him and also when he signaled that he had to go, or else when he had been dry for a very long time. This worked especially well for poops, and we got quite a few pees, too. He was very good at showing his need to go when carried in the sling. He'd squirm and get restless in a very specific way. I also discovered that he could wait a little bit between signaling and going. He almost never wet his diaper while I was undressing him. A nice side effect was that I was never again peed on while at the changing table (this had happened quite a lot before).

We slowly switched to cloth diapers, as I wanted to know whether a diaper was wet or not. With IPT, cloth diapering was not half as much work as I had expected. I usually only had to wash diapers once a week and they didn't even fill the washer.

I didn't know anybody trying the same thing and sometimes felt rather lonely. All I had was a single chapter in one book. I was really happy when I came across an English parenting page that mentioned something called "infant potty training." Following the links, I found several more sites and an e-mail list. I was not on my own after all! Wolfgang was 8 months old then, and we had been at it for half a year already.

My mails to the elimination communication list became our IPT diary, and I've condensed some of them here.

"Wet diapers are quite common, but although Wolfgang poops about 3–5 times a day, I only get a soiled diaper about once or twice a week."

I usually just put him in disposables when going out, as I felt a bit awkward about taking Wolfgang to the toilet when we were not at home. I was also thinking that I wouldn't be able to respond to him very well when out. But reading about others going completely diaperless all the time gave me the courage to try to let him do his business without diapers, even when out. And guess what? It worked BETTER when we were out than at home!

At 8½ months, we started using a potty. I held him like I had on the bucket, so it was a smooth and gradual transition. We also started to use the toilet.

Every year we take a bicycle trip in the summer, staying at a different place each night. Nine-month-old Wolfgang came along in his bike trailer and of course we stopped for potty breaks. I enjoyed not having to take along many diapers. We were away for a week. I used two cloth diapers till they got wet and then continued with disposables (about 2½ a day on average). I washed the cloth diapers at the hotel in the evening and they dried during the night, so I could start over again with them in the morning.

At the age of 10–11 months, we started having quite a few misses due to crawling, teething, a cold, etc. I had been really spoiled up until then because we rarely missed any poops since starting at age 2 months. I kept things in perspective with the thought that, were I using full-time diapers, EVERY poo

Friederike Bradfisch

On our 2007 bicycle trip, we took just 5 undies and 6 training pants
for 11-month-old Carsten.

would be going into the diaper at that age. And of course, things improved after a while. We gradually used fewer diapers. Here are some diary entries:

"I'm so exited! Wolfgang just did some great communicating! I was sitting at the computer while he was playing quietly nearby. Suddenly he started talking angrily, crawled over to his potty and sat down next to it. I took off his pants (no dipes) and put him on it and—peeeee!

"Still no misses! Wolfgang seems to have developed some incredible control almost overnight.

"Wolfgang is 13 months old now and hasn't been wearing daytime diapers for weeks. He wears undies and pants instead."

His starting to walk at 14 months threw us a bit off track, but I was expecting this from what I had read, so I didn't worry. We did not go back to diapers.

"Wolfgang is too busy taking his first steps (7 steps on his own!) to care about anything else, including pottying. He pees in his pants without warning quite

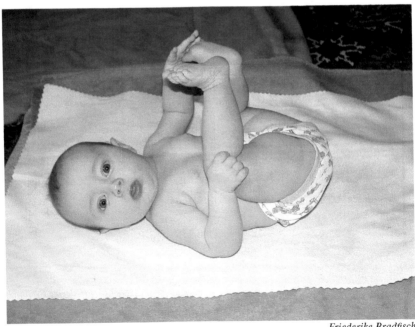

Friederike Bradfisch

4-month-old Jutta, unrestricted by diaper bulk
and free to explore her feet.

often (well, two or three times a day—we're just spoiled, so it seems often). But he also has great communication skills. For example, he crawled out of the room and started banging a wooden block on something. I yelled: NEIN! (no!) because I thought he was hitting the mirror. As I went to have a look, he was standing in front of the bathroom and banging on the door! When we sat down on the toilet, he pooed."

Things got a lot easier when at 15 months, he started signing and using a word for his need to go.

"Yesterday after peeing twice and not going to sleep while nursing and also not going to sleep in my arms, I finally put him in his bed. He sat up, waved his hand, said 'dede' (his word for toilet) and then wet his diaper. I hadn't thought that the need to pee was keeping him awake since he had peed twice shortly be-fore. After changing him, he went right to sleep."

After many ups and downs concerning nighttime, we stopped using diapers at night at 16 months. I wrote this about nights:

"There is one word for how we are doing, and that is 'fabulously!' When doing laundry today, I realized that Wolfgang has been consistently dry at night for at least a week, as there was not a single diaper in the load!"

At 18 months, we were nearing graduation.

"Accidents are VERY rare. Wolfgang consistently announces his need to go by saying 'dede' and waving his hand in that special way. I don't really have to keep track of his timing anymore. Of course, he cannot pull down his pants yet. but that's not elimination control per se. It's 'dressing and undressing,' and that's another chapter."

I considered Wolfgang finished with toilet training at 20 months:

"Now I don't even have to think about the last time Wolfgang used the toilet. I can trust him to tell me. We still have an occasional accident when he is very distracted and tired, but who cares! We just had our first 100 % accident-free week (actually 8 days)."

When pregnant with our second child I looked forward to using IPT again. Can you imagine someone looking forward to toilet training? Well, I was. And after the birth, we started right away while still in hospital:

"They have a diapering room with several changing tables and a sink. The nurses advised to use the sink to rinse baby's bottom after a poo, so I didn't hesitate to let Jutta use that sink as a toilet. I held her in a squat in my arms over

the sink for about half a minute and made the 'sssss' sound to get her used to the procedure. On the third day, she peed for me a few times. I didn't put a diaper back on, and after a short time she started to poo. I lifted her gently, held her over the sink and she pooed again! In the afternoon when I held her over the sink and made the 'sssss' sound, nothing happened. Then I tightened my abdominal muscles (she could feel it) and grunted. She responded immediately and pooed in the sink. Wow!"

At 4 weeks she wore the same cloth diaper for more than 12 hours! And at around 7 weeks we started to slowly, slowly go diaper-free:

"Sometimes Jutta goes diaperless in the morning. I put her in undies and pants until they get wet, then use diapers again."

We started nighttime right from the beginning as well. At first it would take me about 45 minutes to nurse her, then I'd take her to the bathroom where she would pee and poo in the sink in several spurts. We soon got the hang of it and only needed 15 minutes for nursing and bathroom.

"Jutta (6 months) is not wearing diapers about half of the nights right now and staying dry half of the nights, too, mainly depending on how tired and committed I am."

We completely stopped using diapers with Jutta at 7 months—day and night, at home and out.

"What do we need diapers for? You can do without them, and a 'miss' is not more of a mess than other things, like spitting up and leaking diapers, that always happen with a baby anyway. Still, diapers are so ingrained in our perception of babies that it took me 12 months to get rid of them with Wolfgang (daytime!) and 7 months with Jutta."

At 13 months she started to use the potty by herself:

"The last few days when Jutta had to go, I'd just take her pants off and place the potty nearby. She now handles the rest by herself."

We went on one of our bicycle trips again, travelling with a 3½-year-old and a 13-month-old without taking a single diaper! Jutta only had one or two accidents a day, and we would just wash her pants and dry them on our trailer.

At 19 months we had around 1–2 accidents a day (some days none!). I used timing and intuition, and Jutta signaled by making a farting sound with her lips. She learned to pull her pants and undies down by herself and only needed help pulling them up. She was close to taking full responsibility for her elimination needs.

At 21 months she started talking and was a reliable grad at 22 months, with no regressing—even when I later had another baby and she started Kindergarten in the same week. And I am happy to confirm that IPT was as much fun the second time around as it was the first!

My youngest child, Carsten, was born when Jutta was 3 years 2 months old, and I was excited to EC him. He forced me to start even earlier than I had anticipated. When he was just 5 hours old and the only thing I wanted to do was sleep (it was half past three in the morning), he wouldn't stop squirming and complaining. I had nursed him, but that did not change anything. I took his slightly wet diaper off, sat across the front of the toilet while holding his legs up and leaning his back against my thigh, and seconds later he relieved himself, depositing his first poo ever right into the toilet! I dressed him and put him in bed, and within a few minutes he was sleeping peacefully.

Doing this the third time around, I couldn't imagine not responding to a baby's elimination needs, which are so blatantly obvious. Why on earth would you purposefully let a child soil a diaper and then change it? Of course we had lots of misses in the beginning and used homemade cloth diapers, but we had lots of catches too and he obviously enjoyed going potty into a receptacle much more than into a diaper. And he, like his siblings, showed me again what baloney common "potty readiness wisdom" is. At 8 days old, I wrote:

"Today I was cleaning Carsten's navel. He started to pee and I said, 'Stop, wait!' and he stopped. I picked him up, held him over the sink and he immediately finished the pee. Later I heard him start grunting in his bed. I said, 'Wait, I'll take you to the sink!' then took him to the bathroom, undressed him, and there was a tiny spot of poo in his diaper. As soon as he was over the sink, he let loose a big explosive poo. In the evening I was working on his navel again and the same thing happened only I was quicker. And people say babies don't have any control?"

It all went smoothly and uneventfully. I had some new gadgets that made it even easier this time. First I had three old felted wool blankets strategically placed around the apartment to lay him on when I was not wearing him. If I was quick enough, I could simply wipe a missed pee off them and did not have to wash them. Then I got a transparent potty, which gave instant feedback. While I had used diapers and undies with my first two, I used training pants for the first time with Carsten. When he was 5 months old, I made 7 trainers with side snaps and was able to completely stop using diapers. Trainers are so much trimmer and easier to pull down! Homemade leggings (made from our old socks) are fantastic— they kept his legs warm and gave easy diaper access.

As with my other two we never had a long "strike." He sometimes would refuse a pottytunity, but most of the time would be fine with trying a little later or in a different position or location.

He's 23 months now and a grad. Like his brother he announces "Pipi dede" when he has to go. My diary entry:

"Taking over responsibility to get to the potty in time has developed over the last few months, starting with being fairly reliable on his own if he was "nakey-butt" with a potty nearby. Then he started to verbally announce his needs by saying 'Pee-Pee' or sometimes 'Popo puzzen' (wipe butt) and finally 'Pee-pee dede.' And since the day he was 23 months old he tells me when he has to go each and every time. I don't offer the potty anymore, not even after naps. Sometimes at those times he surprises me and plays for half an hour before going."

We continued to go on bicycle trips each summer. One of the assets of EC is that it allows us to really pack light. On his first trip, when Carsten was almost a year old, I packed five undies and six trainers for him—no diapers to lug along. If something got wet, I'd rinse it as quickly as possible and hang it to dry on the flagpole on our bike trailer. We never even had to use most of the trainers! Now we've just returned from this year's trip, shortly before Carsten turned 2. We took just 5 undies for him—no diapers and no trainers. In the 11 days we were traveling—520 kilometers with two tandem bikes and a bike trailer—he only had four accidents, two of which happened on our last day. That was a sure sign it was time to return home.

Carsten was playing upstairs at my parents' home recently while I was out, then at some point came down the stairs unprompted, told my father "Pee-pee dede" and then peed and pooped in the potty. So now with being verbal and so self-reliant, he can even come down the stairs and still hold it long enough. He's not only a grad with me, but also with other caregivers who are not as tuned in as I am. Wow!

Last night he ran around in pajamas but didn't go to sleep. Shortly before midnight he went potty and I asked him to pull his pants down. He did it all by himself and afterwards pulled them up again, too—so he is now totally independent with simple pants on!

Freddy's German web page is at:
http://www.continuum-concept.de/windellos.htm
Her German-language TopfFit e-mail list can be found at:
http://de.groups.yahoo.com/group/TopfFit

chapter 5

australia

Sarah Buckley is trained as a family MD and lives in Brisbane, Australia, where she is currently a full-time mother and part-time writer on pregnancy and birth issues. Together with her partner Nicholas, also an MD, they have four children, all born at home. It is her faith and interest in the natural processes of birth and mothering that lead Sarah to choose infant potty training with her fourth baby Maia, and she found it a lot of fun, with unexpected rewards: Maia was out of nappies from 13 months, and independent in her toileting from about 18 months. Sarah gave her initial testimonial in 2002 and updated it in 2007.

I heard about infant potty training, or elimination communication as I call it, when my fourth baby Maia Rose was 3 months old. I was very excited about it, and the timing was perfect, as I had read a few years earlier that African women cue their babies to wee and poo with a "psss" sound, and I had begun to do this with Maia from birth. It made sense to me because it felt closer to our genetic imprint, and I was drawn to the idea of a deeper physical and psychic connection with my baby. The first time I tried it, I held Maia (aged 3 months) over the laundry tub and made the "psss" noise. To my delight, she weed straight away, and we have been doing it ever since.

For our family, doing this has been more fun and rewarding than I could have imagined. It has given us more skin-to-skin contact, less washing, no nappy rash, and, best of all for me, a deeper respect for Maia's abilities and knowledge of her body, and a finer attunement to her rhythms. As well as these advantages, there is obviously less waste and a better time for Mother Earth. And it's fun! Having had three babies in nappies, I have been constantly delighted at Maia's ability to communicate her needs—and to keep telling me until I get it.

Elimination communication also makes a beautiful contribution to my experience of mindfulness in my mothering. Like breastfeeding, it keeps me close to my baby, physically and psychologically, and provides very immediate feedback when I am not tuned in.

As a GP (family MD), the physiology is interesting to me and is totally counter to what I was taught at medical school, where it is asserted that babies do not have sphincter control until close to the second birthday. Obviously the paediatricians didn't consult the global majority of mothers and babies, for whom knowing their baby's elimination needs is as simple as knowing their own.

From the start, I've had a lot of support from Emma (11), Zoe (8) and Jacob (6), who tell me how much they disliked sitting in wet or soiled diapers as babies. Some believe that we set up our society for sexual problems by encouraging our babies to dissociate, or switch off from their genital areas because of the unpleasant sensation of wearing what some have called a "walking toilet." My partner Nicholas wondered about the extra effort that I went to in the first year, but has been very happy to reap the benefits of a nappy-free toddler.

Reflecting on my experiences with babies in and out of nappies, I've come to the conclusion that probably ALL babies signal their elimination needs from an early age, but because we're not listening out for it, we misinterpret it as tiredness, needing to feed, or just crankiness, especially if our baby is in a nappy and we don't observe the connection with eliminating.

In the first few months, I learnt Maia's signals by observing her closely. This was fairly easy, as she was very much "in arms" for her first six months. I discovered that she would squirm and become unsettled, sometimes with a bit of crying, especially if it took me a while to "get it." At other times, it was more psychic, and I found myself heading for the laundry tub, where we usually eliminated, without really thinking. When I was distracted, or delayed acting on my hunch, I usually got peed on. (However, she very seldom peed on me when I carried her in a sling.) Her signal for poop was usually a few farts, or sometimes she'd even pull off the breast as a means of signalling that she needed to go. She didn't want to sit in her own poop!

Learning Maia's daily pattern was also useful. She usually pooped first thing in the morning, and, as a baby, tended to pee frequently (about every 10 minutes) in the first few hours after arising. (My husband found this really tricky when he was "on duty" in the morning.) I noticed that she would also pee about 10 minutes after breastfeeding or drinking. She still almost always pees on awaking; I think it is the need to eliminate that actually awakens her.

In her first year, we used the laundry tub by preference. I'd hold her upright by her thighs, with her back resting on my belly. I also used a small sandpit-type bucket, with a conveniently lipped top, which came into its own at night later on (see below). As she got older and heavier, I found that sitting her on the toilet in front of me worked well—sometimes we'd have a "double wee," which was always successful if nothing else worked!

Along with the position, I cued her with my "psss" noise, and sometimes, when I thought she had a need but was slow to start, I'd turn on the tap as well. After three months or so of doing this, I became more sure of my interpretation and I sometimes gently persisted even where she was initially reluctant, and usually she'd go in half a minute or so. However, for me, it's a fine line, and I think it's vital to have cooperation, and not a battle of wills, which can sometimes develop around "toileting." It's more a dance of togetherness that develops, as with breastfeeding, from love and respect for each other.

On a practical level, I used nappies when we were out and about, and peed her as much as I could, but I didn't expect to be perfect in these, or any, circumstances. We used toilets or took the bucket in the car. When we missed a pee, my reaction was just, "Oh well, missed that one." On hot days, I just lay a nappy on the car seat. If it wasn't convenient to stop, I'd say to her, "Oh, Maia, you'll have to pee in the nappy, and I'll change it as soon as we stop."

Maia didn't like to be disturbed at night in the early months, so I'd lie her on a bunny rug and just let her pee. I changed this whenever I woke up. Or I'd wrap a cloth nappy loosely around her bum and change it when wet. I found that, as with naps, she usually peed on awaking and then nursed.

Around 6 to 7 months, Maia went "on strike," coinciding with teething and beginning to crawl. She stopped signaling clearly and at times actively resisted being "peed." I took it gently, offering opportunities to eliminate when it felt right and not getting upset when, after refusing to go in the laundry tub, she went on the floor. Even on "bad days," though, we still had most poops in a bowl, bucket or the toilet. At nearly 10 months, we were back on track. I noticed that as she became more independent and engrossed in her activity, she was not keen to be removed to eliminate, so I started to bring a receptacle to her. She preferred a bowl or bucket on my lap, and later we began to use a potty: I initially held her while she used it.

At nighttime, I started sitting her on a bucket (and on the breast at the same time, tricky to lie down afterwards and not spill the bucket!). When I was less alert, she peed on a nappy between her legs and/or the bunny rug underneath her.

There was a marked shift in things soon after she began walking at 12 months. At 14 months, to my amazement, Maia was out of nappies completely. She was now able to communicate her needs very clearly, both verbally and non-verbally, and her ability to "hold on" was also enhanced. When she needed to eliminate, she said "wee" and/or headed for the potty—we had several around the house. Nicholas, her dad, was so delighted when she first did this that he clapped her, and so she would stand up and applaud herself afterwards. She began to be very interested in the fate of her body products, and joined me as we tipped it onto the garden or into the toilet. (Later she wanted to empty the potty herself.) She even began to get a cloth and wipe up after herself!

With this change, I stopped using nappies altogether and switched to trainer pants—the Bright Bots are great and come in small sizes—for going out. Dresses were great too, for outings with bare-bottomed girls in our warm summer months.

By 19 months, Maia was totally autonomous in her daytime elimination. She could tell us her needs and/or go to the potty herself. Although I would take a change of pants when we went out, it was very rare to need them—compared to my other children, she was about the 3-year-old stage with her toileting.

Nighttimes were busy for us up to age 2 or so, when I began to wean from night nursing. Although peeing Maia frequently at night was a big commitment, it was worthwhile for the daytime benefits. Once we cut down on her nighttime intake, her output reduced as well, and she peed infrequently after that.

Reflecting on my experiences, it interests me that babies learn to release before they learn to hold on. This makes it very convenient because, when cooperative, a baby can empty even a small amount of pee from the bladder. (This means, for example, I can know that we are starting a car trip with minimal chance of Maia needing to wee for at least half an hour or so.) In contrast, conventional toilet training is built around the child's ability to "hold on" to their pee and poop, until they can release it in a socially acceptable place.

I wonder, then, about the mind-body implications of this subtle but important difference. Aren't we a society where we tend to "hold on" to our "stuff," often needing the help of others (e.g., therapists) to encourage us to "let it out." One of my friends commented on Maia's relaxed mouth, and this made me wonder if the process might relax the whole digestive tract. I can also feel, in my mothering, the beauty of supporting her healthy eliminative functions, which many of us feel shameful about and would prefer to deny—hence nappies, which hide the eliminating act itself.

Furthermore, the "toilet training stage" is, in Erik Erikson's psychological stages, centred on the issue of "autonomy vs shame and doubt," and it seems to me that Maia has mastered these issues already—she is incredibly autonomous, not to say bossy at times! I wonder if this might be in part due to being an early mistress of her elimination.

For me, the beauty of elimination communication has been in the process, not in the outcome, however remarkable or convenient. Yes, it's been great to do less than a full load of washing each day for a family of six, but much more significant is the learning that mothers and babies are connected very deeply—at a "gut level"—and that babies (and mothers) are much more capable and smarter than our society credits. As a mother and as an MD, I highly recommend this very satisfying practice.

You can learn more about Sarah's views and teachings from her book *Gentle Birth, Gentle Mothering: The wisdom and science of gentle choices in pregnancy, birth and parenting*, available from www.sarahjbuckley.com

chapter 6

canada

Ingrid Bauer is a writer, nonviolent communication workshop facilitator, parenting coach and parent. She writes and speaks regularly about compassionate parenting and communication and natural living practices. To respond to her baby's needs for consistent skin-to-skin contact and comfortable, hygienic elimination, Ingrid decided in 1997 to raise her second child without diapers. She was amazed to discover that she could learn to distinguish intuitively when he needed to go. She then wrote a book about her experiences and research on raising babies diaper-free. Her next two children were born in 2001 and 2007 and were both raised diaper-free. Ingrid lives with her children and partner on an island in British Columbia, Canada and submitted the following in 2007.

In the fall of 1996, when I was expecting my second child, my partner and I reexamined the diaper issue from a completely different perspective. The question we asked ourselves, as we prepared for our baby's birth, was not "single use or cloth?" It was: "Is it possible to minimize, or even eliminate altogether, the need for diapers?"

Neither my partner nor I had any desire to rush our child in his growing process, nor were we repulsed by body functions. We definitely wanted our baby to relieve himself whenever he needed to. Diapers felt like an impediment to the awareness of these needs. Eliminating diapers, by tuning in to our baby's rhythms, seemed like a natural extension of our parenting philosophy, which is to try to understand, to value and to respond to all our child's needs.

We didn't relish the thought of our baby lying or sitting around in a soggy or poopy diaper, even for a short while. Waste was meant to be eliminated from the body, not plastered to it! We couldn't imagine anyone choosing to spend 24 hours a day with a restrictive bulk between their legs. We wanted our baby to be free to enjoy as much skin-to-skin contact as possible. We were perfectly willing to change diapers, if need be; but at this point, we were wondering if it was really necessary or beneficial.

On our journeys in India, we had seen diaperless babies everywhere. I had also heard about baby-wearing cultures, where mothers were so in tune that they knew exactly when their infants were going to pee or poop and just held them away from their bodies at the right moment. For these women, being peed on was almost unthinkable. How I longed to be this connected to my baby! How did they do it? Was it possible in our culture? Even if I managed to attain this closeness, I couldn't just hold my baby away from me and let him pee on the floor! A friend, who had also traveled in India, gave me a clue. She spoke of naked babies whose mothers just took them off the bus at each longer stop and "peed" them on bus trips that lasted several hours. Based on this tidbit, and convinced that this intimate communication was natural and possible, I set out to rediscover what, for millions of people worldwide, is common knowledge. I learned through observing my son's patterns, by following his cues and my intuition and from the occasional anecdote of someone else's experience.

With no plans or models to follow, things evolved in their own natural way. Early one January morning, after an intense and blissful two-hour labor, our son was born into his parents' hands. The thought of dressing or diapering him never even entered our minds. Outside winter raged; inside the wood stove was stoked, and baby and I lay skin-to-skin, and absorbed each other's presence. Forget about the prescribed hour of bonding! We indulged sensually for weeks on end! Visitors speculated on how old our baby would be before he wore his first clothing.

In fact, he was about 3 weeks old when we first dressed him to go for a longer outing. Until that time, and for much of the following weeks, he was carried naked against us or lay on our bed with flannel pads beneath him, to protect our clothing and the bedding. These I changed the moment they were wet or soiled during the day and several times at night. Gently lifting him to replace the padding was much easier than changing a diaper in the middle of the night. A soft flannel blanket over him prevented the fountain effect, for which little boys are famous.

I started exploring natural infant hygiene with him from birth by making sounds and holding him in position but didn't take him to a toilet place till he was about 4 months. When he pooped, I held him in an upright squatting position by supporting him under his knees, over a change pad, cloths or a diaper. In an improvised approach to my friend's account of the Indian babies, I simply repeated a "cueing sound" two or three times during his efforts. Because we are a bilingual family, I chose *caca*, which is the French equivalent of "poop." (For pee, we used the French word *pipi*.) Sometimes I imitated his soft grunting sounds. Later, I was to learn that mothers in traditional cultures, from Korea to New Guinea, also do this to stimulate a bowel movement.

By 4 months, our son clearly understood our cueing words. He would bear down slightly when I said *caca*. I asked myself whether he really still needed to poop in a diaper, which he was now wearing more regularly. On a whim one morning, I removed his diaper, held him in position and said *caca*. He responded by having his first diaperless bowel movement! I figured it was lucky timing. In fact, it signaled a total end to the washing of soiled diapers. Except for once, in the car, he never pooped in a diaper again.

Tuning in to our baby's need to pee was a longer, subtler process that required deep listening. It started with the "technique" of cueing him and watching for his signals. Gradually, the linear concept of cause and effect gave way to a more synergetic way of being together, and I became as aware of his need to eliminate as I was of my own.

We used various receptacles and locations. Indoors, it was mostly the toilet (always for poops), sometimes the laundry sink (for pee only), occasionally another sink, a bowl or a bucket. In the summer, I took him outside a lot and fertilized the bushes. I always carried him to the bathroom until he chose to begin using the potty on his own, which occurred naturally and gradually over time, between about 14 to 20 months.

At night, although he stirred and partly awoke when he needed to pee, he often really disliked being removed from the bed to the bathroom (I think using a potty by the bed might have worked, but I didn't try). So I tried to pee him before nursing him to sleep, and I used a cloth diaper. He would awaken when he wet it, after which I would remove it immediately (we have a family bed), and he would be naked and dry the rest of the night. He was usually dry through the night, though not consistently, when he 12–18 months.

Sometimes I'm asked at what age my son completed toilet learning. Like weaning from the breast, I don't see natural infant hygiene as a linear process with a specific end point. He first began using the toilet independently at about

12–14 months, but still wanted me to take him to pee many times. Even when, at 2, he rarely needed me, he still wanted me to "pee" him in public rest rooms, when he was sick and in a few other situations.

By the time my daughter was born, I had done lots of research, interviewed dozens of people and written my book about this whole process. Whereas with my son I'd never talked to anyone who'd done it when I started, I had now talked to hundreds of experienced mothers. I am so grateful for the support, the companionship and the opportunity to share the joy of this special communication. With my daughter, I again spent the first precious weeks in retreat, enjoying skin-to-skin contact and getting to know her rhythms. I held her in-arms to go until she was about 7 months when she began to prefer sitting on a little potty. She slept diaperless from birth—we used a bedside potty quite successfully most nights. I used a cloth diaper for backup occasionally on outings, especially with cold weather outerwear, to minimize stress. Otherwise she enjoyed diaper-free comfort. The second time around I felt so much more relaxed about the whole thing. Rather than focusing intently on her elimination needs, it became simply a part of what we do, like nursing or sleeping. I relied even more on intuition and thought about the process less, yet misses were much rarer. And I was far less concerned about misses if they did happen. I accepted that it can be hard to get to a toilet place during outings and that the backup diaper sometimes got wet.

She started walking the day she turned 9 months, and three weeks later, she used her potty without assistance for the first time. Her brother saw and announced it with delight! Sometimes she put things in her potty or called to me to tell me she had to go. Other times, she didn't signal at all and I relied on intuition, cueing or timing. She was toilet independent quite early, already dressing herself before one year old, which is very much her personality.

My youngest is 4 months old as I write this, our third diaper-free baby. I'm quite in awe of how relaxed and easy the process has been with her since birth, despite a very full life. Again, I started with a 6-week "babymoon," have had her diaperless at home from birth, and was catching all her poops by the second day and most of her pees by the first couple of weeks. I'm convinced that this early bonding and diaper-free time has contributed enormously to the ease of our elimination communication. Although she will signal me by fidgeting and vocalizing when she has to go, I rely mainly on intuition, cueing and timing. If we're going somewhere or I'm about to put her in the sling, I simply take her to pee before, and she will, if she has to. She does wear a cloth backup diaper sometimes when we are out or traveling, and when I am in the middle of teaching a large group I may choose to let her go in a diaper and change her immediately in my arms—I've perfected the discreet one-handed change!

One difference I've noticed is that people now seem to know more about diaper-free babies. Many times, I've been approached in public by people who notice that my baby is diaperless or that I'm taking her to the bathroom and heard some version of "Oh, are you doing the diaper-free thing? My sister/ daughter/friend read a book about that and it's been really great!" Sometimes I tell them I wrote one of those books, and sometimes I simply smile and marvel quietly at how wonderfully times are changing.

What I have chosen to call "natural infant hygiene" (I first called it elimination communication) is far more than a practical method for keeping babies clean, dry and happy without diapers. It offers an opportunity for a deepened intimacy between parent and child and a loving way to communicate with your baby and respond to his or her needs. Our babies are so utterly dependent on us to care for them. Natural infant hygiene offers us a beautiful opportunity to understand and respond compassionately to our baby's needs. It serves to strengthen our own intuition and our intimate connection with both our child and ourselves. With natural infant hygiene, as with breast-nurturing, I appreciate the possibility for a respectful and loving two-way interchange, long before that first word is spoken.

You can read more about Ingrid Bauer, her philosophy and teachings, in her book *Diaper Free! The Gentle Wisdom of Natural Infant Hygiene*. Ingrid describes four integrated approaches to tuning in to your child's natural elimination needs: timing, signals, intuition and cueing. With an emphasis on strengthening the bond between parent and child, the book promises many practical tips as well as insights into the parenting journey.

chapter 7
short reports

Japan

Ai Nozawa brought up five children using her own version of infant potty training. She has one son, four daughters and fourteen grandchildren. She was 65 years old when this report was filed in 1988 by one of her relatives, Kumiko Iwamoto:

I have heard from Ai Nozawa that she began the training from birth with all her children. She opened the diapers at the right moment and called to her children, *shii shii* (which means "pee pee") while the children were urinating, and as a result she completed the training before her children were one year old. She was satisfied with this method.

She began the training from the 7th day after birth. She spread newspaper on the floor (the passage which is usually boarded in Japan) and put a diaper on the paper. She made her baby sit on the diaper, called *shii shii* and observed the intervals of urination. At 6 months old, she held the baby on a stool over a toilet. She devised a way to make the atmosphere in the toilet joyful; for example, she decorated the toilet with flowers.

Her husband and her husband's mother assisted her with the training. She did not wake the babies at night. The method was time consuming.

She later helped toilet train all her grandchildren, and they all completed the training around one year old. The mothers enjoyed it and found it a good method.

It was easier with the girls than the boys, because generally boys are less sensitive than girls and also because the intervals of urination of girls are longer than those of boys. The intervals of urination for boys were 20 or 30 minutes at the beginning.

This method is not widespread in Japan. Japanese mothers usually begin toilet training in warm seasons after their children turn one year old. They spread thick rush-woven matting called *tatami* on the floor. In the winter, the matting is hard to dry if the children have an accident. The traditional Japanese method is to sit a child on a stool or a pot called *omaru* at the right moment, when the diaper has been dry for a long time, and say to the child, *shii shii*. The infant word for "urine" is *shii shii*, *shikko* or *chikko*. The mother gives the highest praise to the child when the child urinates in a toilet.

Myanmar (Burma)

Dr. Nyo Nyo Any Mrcog, consultant obstetrician and gynecologist from Ottwe, responded to my inquiries by providing information "based on my own experience and also by inquiring of other mothers" in 1988:

The traditional method of toilet training in the villages of my country is to make the child sit on the feet of his mother, whose feet would be about 6 inches apart, while she is sitting on a low stool, either knees flexed or knees stretched.

This type of training is started by the age of 6 months and completed when the child is able to communicate and picks up the habit; i.e., about the age of 18 months. This has been passed on for many generations. No research work has been done in this field to say how many centuries it has been used.

Some mothers do begin the training at birth, at about 2 weeks of age. The mother holds the infant's feet while it is lying on a diaper. Then the mother makes sounds like *inn-enn*. In fact, I used this method with my babies. Whenever they wanted to pee or pass a stool, they became restless and at that time, I made the sound and the baby started passing.

Philippines

Eric Dedace interviewed several mothers and grandmothers in the countryside near Sariaya and filed this report in 2002:

In rural Philippines, especially areas of low-income families, toilet training is casual and relaxed and is begun when a child is old enough to sit and hold its head upright. Babies are considered too young to start before this. Cloth diapers, often hand-me-downs, are used. Babies and children from the poorest families go naked. Small children are generally taken outdoors to eliminate. In traditional houses with slotted bamboo floors (these consist of bamboo strips with spaces in between and raised a few feet from the ground to facilitate added ventilation), babies and small children are allowed to urinate on the bamboo floor. The urine falls directly to the ground and seeps into the dry soil.

One way to determine if a boy is ready to pee is to see if his penis is hard and if so, the mother gently shakes the organ while saying "shh-shh" to encourage urination. A Filipino father reported that if his infant sons were asleep, he could ascertain when they needed to pee by lifting their diapers to see if the testicles were closer to the groin area, rather than limply hanging downwards. He would then hold a potty in position and make the "shh-shh" sound.

Before defecation, the mother fills the potty with just enough water to cover the bottom and prevent the waste matter from sticking. Those who do not have a potty simply let their babies defecate on a piece of paper which is then thrown away in a ditch with running water or else into a makeshift toilet dug in the ground and surrounded by coconut palms arranged for privacy. Cues for defecation include "oo, oo, oo" and "mmmm." Mothers know when their babies have to go, based on instinct, timing and body language, especially facial expressions.

When I asked some mothers if they ever get angry over accidents, they looked at each other and laughed, amused at the question. They said, "How can you get angry if there is an accident, much less get angry at a child who still doesn't understand how to communicate fully?"

If the notion of a baby being properly toilet trained means being able to communicate so there won't be any mess, then this happens around the age of 2–3 years. At this time, babies can imitate the cue sounds their mothers make and advise in advance that they need to go.[1]

South Africa

The following four reports were furnished by the Department of Health Services and Welfare, Pretoria, South Africa, in 1988, in response to a 10-question survey I developed and distributed via legal firms abroad in 1988–1989:

Lady of European origin, registered nurse, Pretoria

The practice outlined below is the usual one and is taught by the nurse in the health clinic for her community.

The traditional method was to begin toilet training at about 3 months of age, to achieve success at about 6–9 months, all going well.

The baby was supported over a tiny potty, at first once a day after bath and feeding time in the morning. Later, with some success, the mother would try at other times in the day, if possible before the baby was found to be wet, e.g., upon waking in the morning and before going to sleep at night.

Sometimes, I woke the babies who were staying at the clinic at night until they remained dry. Some mothers tried to catch the bowel action first.

The method of early training was not stressful. The mothers would show pleasure in "success" but no displeasure in "failure" if there were accidents.

With regard to three of the children in question, one girl was trained (day and night) at 9 months; one girl and one boy were trained at one year. It was easier to train girls than boys and, in general, girls finished the training sooner. The method was unsuccessful for only one child at the clinic.

Indian lady, Asian origin, Pretoria

Training from infancy is commonly used in her area. Her parents and many of her friends used it. She felt that there is no difference in training time for boys and girls. Reassurance is very important. Everyone she knows who used the method found it to be satisfying. No one found it to be inconvenient or frustrating. Her feeling was that it all depends on the reaction of the parents—if they are anxious or upset, they will find it frustrating.

Lady of the Xhosa tribe, registered nurse

1. Among Xhosas, toilet training starts from between 5 and 6 months of age. In the olden days, huts were smeared with cow dung.[2] The mothers used to take dry mashed cow dung and put it on the floor. First thing in the morning (at about 6 a.m.), the baby is held in the squatting position on this cow dung until he urinates or defecates, and then the cow dung is removed. This method is repeated after about every hour until the end of the day.

   As time goes on, the child will show signs of restlessness and crying as a sign of wanting to pass urine or defecate. Toilet training is usually completed by about 7 to 8 months. It takes about one month, at the most 2 months.

2. This method has been in use for centuries. Nowadays, some people with economic means use potties and diapers.

3. There is basically one main system, training from infancy, but not from birth.

4. I learnt this system from my own mother.

5. The method is common.

6. Every female member in the family must cooperate and helps if the mother is busy.

7. The babies are woken at night, but not as frequently as in daytime—roughly about twice per night.

8. They are successfully trained around 7–8 months of age.

9. The method used was the same with all the children in my family.

10. It is successful if family members are cooperative and do the same even if the mother is away.

11. The method is satisfying.

12. This method is time consuming. It needs a lot of patience. If the baby takes too long, you must even make the sound of urine coming out, by saying "pssssss."

Lady of the Tswana tribe, registered nurse

1. Toilet training with Blacks starts very early. They have no nappy to catch the stool for sometime. To have the problem over and done with, outdoor methods are used. Thus the infant learns at an early stage.

   As time goes on, the mother learns to notice how the strict routine mealtime regulates the bowel motion times as well.

   Babies are encouraged to pass water and stools as the first thing at bedtime and first thing in the morning.

2. This method has been in use for a long time. The material used is soft grass, dry dung, leaves and water.

   Mother sits with her legs stretched out slightly apart. Baby is then put just below the knees with a little dry dung underneath that would serve as baby's toilet.

3. A similar type of training involves squatting outside on the soil for the infants who are old enough to already understand.

4. Mothers usually start training from 4 to 5 months of age.

5. I learned this from my own mother and culture.

6. The method is commonly used.

7. A family member helped me with the toilet training.

8. Early on, I woke the baby at night. Later, the baby would wake up dry in the morning.

9. My children completed their training at about 20–24 months.

10. Girls were easier to train than boys.

11. The method was satisfying.

12. The method was time consuming, but otherwise not frustrating.

Taiwan

Henry Chen, Jr., (Attorney in Taipei, 1988)

1. We usually use diapers with infants between 1–3 months of age. This is because infants are not so reactive to outside circumstances at that stage.

   After the 3rd or 4th month, diapers are still used, but parents will untie the diaper every 3 or 4 hours and hold the baby in front of a spittoon (pot, close-stool) or a flush-toilet (no matter if the baby is asleep or awake) and then whistle a special single tone (a sound like "hsu") for about 2–3 seconds and repeat the whistle till excretion. If not successful, we'll wait 5–10 minutes to do the same action again. After 4–6 months training, most of the babies grow used to it and excrete on time.

2. I believe this method has been in use by the majority of Chinese families (over 80%) over hundreds of years. Equipment used is the same except flush-toilet.

3. The "whistle" system is the main system. As far as we know, some of the parents (less than 10%) let their baby listen to music instead of a whistle sound when they use the method.

4. We learned the method from our family. As a matter of fact, my two daughters were trained by their grandmother since their 1st month of life.

5. The method is common.

6. Generally, grandma will help with toilet training the children.

7. Toilet training is completed at about 10–14 months of age, depending on the patience of the parents when they train the baby.

8. There is no difference in training girls and boys.

9. I questioned three couples and was told that all of them use this method and were all very successful.

10. We were satisfied with the method.

11. The method was very convenient, but at night it is annoying, since parents have to get up at night.

Mrs. C. S. Chen (Magazine Editor, Taipei, 1988)

Mrs. Chen was kind enough to include some of my questions in a poll she conducted for Woman-ABC magazine:

What are the primary methods of training used in China?
- Train the child to utter sounds when he (she) feels like evacuating.
- Whistle or hiss to provoke the child's desire of evacuation.
- Say "hmmm" when holding the child on the toilet.
- Train by calculation based on feeding time.
- Turn on the faucet.
- When the child can sit, use a small potty.
- Have the child sit on the potty at the proper time of day.

What kind of device did the ancient Chinese mothers use?
- any available place
- squatting style toilet
- grass toilet paper
- spittoon
- washing basin
- bottle (for boys)
- small round basin

- open-crotch pants (split pants)
- no device at all

What method did mothers then use for training their babies?
Lay the child on its back. Unfasten the diaper. Hold and slightly raise up the baby's legs. Make hissing or "hmmm" sounds to prompt the baby to urinate or defecate.

The Whistling Sound in Adulthood

If the whistling sound is used for many months into toddlerhood, adults who grew up eliminating upon this cue sometimes still react to the conditioning in adulthood. (The same applies to babies who hear the "sssss" sound for a long time.) Here are comments made in 2000 by three people who speak from experience.

1. My husband is furious about me making the "shhhh" sound for our baby because he feels when our son hears the sound later in life that he will need to go to the bathroom. This happens to my husband every so often and he doesn't like it.[3]

2. In Taiwan, many people use a particular whistle. To this day, when I hear it, I feel like going. When we started toilet training our girl, most of the time I ended up going before she did! I hear a lot of people joke about having the same response, but more like suddenly realizing that it may be a good idea to go to the restroom.[4]

3. An American friend of ours who was teaching a class to Chinese students would occasionally whistle absentmindedly out of habit. He noticed some of the students started squirming and then they asked him to please not whistle, as it made them afraid that they were going to pee.[5]

Turkey

The following 1988 report was submitted by Seyma Dogramaci, a psychologist in Istanbul, Turkey:

I have been in the field for 10 years. I work with children and families on different issues, including bedwetting problems. I am therefore pretty much acquainted with the toilet training methods of urban parents. My answers to your questions are based on the knowledge I gathered from my clients, my relatives and, being the mother of a 10-month-old son, direct from my own personal experience.

Mothers tend to toilet train babies as early as they can. They mainly want to accomplish this before the baby is a year old. The usual way of toilet training is to put the baby in lukewarm water after he is washed and whisper "shhh" in the ear of the baby, which will hopefully motivate urination. If this is done repeatedly at the appropriate intervals, the baby acquires a rhythm. What I mean by "appropriate intervals" is the frequency of the baby's urination, which is mostly determined by keeping him nude in the summer months to see how often he urinates. Once his frequency is obtained, the mother will have to invite the baby for urination at slightly shorter intervals.

It is often the case that daytime toilet training is completed before nighttime training. Mothers leave the diapers off in the day, but keep them on at night for some time more. Most children I have worked with have been reported to have their toilet training complete between the ages of 1 and 2.

As the baby grows older, potties are introduced around 8–9 months. Mothers and grandmothers are the ones to initiate the training. I do not think there is a significant difference between boys and girls in being toilet trained.

The method is usually learned from the elders of the family. Babies are not awakened at night for training purposes, but it is advised to do so when bedwetting is an issue at older ages.

Zambia

Kira Rowat and her husband Stuart Taylor spent 2½ years in Zambia (2004–2006) with their young daughter Iona doing volunteer work in agricultural and nutritional development. They lived in the town of Choma in the Southern province of Zambia which is home to the Tonga people. Stuart returned to Zambia for work in 2006 and also in 2007 when this report was filed:

With the Tonga people in Zambia, the method of toilet training is basically avoidance. Babies and toddlers can pee anywhere they like—on your lap (and quickly held off the lap to finish peeing), outside on the dirt, inside on the dirt or polished cement floors, wherever until they are somewhere between 2 and 3 years old when they know to go outside off the main path.

They start bowel "training" or positioning when they are somewhere between 4–6 months old. It simply involves placing the baby's bottom between your calves while you are either sitting on the ground or on a rock or stool. It is referred to as "helping the baby." The poop is then either buried right there in the field or put down the latrine. As the hole in a latrine can be sizeable, toddlers do not use the latrine until they are around 4–5 years old and not at risk of falling in.

The women put their babies in flat gauze diapers and plastic pants when they go to church, travel on buses or the backs of trucks, when they visit the health post and anyplace where eliminating would not be easy to deal with or if a mother is in nice clothes. They also use diapers right after the baby is born for the first little while.

At night, when babies are small, they keep some diapers or cloths handy for the baby to poop in during the night. Once night pooping stops, they stop using these. For urinating, I was told that when a baby starts fussing in the night, the mother holds her baby over the side of the bed. In the village, a small pile of sand is kept by the bed or sleeping mat and swept out in the morning.

Everyday mothers hang their blankets on the line. My guess is that the blanket protects the bed. Given the daily trek to get water (20 liters at a time in a bucket on your head), diapers are not very practical. While hand washing is the norm throughout Zambia, the average top-loading washing machine in North America uses upwards of 200 liters for one load of laundry. That would equal 10 trips to the well just to wash diapers!

In bigger towns, women use cloth diapers most of the time, although in some of the very poor neighborhoods the village approach still stands. In the big modern capital city of Lusaka, cloth diapers are still the norm although you can easily buy disposable diapers which the wealthier residents and expats use.[6]

part **4**

CROSS-CULTURAL
STUDIES

chapter 1

cross-cultural comparisons

Part 4 of this book offers a selection of information and writings on infant elimination training gleaned from various reports and field studies around the world. This chapter begins with a description of the main methods of infant elimination training, then describes some cultural differences between industrialized and nonindustrialized societies vis-à-vis basic infant care practices.

Infant Elimination Training Methods

There appear to be two main methods of elimination training in nonindustrialized societies, with a third possibility being a hybrid of the two in the form of progressing from one to the other. Diapers are generally not a part of these methods. Nurturant care is the norm.

Method 1 – Mother-Baby Training

Mother-baby training is similar to IPT. The mother or caregiver becomes familiar with baby's cues, timing and patterns; anticipates when to take baby to go; holds him in a particular position; and encourages elimination with a vocal cue such as "sssss." The child quickly learns to associate the position and sound with elimination and responds to these stimuli by eliminating on cue. Mother and baby synchronize, and the child at some point begins to signal the need to eliminate. The mother is attentive; communication, intuition and responsiveness play important roles; and mother and infant function as a symbiotic unit. The word "training" applies to the mother-infant dyad in that both undergo a reciprocal learning process, teaching and learning from each other.

Method 2 – Avoidance

With avoidance, the mother or caregiver is not concerned with elimination training in early infancy, since in some societies, tradition has it that a baby is developmentally too young to understand or do anything about elimination. Instead, the mother focuses on avoiding messes in the home or on the child and herself. She keeps her baby in light underwear or bare-bottomed and uses "baby-aiming." When he starts to go, she aims the child away from herself and in a favorable direction in terms of keeping the living quarters clean. If he eliminates inside a dwelling, she nonchalantly cleans up and carries on with her activities, almost as if nothing has happened.

When the baby reaches toddlerhood, he learns by observing and imitating older children and adults and by gentle encouragement from his mother. In some societies, punishment and peer pressure are used when toddlers eliminate in the wrong place.

Method 3 – Hybrid

The mother starts with avoidance by aiming baby away from her to eliminate (per Method 2) then eventually begins mutual training with baby (per Method 1) when she feels her baby is old enough to understand. In other words, baby-aiming and avoidance transition to mother-baby training. There is no set age for the switchover, but it can occur as early as 2 months.

Cross-Cultural Child-Rearing Practices

There is not one child-care philosophy that is superior to all others, nor is there one inferior to all others. Each has its pros and cons. Through cross-cultural studies and research, parents are able to select or reject individual practices and thereby customize and hone their own child-rearing style, calling on wisdom from the past and from around the world.

The biggest difference between Western child-rearing practices and those of many other parts of the world is the amount of close, physical contact between mother and baby. In rural areas of most developing countries, infants are:
- born at home (sometimes in a clinic) via natural childbirth and immediately held by mother or caregiver
- closely bonded with their mothers during a postpartum honeymoon ("babymoon"), often in seclusion, lasting from 7 to 80 days

- in constant and close physical contact with their mother or caregiver(s) until they walk
- held or carried throughout most of the day
- kept in bed, or on a mat or cot, beside their mother all night
- nursed on demand for 1–4 years, sometimes longer
- immediately soothed and never left to cry
- never alone
- rarely disciplined or punished
- generally not diapered (except in some affluent families or when using natural materials)
- not pressured to be toilet trained

A caretaking model along these lines was coined the "continuous care and contact model" by Edward Tronick in 1985. One person, usually the mother, is the primary caretaker, responsible for providing continuous care, constant contact and frequent, short periods of nursing.[1]

Margaret Mead classified children into four age groups based on her research on childhood in six societies. The first is the lap child, from birth to 1 year of age. Next comes the knee child which consists of toddlers from 2–3 years of age. The yard child is the preschooler aged 4–5 years, and the community child is 6–10 years old. "Since the lap children in most of our samples are in close physical contact with their mothers during both day and night (they sleep in body contact with their caretakers), much of their communication with caretakers is nonverbal. Caretakers learn to read the cues of their charges. . . . The best demonstration of this kinesthetic style of communication is the caretaker's ability to foresee the lap child's need to urinate or defecate; the caretaker then holds the baby out before it soils the caretaker's clothes. In contrast, the style of communication of American mothers is more verbal and less kinesthetic."[2]

Anthropologist Robert LeVine theorizes that the attentive infant care practices of Africans and others are a cultural adaptation to high infant mortality rates. He refers to this type of maternal behavior as a "folk pattern of preventative medicine in infancy" and a "constant medical alert, a chronic emergency mobilization to save the child at risk." By being held or kept close to a caregiver at all times, a baby is kept out of harm's way and closely monitored for illness. A quick response to crying provides immediate feedback about baby's condition. Minimizing crying from other causes heightens the value of crying as a signal of more serious problems such as disease. Continual breastfeeding assures that baby's fluid level is always sufficient, thus alleviating dehydration from diarrhea, which is one of the main causes of infant death in the tropics.[3]

Different societies have different ideas about what constitutes essential care and what is considered indulgent. LeVine and others postulate that certain behaviors by Western parents, such as a desire for intimacy in social relationships, seem indulgent to parents of lesser-developed areas. In the West, parents lavish their babies with physical and verbal affection, often in public. They believe verbal stimulation will encourage learning and cognition. They spend considerable time smiling at their babies. They make eye-to-eye contact, kiss, cuddle, sing, chat (high pitched or baby talk) and coo a lot, whereas mothers in other cultures typically do not and find these types of behavior indulgent. Westerners feel that mothers in some other societies are aloof in that they do not kiss and cuddle their babies. Gusii mothers do not speak to their babies, considering it a waste of time. Instead, they soothe and nurse.[4]

Most American and European parents believe that behaviors such as maintaining constant physical contact, nursing on demand and quickly responding to crying will spoil a child. Importance is placed upon rearing independent children. It is believed that this goal can be accomplished by instilling separateness, self-sufficiency and self-confidence in the child, starting at birth.[5]

Whether carrying on conversations or performing labor or other tasks, a typical baby-wearing African, South American, Asian or Eskimo mother is aware of the needs and state of her infant. It is never necessary to "go look and listen" the way American mothers do when the baby is at a distance or in another room.[6]

Another component of nurturant cultures is the casual and relaxed attitude towards infant elimination and toilet training. Although the odor of feces can be unpleasant, there are no hysterically negative feelings about excreta. By way of comparison, Westerners often feel that dealing with elimination is disgusting and "yucky." Some resent or punish infants for making a mess. In extreme situations, these negative feelings lead to abuse and even murder.

Western babies are typically surrounded by toys and other possessions— another example of indulgence in the eyes of third world peoples. Most of the toys are for entertainment or learning purposes. Many also serve as a substitute for attentive care. A Western child quickly becomes bored and is at a loss without his toys and electronic gadgets and games, whereas children in many other societies are entertained without these things. I once proudly presented the latest American toys and gadgets to some small children in rural India, but they preferred to play in the fields or to collect rocks and pieces of kite string from the village streets. Their mothers ended up putting the shiny new toys in a display cupboard since the kids, including babies, had no interest in them.

Since the late 20th century, more and more Western families have been adopting a number of nurturant practices such as babywearing, family sleeping, quick response to crying and nursing on demand. At the same time, a number of families in third world countries are abandoning traditional ways and swapping some of their customs for Western ones, such as bottle-feeding, early weaning, diapers and leaving baby alone in a crib or other location—mainly in the case of affluent or well-educated families, but there are exceptions. Letting children run around diaperless is viewed as lower class by the upper class in some third world countries. In an effort to avoid criticism, some poorer families are abandoning infant toilet training and using diapers.

Precocity vs. Cultural Factors

Marcelle Geber spent considerable time studying African infants, especially Ugandans, in 1954–55 and concluded in a 1958 report that Ugandan babies are precocious in some aspects when compared with Western babies. She was amazed to find that Ugandan babies smile and sit months ahead of their Western counterparts. Geber attributed this precocity to several factors, including the placidity, greater physical activity and positive view of motherhood of Ugandan women during pregnancy as well as the quality of mothering in infancy. Both earlier and ensuing observations and studies by others found that African babies develop faster and are more precocious than the children of European races.[7] The current consensus, which includes Geber, is that: (a) Genetics is not the cause of African precocity[8] and (b) The cause of faster development of sensorimotor behaviors in African infants during the early weeks of life is predominantly due to socioenvironmental factors. African babies receive far more physical and social stimulation than Western babies.[9] Whatever the case, in the long run, it does not seem to make much difference in North America and Europe whether a baby learns to sit at 2 months or 6 months of age.

As parental expectations, training and handling of infants interact and feed off one another, they can contribute to improving muscle tone and motor control in developing infants.

Parental and Cultural Expectations

Every society has some sort of guidelines for how to handle a newborn, what precautions to take and when to expect what from baby. Different people around the world have different expectations, training methods and time frames. The age at which a mother and a society expect her baby to learn certain skills can influence the way she interacts with the baby. For example, most Baganda mothers believe a baby does not hear sounds until the age of 3 months. As a result, these Baganda mothers do not begin singing to their babies until they are 3 months or older.[10]

In his 1977 study of the Digo tribe in Kenya, Marten deVries reported that cultural expectations and attitudes lead the Digo to view their babies as relatively hardy beings and active participants in life. Where toilet training is concerned, the Digo are close to their infants and use a series of reciprocal cue-and-rule learning starting around the age of 2 months.[11] The tribe believes and *knows* their babies are capable of toilet conditioning in infancy. They therefore *expect* to watch for, learn and respond to elimination signals from their infants, then reciprocate with their own cues, in turn expecting baby to respond, effectively creating a snowballing of give-and-take between mother and infant.

Cultural attitudes and mores concerning modesty, shame and embarrassment also influence the time scale and method of teaching toilet training. Some peoples are fairly laid back and immodest in their attitudes while others are extremely shy and prudish. In many of the societies portrayed in Part 4, local tribes base their toilet behavior in part on fears related to witches, evil spirits and magic.

Parental Handling

Another contrast between Western-style parenting and that of many developing countries is in the way babies are handled. Surprisingly, parents in societies more attentive to baby are generally rougher in their handling of babies. In India, mothers and caregivers give daily massages and tend to an infant's needs with quick and abrupt movements. In a study in Karnataka state in India, infants received a rough and vigorous daily massage and other forms of motoric stimulation with the result that at 3 months of age they were above U.S. standards for motor development (Bayley Scales), including 2–3 months ahead of U.S. norms where certain head-control items were involved. For example, 1-month-old infants demonstrated good head control during a pull-to-sit exercise.[12]

The Gusii of Kenya and many others toss their infants in the air or between adults. Babies are handled with much more forcefulness than is tolerated with American infants, "without gasps of 'watch her head, you'll hurt her neck' from grandparents and other protective adults."[13]

By the age of 3 months, Gusii infants are lifted by one arm and swung onto their mothers' back, without loss of head or trunk control.[14] Mary

Ainsworth reported that Baganda mothers do not support the heads of newborn babies. A mother hurries along and takes no notice of the fact that her infant's head is bobbing about.[15] The fact that Baganda babies are carried in a sling may reinforce the infant's ability to hold his head firmly since he learns to compensate for his mother's movements.[16] Baganda mothers typically pick up their babies by grabbing hold of an arm near the shoulder and swinging the baby up onto their back, taking no precautions to support the head. Ainsworth comments that some of the precautions we take in our society to support an infant's head may be unnecessary, overprotective and a cause for delayed control of head and trunk muscles.[17] Crossing into the realm of toilet training with this theory in mind, perhaps the precautions we take in our society are a cause for our relatively late completion of toilet training. Evidence from abroad indicates that by encouraging, working with and training a baby to control his sphincter muscles from the early months of life, we may be able to advance the age at which a child gains control of these muscles.

Parental Training

Many African babies receive training in certain skills at a relatively young age. !Kung parents believe that certain parts of motor development, such as sitting, crawling, standing and walking, will not take place without training. They routinely begin early training in these areas, with the result that !Kung babies learn these skills at a younger age than Western babies.[18]

In 1973, Charles Super tested 20 Kipsigis infants in Kenya during the first year of life and found these infants were advanced in skills which were either specifically trained or encouraged by caregivers. These skills included sitting, head control, grasping, and strength and coordination of the legs.[19] Skills such as crawling and rolling from the back to the stomach, for which the Kipsigis infants were not specifically trained, did not show advancement on the Bayley Scale of Infant Motor Development.[20]

In a study comparing the sitting skills of Baganda and Samia infants in Africa, both received intensive and prolonged training to sit in infancy. The Baganda trained their infants to sit around the age of 2 to 3 months, purely for social reasons. Samia infants were even more advanced, perhaps because there was more urgency for them to learn to sit early. Samia mothers needed to be free to work in the fields and were able to do so once their babies could sit nearby.[21]

Expectations, training and handling of infants set the tone and pace for learning. Marten deVries sums this up nicely. "Infant capacity, cultural goals, the physical and social environment as well as maternal behaviour and experience all fit in a web related to neurodevelopment, maturation and outcome measures." He stresses that neurodevelopment follows on a blueprint of both genes and culture. "Every culture and every social niche provides its own signature to the maturation and development of its offspring." He refers to "mechanisms that push or retard the rate of development and train for specific tasks as well as particular psychological characteristics, that have historically provided a survival advantage. Much research in infant development has shown that the neonate is ready and capable for these early learning transactions."[22]

Scant Research

The topic of infant elimination training has received very little attention by Western medicine. It has been ignored despite the fact that toilet training is at best an emotional ordeal in Western society. I believe the reasons that Western medicine and academia have avoided this subject are mainly cultural. The attitude seems to be that infant elimination training is considered:

- impossible by Western medicine
- dangerous by Western medicine
- too time consuming for Westerners
- too inconvenient for Westerners
- an uneventful process in many non-Western societies where it is rarely a problem for parents
- a female issue of little or no interest to men

Since no scientific or academic studies, scales or other means of measurement and testing exist, there is no way to reach a scientifically sound conclusion, but this does not mean that a general conclusion and impression about the efficacy of IPT cannot be reached. The practices, preferences, cultural tendencies and claims of a number of peoples described in this book all lead to the conclusion that infant elimination training is not only possible and practiced in many societies, but it is also gentle and effective. It should also be noted that there have not been any in-depth studies conducted on traditional toilet training either.

Field Studies in Anthropology

Generally speaking, anthropology has been more helpful to the cause of infant toilet training than has medicine. Field studies and research in anthropology provide interesting material on infant elimination training, not so much because anthropologists or journalists expressly seek this type of information but because it has long been an integral and undeniable part of life in many parts of the world. Field studies would be incomplete without including toilet training, and professionals are required to publish accurate and objective reports. Many of the pieces in Part 4 come from anthropologists and journalists. Here, author Judith Goldsmith compares toilet training in Western and traditional cultures:

"In Western society, toilet training is usually delayed until after a child can walk and talk, much later than in traditional cultures. This leads to further frustrations in child raising, greater dependence on consumer products, and sometimes traumatic attempts at pattern altering. Traditional mothers end their time of cleaning up after their child much sooner, in a much gentler way. Here is yet another area of the childbirth-child nurturing process in which new investigations into old ways would be greatly welcomed.

"As we can see, just as with childbirth, we have often made child nurturing a more complicated process than it needs be." In tracing the development of a child from fetus to toddler, Dr. H.M.I. Liley noted that in the distant past, a "'child was born into an environment so similar to the one that he had just left that he did not need clothing, diapers, playpens, toilet training, spoon feeding, cribs, or any of the other paraphernalia we associate with infant care today. . . . There would be no bottom rashes or routines or formulas and very little crying. . . .This shows that many of the problems we have with our babies have been created by ourselves.'

"When American actress Jane Fonda visited Vietnam in 1974, she left her two-year-old son with a Vietnamese woman doctor while making a tour of the country. During the two weeks of travel, she received reports of what he had eaten, how he had slept, how much weight he had gained. However, a big surprise awaited her on her return. She writes, 'It was only when we got back that we discovered that he'd been toilet trained. Dr. Huong would hold him over a pot at regular intervals, making a hissing sound like running water and sure enough, nine times out of ten, it would work. It still does. It occurred to us that all the talk about how early toilet training creates psychological problems may be just a myth to protect the diaper industry. Vietnamese kids are toilet trained by the time they can sit and they don't seem to have problems.'

"This training of a child to respond to a particular sound was practiced throughout much of the traditional world, with great success, and often from a very early age (much earlier than the one to two years at which toilet training is commonly begun in modern Western societies). For example, in Korea, the child was placed on a jar early in the morning. The mother would say 'shhh . . .' and touch the genitals to suggest urination, or say 'ung-ga' to encourage defecation. In Japan, at about three months, the mother started training the child by whistling low and monotonously as a signal. In Sikkim, again at three months, the Lepcha baby was taken out on the balcony to eliminate at regular intervals and soon learned to cry when it wanted to be taken out; by crawling time, it simply crawled out by itself. In Busama, New Guinea, also from the third month, the mother would hold the infant over the earth floor as soon as it awoke in the morning, while she grunted and strained to indicate elimination.

"Asia was not the only area in which this technique was used. In Peru, toilet training began when the infant's diet was supplemented with food other than milk (about six months). There, too, the child was held over the floor, at a set time each day. The Gros Ventres of Montana, who began toilet training between the sixth and twelfth month, estimated the times of elimination, opened the baby's cradle sack, and held the baby out, supporting it under its knees and thighs; according to reports, the child would usually respond to this, but if there was a delay, the adults would talk to it and make a hissing noise. Similarly, the Eskimo mother of Alaska held her child on a pot on her lap, and cued it by blowing gently on its head; Eskimo children were toilet trained before their first birthday.

"These practices must have been very common, for there are similar accounts from Africa. At first, the Kgatla mother of Botswana simply cleaned her back after the child eliminated. Before the child was returned to her back she held it and said 'sss, sss, sss,' until it relieved itself. She would take the child down from time to time and repeat this procedure, until the baby had learned to cry when the need arose. When a mother among the Bafut of the Cameroons wanted her baby to urinate, she jiggled it up and down; if she wanted it to defecate, she held it steadily on the floor.

"It seems, then, that 'diapers' were not necessary for as long a time in traditional cultures as they are today; nor was the process of toilet training as complicated as it sometimes is for us."[23]

chapter 2
africa

Botswana – the !Kung (Konner)

In 1972, Melvin Konner reported that among the hunting and gathering !Kung (also referred to as San or !Kung San and formerly called "Bushmen")[24] of the Kalahari desert in northwestern Botswana, "Elimination has no social consequences for Zhun/twa infants (though it does for problem 'bedwetters' in later childhood). Before he can crawl easily the infant routinely urinates and defecates in someone's lap. Usually he is not even moved until it is finished, and it is cleaned up with no comment whatever. Gradually, as he acquires control and mobility, he is told to leave the house and, after he is walking well, to leave the village. In many observed episodes, no infant or child has ever been in the least upset in connection with elimination (except infants in the first two or three months upset by the change in position required for cleaning), nor, for that matter, has any adult. . . . Since infants are unclothed and soiling attended to immediately, wetness is never a cause of crying."[25]

Joseph Chilton Pearce presents a slightly different rendition. "Konner, in his studies of the Zhun/Twasi, an African hunting-gathering culture, found the infants carried in the Ugandan fashion. These mothers always knew when the infant was going to urinate or defecate and removed the child to the bushes ahead of time. The mother sensed the general state of the infant and anticipated the infant's every need."[26]

Melvin Konner has confirmed that both of these descriptions agree with his observations. "I would say the mother's response might be either to anticipate and hold the baby away from her; or if she missed the cue, to hold the baby away from her after the baby begins urinating or defecating." If she misses the chance completely, she cleans up afterwards. "In any case, the nonchalance is what impressed me, coming from a culture where we are anything but nonchalant!"[27]

Botswana – the !Kung (Marshall)

"Babies are naked and, since there are no floors but the desert sand, not much is made of their urinating wherever they are. When they defecate, they are wiped with grass and the fecal matter is cleaned up at once by some older child or adult and carried off. As soon as children can walk fairly well, they are led by the hand and encouraged to go out of the werf for their toilet needs, at first for the sake of cleanliness and, as they grow older, for the sake of modesty as well."[28]

Kenya – the Digo

In 1974, Marten deVries, M.D., conducted research that included infant elimination training as used by the Digo tribe inhabiting the coastal plain along the Indian Ocean from Mombasa, Kenya, into Tanzania. DeVries reported that 30 of 34 mothers in a random sample of families stated that they started bowel and bladder training at 2 to 3 weeks of age and had succeeded with all aspects reasonably well by the age of 4 to 6 months. DeVries attributes the Digo's early effectuation of elimination training to specialized cultural programming that he calls a "cultural blueprint" for child-rearing behavior. "A network of complexly related factors shapes a culture's ideas of what infants are and what they can do. Training behavior is carried out in light of these expectations." The Digo place importance on infant toilet training. They believe and *know* firsthand that infant elimination training is effective.

Since Digo mothers spend most of their time with their babies during the early months of life, it is a logical and ideal time to toilet train their babies. "The mother takes a teaching role and assumes all responsibility in the initial phase of the training process. She places the infant in a special training position outside the house, at first at times when she senses that the infant needs to eliminate (after feeding, when waking from naps, etc.), with the idea that he will soon learn to let her know more independently. . . . For voiding, the mother sits on the ground outside, with her legs straight out in front of her. The infant is placed between the mother's legs, facing away from her, in a sitting position, supported by the mother's body. The mother then makes a 'shuus' noise that the infant learns to associate with voiding. This is done many times during the day and at night."[29]

The infant is rewarded if he voids upon hearing the "shuus" sound. He gradually learns to signal his elimination needs and then to climb into the elimination position just before he needs to void.

A different position is used for bowel movements. The mother sits on the floor or ground with her legs in front of her bent at the knees, heels touching ground, toes touching each other and pointing up. The infant faces her and sits astride her ankles. The area beneath her ankles serves as a little potty. Instead of using a vocal cue, the position serves as the stimulus to encourage the baby to defecate. If the baby evacuates, he is rewarded. If he does not, he is matter-of-factly returned to his previous position or activity, and the session ends.

After a month or two of training, young girls aged 5 to 12 years help with the process. Throughout the first year, occasional accidents are expected and handled casually. The mother or caregiver clean up excrement immediately. Around the age of 1 year when the child can walk independently, he is expected to eliminate away from the living area. If he eliminates in the house, he is given a warning. If he repeats the behavior, he is physically punished.

DeVries found that variations and delays in training were due to negative caretaking attitudes or illnesses such as diarrhea, and in a few cases due to a child's individual characteristics.

In 2007, he returned to conduct further studies of the Digo and some other tribes in East Africa. In initial interviews with young mothers during the most recent field visit, significant changes in childcare practices came to light. The degree to which these changes have effected toilet training and the context of the Digo practice of early training in general awaits further study. Dr. deVries speaks about the Digo, the power of parental expectations, toilet-training dogma and more in the *Potty Whispering* DVD.

Kenya – the Gusii

Robert and Barbara LeVine wrote a piece on the Gusii in the 1960s and had this to say about toilet training. "Feces and urine are wiped away with soft fuzzy leaves collected by the mother for that purpose, but the mother does not try to anticipate the child's excretion. Most mothers are very casual about it and show no sign of disturbance when their infants soil the cloth and the mother's person as well. Sometimes their response is not immediate, but eventually they wipe up the excrement with the leaves, cleaning the infant, cloth, and themselves. No attempt is made to effect sphincter control during infancy."

Training in sphincter control usually begins shortly after the birth of a younger sibling, the median age being 25 months. When the mother feels her child has had enough instruction, she will cane him for infractions. Another form of punishment is to make the child sweep out the feces himself while the mother tells him what he has done wrong. "The amount of time mothers reported for this training ranged from a week to a year, with the majority around a month. Some mothers who trained quickly attributed it to the fact that they were 'serious' about it and punished severely for infractions."[30]

Kenya – the Tiriki

Anthropologist Walter Sangree conducted field research among the Bantu Tiriki of Kenya from 1954 to 1956. He has published several articles and a book on the Tiriki and made the following observations on toilet training.

"Toilet training is permissive and gradual; in Tiriki huts, which mostly have floors of pounded earth smeared with dung, accidental soiling by a baby does not pose much of a cleanup problem. Babies are not diapered, and the adult or the child nurse is quick to hold the infant away from her body at the first sign of evacuation. Babies astride their nurses' hips are conditioned to going outdoors to a secluded spot, such as the banana patch, to defecate even before they can walk, and after they are walking they soon learn to head for the out-of-doors on their own through being verbally reminded or, if necessary, picked up and carried to the door. When they are a bit older children learn through the example and admonitions of their elders."[31]

Madagascar – the Tanala

Anthropologist Ralph Linton visited the Tanala ("people of the forest") in 1926–28 and reported that small children were carried in-arms almost constantly by mothers, fathers and siblings. From the age of about 4 months, a baby was carried in the back of his mother's dress, sitting with his legs on either side of her body. He remained on her back except at night or when he was being nursed.

"No clothing is worn under the age of about three years. Even when carried on the back, there is no equivalent for the European diaper. As soon as the child begins to be carried in the mother's dress, it is slapped for befouling her and it learns to control its functions at a surprisingly early age. This was the only offense for which I ever saw a Tanala child punished.[32]

"Diapers are not used, with the result that the child is constantly soiling its mother, and since the clothes that the mother wears are difficult to replace, we have here an incentive for premature sphincter discipline. In fact, anal training is begun at the age of two or three months, and the child is expected to be continent at the age of six months. If after this time the child soils its mother, it is severely punished. In other words, the child is taught to be continent while on its mother's back. The child is however, permitted at intervals to leave the mother's back. It may be interesting to note that the woman is expected to be sexually abstinent for six months after the birth of her child. Thus the period of anal training of the child and the mother's sexual abstinence after the birth of the child coincide."[33]

Mali – the Dogon

Nadine Wanono has worked among the Dogon on a part-time basis since 1977. She returns to Mali on a regular basis, for 2–3 months every one or two years. She is an ethnologist, filmmaker and researcher at the National Center for Scientific Research in Paris, France. She made the following observations about toilet training in the region of Sangha, "A child is carried on his mother's back for approximately the first 3 years of life. Around the age of 6 months, the mother sits her baby between her legs and encourages him to defecate either on the ground or into a little pot. Some mothers make little noises to encourage the elimination. These vocalizations are more systematic among the Bambara, who comprise the ethnic majority of Mali. Dogon mothers never scold their babies about elimination. A mother sometimes receives assistance from her older daughter(s), sisters and aunts but generally not from her brothers or other men.

"I believe Dogon babies finish toilet training around 18 months, depending on their position in the sibling hierarchy and also on the mother's desires. Dogon women have very heavy workloads, and the time they have to dedicate to their babies depends on the degree of maternal fatigue and also on how much time they have available after work. Their available free time can also vary with the seasons and the time of day in question."[34]

Nigeria – the Dahomeans

Melville Herskovits and his wife conducted field research on the topic of native life in Dahomey, during a period of five months in 1931. Dahomey was selected in part because it represented a West African civilization more or less in a natural state, one that had hardly been affected by the circumstances of European control.

The Herskovits' colorful account states the following about toilet training, "Very young children are carried most of the time on the backs of their mothers or, in rare instances, of nurses. Unless prevented by special circumstances, a mother takes her baby with her wherever she goes, and women may be seen selling in the market, carrying burdens on the road, working in the fields, or dancing in ceremonial dances with their infants straddling their backs. A child is trained by the mother who, as she carries it about, senses when it is restless, so that every time it must perform its excretory functions, the mother puts it on the ground. Thus in time, usually two years, the training process is completed. If a child does not respond to this training, and manifests enuresis at the age of four or five, soiling the mat on which it sleeps, then, at first, it is beaten. If this does not correct the habit, ashes are put in water and the mixture is poured over the head of the offending boy or girl who is driven into the street where all the other children clap their hands and run after the child singing, *Adida go ya ya ya* ("Urine everywhere.")

"In Whydah, the child is taken to the lagoon and washed, this being repeated a second time if necessary. If the habit is then not stopped, a live frog is attached to the child's waist, which so frightens the offender that a cure is usually effected. In Abomey, however, beating is the customary punishment.[35]

Nigeria – the Kanuri

Anthropologist Ronald Cohen conducted fieldwork in the 1960s among the Kanuri, a tribe residing in the northeastern corner of Nigeria. Cohen published papers on aspects of Kanuri society and history. His book on the Kanuri includes information on toilet training.

Toilet training for the new infant is minimal. "The mother tries to learn when the child is likely to urinate. At first the child is merely wiped clean by the mother, but as soon as it can sit up, it is placed astride her ankles with its back resting on her upturned feet. A little hole is dug in the sandy soil between the ankles and the infant then has a simple and comforting toilet ready made for it by the mother. Afterwards its loins are washed and the hole covered up with sand."[36]

"Toilet training is geared to the acquisition of walking skills. As soon as the child is able to toddle on its feet, the adult woman in whose hut it lives starts enforcing the rule that the child should go outside of the hut, stoop on the ground and use only the left hand for any function having to do with toilet activities. Failure to learn these skills is met with more insistent pressure as time goes on. A young child only recently weaned who cannot accomplish facile toilet functions may not even be scolded. However, with increased age and language skill, admonitions soon begin and are given with increasing frequency; the child is told that it is dirty, bad, and that it must not do such things as urinate on the hut floor."[37]

Senegal & Central African Republic

Alain Epelboin is a medical anthropologist and researcher at the National Center for Scientific Research in Paris, France. He conducts fieldwork in Senegal, the Central African Republic and among children of African immigrants in the region of Paris. His research focuses on the anthropology of sickness and healing, with an emphasis on the effects of (the lack of) sanitation. In March 2000, he replied to my request for information about infant elimination training in Africa.

"In my experience, sphincter-control training begins as soon as a mother comes out of seclusion with her infant—in general, around the age of 1 week. At this time, the infant transitions from lying alone on its mother's bed (covered with cloths which serve as a sort of incubator) to being constantly carried, taken outdoors and passed from person to person—in short, he transitions to being socialized.

"I would say that in the beginning, there is an attentive observation of the infant by the mother, which gradually enables her to coincide the spontaneous voiding of her baby with auditory stimuli, visual interactions and traditional positioning—all stemming from the mother's society and family culture. Later, the mechanism of stimulus-response comes into play (I don't like comparing this to the Pavlovian model, as it is too restrictive and simplistic.)

"In my observations in West Africa, a favorite position involves sitting the infant on the mother's ankles. In corresponding urban areas of Africa and France, the same position is used, but the mother sits her baby on a plastic (chamber) pot which she holds in position between her feet."

Among the Aka Pygmy hunter-gatherers of the Central African Republic and Northern Congo, infants are carried and cleaned by their mother or sometimes by another adult. "When a mother senses that her infant needs to defecate, she sits on the ground, holds him in position and has him eliminate next to her. No force is used."[38] "Stools are immediately thrown outside the encampment or village. When he's able to stand, move about and later walk, a child learns to defecate behind the huts or outside the encampment. If he goes in the wrong place, the mother or sister grabs a machete or large knife for scooping up the stools and soiled dirt, places it on a bed of dried leaves, then wraps it up in the leaves and throws it as far as possible into the vegetation outside the encampment or village. The rules are more strict in permanent encampments and shelters. The emphasis on toilet training is not as great among the Aka Pygmies as it is among the peoples of West Africa."[39]

"In some other societies, a regular daily enema is given (via the mother's mouth or a device) for hygienic, therapeutic and preventative purposes. Once the cleansing liquid has been injected, the mother sits on a stool and seats the baby on her thighs above a receptacle.

"As in all societies, African mothers express their satisfaction with their babies. This is sometimes done in a different fashion than elsewhere, in that it is not always apparent to outsiders. In public, the mother is very reserved and adopts a mask of impassivity which conceals her satisfaction. This is done out of fear that too much praise of her baby will attract the attention of malicious and other jealous evil spirits. In contrast, the entourage of siblings and female relatives and neighbors never misses a chance to loudly acknowledge each new "performance" of the baby. Praise and approval are thus always present, though not necessarily displayed by the mother. "Mommies," "aunties," grandmothers or the entourage (especially women and children) play a preponderant role in teaching everyday social conventions. In this respect too, traditional roles fluctuate, delegating roles of authority to some and roles of tenderness to others.

"As for the role of the father, situations vary greatly, depending largely on his personality and on the status of the baby (first born, last born, boy, girl). There are societies where a father takes no part in the daily care of his babies and others, such as the Pygmies or the Bassari of Senegal or in Asia, where the presence of men in their babies' lives is ubiquitous.

"In Africa, toilet training is completed at as young an age as possible. When ascertaining the age of completion, it is necessary to distinguish between bowel and bladder training, as well as between normal bowel movements and diarrhea (unfortunately fairly frequent in these regions).

"In general, whether it be toilet training or its corollaries (for example, many cultures restrict wiping to the use of the left hand), African cultures are very precocious in this regard, with remarkable results. The early accomplishment of sphincter control corresponds to the rapid psychomotor development of babies up to 12–18 months and has been emphasized by experts on infancy. It is my opinion that this precocity is related to the incessant social stimulation to which infants are subjected, not only by their mothers until weaning/separation but also by the many other people involved."[40]

Senegal – the Wolof

Jacqueline Rabain is a researcher at the National Center for Scientific Research in Paris, France. Her background is in anthropology and psychology, and one of her specialities is child anthropology. She has done fieldwork among the Wolof in Senegal, starting with a visit in 1965–66 and followed by visits in 1994 and December 1998–January 1999.

Jacqueline Rabain told me that starting at the age of 2 months, a mother sits her infant on her ankles. She holds her ankles spread apart to make a place for the child to urinate or defecate. A baby can hold its head up straight at 2 months. The mother supports him in position on her ankles by holding his arms steady. She encourages the child to eliminate by making a whistling "sssss" noise. A mother does not compliment her baby when he has eliminated for her. She often passes the time chatting with other women during the potty process. This behavior was observed in 1965–66.

A child is not expected to be toilet trained before he can walk. Rabain states that she never saw children under 3 years of age being scolded for urinating on the ground. There is a lot of emphasis for the child to learn to defecate "in the bush" behind the home. This is learned mainly by imitating adults and older children; the baby is trained by their example.

"I made a field trip to the same villages and the same families in January–February 1994 and December 1998–January 1999. At that time, I observed that small plastic potties had been introduced and were available from the local street markets. They are fairly common now. I do not know if the pot is used as early as sitting on the mother's ankles but saw it used by children from 18 months to 2 years of age."[41]

Sudan – the Batahein

Writings published in 1970 about a sampling of Sudanese Arab children belonging to the former nomadic tribe, Batahein, reveal that elimination training was started at the age of 6 to 8 weeks in 60 percent of the families surveyed. Diapers were not used, and training was mild. The baby was held between the mother's knees and learned to make a smacking noise to indicate that it needed assistance. No formal training was used in 33 percent of the cases; these children learned spontaneously to imitate their older siblings. Enuresis nocturna was fairly common but not related to toilet training. The fact that infection of the urinary tract was common seems to explain part of the high frequency of enuresis.[42]

Tanzania – the Chaga

German scholar Otto Raum, whose father was a missionary among the Chaga near Mount Kilimanjaro for nearly 40 years, included the topic of infant elimination training in his 1940 book *Chaga Childhood*. He found an "obvious slackness in training" or overall relaxed approach, except in some situations of long-term enuresis. "As in the case of weaning, no evidence could be found for the traumatic suddenness which psychoanalysts would fain impute to it, so does the interest in excreta lack the morbid glamour ascribed to it by those theorists."

"The control of urination and defecation forms part of the child's learning. That it be done successfully is a constant concern of the mother. Indeed, the marriage ceremonies foreshadow this." Men are discouraged from making disparaging comments about a mother's duty of toilet training her young and are taught to be patient with their wives should they find their clothes soiled by a child.

"A timed habit, absent in the case of feeding, one would expect to be inculcated only by women who have come under European influence. Some of these begin to train their children one or two months after birth to defecate at a fixed time every morning. In the majority of cases, however, regularity is not insisted upon. The child lies on a piece of leather. Any excreta have to be wiped away with dry grass as soon as possible to prevent the rotting of the hide and a bad smell. As long as the child is carried about, the mother closely observes it and develops an almost uncanny knack of guessing its needs. Whenever it wakens, becomes restless, or, in the case of a boy, has an erection of the penis, it is held out. . . . As the child grows up and learns to walk, it is taught to retire into the [banana] grove.

"Enuresis calls forth a variety of measures. The steps taken with smaller children are magical. When a baby is about nine months old, its mother collects drops of rain in the hoof of a goat or the involutions of a colocasia leaf. This she gives to the child as a medicine, saying, 'Take and drink this drug. It will keep you from wetting the bed.' A bigger child is shown the puddle and scolded. . . . Some children never learn to control urination, though they are scorned for their deficiency and told that this will be an obstacle to their marriage. (Enuresis is a ground for divorce.) In such cases a boy prefers to sleep with the hens in a corner of the hut, where he can pass water with impunity."

As in many other societies, Chaga boys have a sense of humor where urine is concerned. "It serves as an ever-ready lubricant when boys make models out of clay, and occasionally they will urinate on each other for fun."[43]

Epelboin/CNRS (all)

A mother in Senegal using classic toilet training position.
Child sits on mother's upturned feet while waiting to go.

After peeing, baby girl wonders
where the water went.
(Ibel, Senegal, 1990)

Togo

In their 1998 exquisite work entitled *Babies Celebrated*, a book rich in photos which are described by anthropologists and other researchers, Béatrice Fontanel and Claire D'Harcourt take us on a tour of mothers and babies around the world. Here is a sample selection that touches first on Africa in general, then on Togo in specific.

Epelboin/CNRS

18-month old Senegalese in her communal home.
For now, privacy is not an issue. (Malicka, Senegal, 2001)

Epelboin/CNRS

Mangutu, an Aka Pygmy mother, holds her infant in position as he defecates. (Bekele, Central African Republic, 2006)

In Africa, it is rare to see a woman soiled by her baby. Africans "seem able to detect the slightest signals of their children's toilet needs. At the most subtle movement or change of breath, they understand the message and take them off their backs and put them onto their ankles in an instant. If an accident happens, the mother is ashamed and embarrassed.

"Some ethnologists qualify the commonly held belief that in Africa babies' bowel movements do not provoke revulsion. Nadine Wanono points out that long deodorant necklaces of cloves are worn by the mothers of young children, and Suzanne Lallemand reminds us that in many traditional rural societies men complain about these smells. In central Togo, there is even a song with the refrain, 'To smell as bad as a woman who has a baby.'"[44]

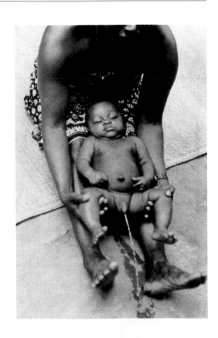

3-month-old Digo (Kenya) baby in standard urination training position: before, during and after.

Mwanasha makes "shuus" sound to elicit urination.

Baby and mother both look satisfied after the fact (1974).

Marten de Vries (all)

Uganda – the Baganda (Ainsworth)

Mary Ainsworth dedicated 11 pages of her book, *Infancy in Uganda*, to the topic of infant elimination training. She studied 28 Baganda infants and their mothers in 1954–55. This took place in six villages about 15 miles from Kampala, in the former kingdom of Buganda (now simply a geographical region of Uganda). Throughout most of her book, she uses the term "Ganda" to refer to the Baganda.

"The method of training consists in holding the baby down in a squatting position, his feet on the ground, with the mother's arm passing across the baby's back, supporting it, and holding him under the arm farthest away from her. The mother's other hand usually was on the baby's body also, but it was not clear to my eye whether it was used to provide support or pressure. The baby is 'held down' immediately after he wakes from sleep and immediately after feeding. Indeed, as one of our old informants told us, the mother might interrupt feeding, if she sensed that he was about to have a bowel movement, and thus avoid soiling."

The Luganda word for holding the child in this position is *okusimba*, a synonym for the verb "to plant." An alternative position observed by Dr. Hebe Welbourn and described as "holding out" refers to holding the baby under the armpits in a standing position, with his feet touching the ground.

The child eventually builds up an association between being held down (or out) and elimination. "Most mothers implied quite clearly that the practice of 'holding down' was designed to catch the child at an opportune time when he was ready to excrete but had not yet done so. They all placed stress on the need for vigilance if the child was to be caught. They attached importance to the convenience of avoiding soiled or wet beds by undertaking this practice, but at the same time they believe it to be a method of training."

The mothers displayed much patience throughout the period of training. Babies were never scolded or punished for accidents; instead, lapses of control were treated in a matter-of-fact manner without fuss.

Ainsworth concludes that "Ganda training in elimination control is at least as effective as the training methods used in our culture. It rests for its effectiveness not so much upon a schedule of holding down but upon the child's own indications of need. Before he can actually signal his needs the mother gears her practices to what she has observed of the child's rhythms, and holds him down at times when he is most likely to defecate or urinate. Soon he is able to signal his needs with special sounds that she recognizes even before he can verbalize. The extent to which control is something accepted by the child rather than imposed upon him is shown by his tendency to take the initiative himself in finding the appropriate place to excrete waste when he is old enough to get there under his own steam. All of this is contingent upon the mother's (or some other adult's or responsible child's) omnipresence and responsiveness which ensure that the baby's signals will not go unheeded."

Mary Ainsworth's book contains a table which details the age at which elimination training was begun and completed by each baby in the study. The ages range from 1 to 6 months. In the past, the Baganda infants of Buganda, Uganda, traditionally began elimination training around 2½–3 months. Training is still begun at or before the age of 4 months, sometimes as early as 1 month old and in most cases is done consistently and conscientiously. Success is dependent upon close interaction with babies; more specifically, it is contingent upon the baby giving recognizable signals and the mother's timely response to them. There were some situations where elimination training took longer than the norms given here, but in such cases, the mother was either not present when needed or failed to pay adequate attention to her baby's signals.

The range of ages at which soiling the bed ceased was from 5–11 months; in addition, mothers whose children were trained before Ainsworth arrived claimed their babies finished this phase at 4–8 months. Bedwetting ceased between 9 and 22 months of age.

Soiling the house generally stopped between 8 and 12 months of age (a few took up to 20–22 months), at which time most of the babies were able to go outside on their own initiative when they needed to defecate. The age for ending urinating indoors was just under 12 months. One 10-month-old child could delay voiding, but if his signals were not heard, he would end up going indoors.

Ainsworth theorizes that "it may well be that the task of learning first of all that the bed is a place *not* to be wet or soiled is an easier one than learning that elimination can take place only in one place—on a potty or toilet. Having grasped this notion it is perhaps easier to take the next step of delaying until the proper place is reached than it would be to learn that all at once without intermediate objectives."[45]

Uganda – the Baganda (Kilbride)

In 1990, Philip and Janet Kilbride published a book about family life in East Africa. They attribute the precocity of Baganda and Samia infants mainly to cultural factors. Infant toilet training practices of the Baganda are discussed as part of the early learning of infants.

"'Toilet training' occurs gradually and casually, although it may be begun as early as two or three months of age. Whenever a mother senses that her infant is about to urinate, she will 'hold him out' in the air and or with his feet touching the ground. This is not supposed to be done quickly or suddenly and, often, if the infant has already begun to urinate, he will be left seated on the lap. He is held in a squatting position with his feet touching the ground in order to defecate. Children are usually not taught to excrete outside the house until they are old enough to understand (i.e., when they can speak). Until then, the child's excretia [sic] is wiped up with a banana leaf and deposited in his latrine. Most children are 'toilet trained' and use their own latrine by the time they are three years old. Many urban mothers use diapers, but because they are expensive, they have few of them; therefore, they are likely to remove the diaper and squat the child if they anticipate an elimination."[46]

Uganda (Geber)

In her study of African children, Marcelle Geber observed that Ugandan mothers were attentive to all the needs of their infants, including elimination. She noted that Ugandan babies never leave their mother. At night, they sleep on the same mat, skin-to-skin with their mother. During the day they are carried on her back wherever she goes, without urinating or defecating upon her.

The Ugandan mother "never misreads the needs of her infant, whether he wants to suckle, urinate, defecate. In a quick and tender movement, she rolls him from her back onto her hip, then holds him against her chest with her wide hand; or she slides him to her side and holds him out by his arm so he doesn't get her wet; or else she takes him out of the cloth sling and holds him seated between her two hands so he doesn't soil himself and doesn't soil her."

A Ugandan mother is so intimately connected with her infant that she senses and responds to "the slightest movement, the tiniest whimper and the most subtle gesture" which communicate the child's needs. The same is true on occasions where she is not carrying him but has, in accordance with tradition and duty, offered him as a sign of welcome to a visitor to hold.[47]

When the babies were old enough to walk, Geber observed them going outdoors, without prompting, to relieve themselves. She reported that Ugandan children completed toilet training between 15 and 24 months.

Uganda (Pearce)

In his book *Magical Child*, Joseph Chilton Pearce writes, "Jean MacKellar told me of her years in Uganda, where her husband practiced medicine. Local mothers brought their infants to see the doctor, often standing patiently in line for hours. The women carried the tiny infants in a sling, next to their bare breasts. Older infants were carried on the back, papoose style. The infants were never swaddled, nor were diapers used. Yet none of them were soiled when finally examined by the doctor. Puzzled by this, Jean finally asked some of the women how they managed to keep their babies so clean without diapers and such. 'Oh,' the women answered, 'we just go to the bushes.' Well, Jean countered, how did they know when the infant needed to go to the bushes? The women were astonished at her question. 'How do *you* know when *you* have to go?' they exclaimed."[48]

West Africa

Hélène Elisabeth Stork is a professor of clinical and anthropological psychology at the Institut de Psychologie de l'Université René Descartes in Paris, France. In her 1999 book *Introduction à la psychologie anthropologique*, Hélène Stork describes the method of toilet training used in West Africa. Sphincter training is ". . . very permissive. Adults never force anything that would surpass an infant's level of sphincter maturation. An infant gradually learns toilet behavior by imitating siblings and adults. No timetable or device such as a Western potty is used. The young baby wears no diapers, yet his mother, who carries him everywhere with her, is never wet. Being in constant contact with her baby teaches a mother to sense, through empathy, the meaning of the slightest whimper or movement made by her child. She knows precisely when and how to respond, and has the ability to distinguish, for example, between her baby's desire for the breast and his need to defecate. To stimulate this function, the African mother, in similar fashion to the Indian mother (Stork, 1986), sits on the ground and installs the infant on her ankles, spreading them at precisely the opportune moment. Her use of onomatopoeia, which evokes the sounds of evacuation, encourages the baby to go. A mother never expresses any disgust when picking up feces and throwing it out of the area where daily life takes place. Toilet training is not an occasion where a child confronts an adult, as is often the case in the West. Self-soiling is not the goal of any punitive attitude and thus never manifests itself as a means of protest by the child."[49]

chapter 3
asia

French Polynesia – the Marquesans

In 1920–21, anthropologist Ralph Linton spent nearly a year in the Marquesas, a series of islands in the central Pacific. He noted that infants were simply laid on bark-cloth on the stone floor inside the house. The bark-cloth was changed from time to time as needed. "There was no particular effort at anal control for small children until they were a year or so old. The adult merely changed the bark cloth on which the child lay. Later the child might be picked up, carried a short distance, and held out to perform its functions."[50]

On 'Ua Pou in the 1970s, John Kirkpatrick and Mary Martini reported that by four months, a baby typically is cared for while facing away from the caregiver. For example, feeding is done from behind as the infant sits on a caregiver's lap. The undiapered baby is held away from the caregiver when the caregiver thinks he will urinate. All routine caregiving activities are performed while the baby faces outward. . . . The 12- to 18-month-old . . . begins to understand to go outside to urinate and defecate."[51]

India – the Lepchas

The Lepchas are a Mongoloid people living in the state of Sikkim. They inhabit the southern and eastern slopes of Mount Kinchenjunga in the Himalayas. The following account was published in 1938.

"The teaching of sphincter control is meant to start at the age of three months when the children are taken out on to the balcony at regular intervals; they should learn to cry when they want to be taken out and by the time they can crawl should be able to crawl there by themselves. This is, however, an ideal rather than a real statement; sphincter control and bodily cleanliness are not regarded as of emotional importance, and some quite big children refuse to accept the discipline and excrete inside the house, especially if the house has bamboo flooring. Children aged three or over who cannot or will not learn sphincter control are considered to show a bad prognosis; when they grow up they 'will show forth a bad heart (disposition)'. If big children are dirty they may be given a smack or other slight punishment; but as often as not no notice will be taken and the dirt just cleared away by some older person. Only if the child spoils or dirties somebody else's property will he be severely punished. When a child can move about by itself it is taught to go outside to relieve itself; it is always accompanied by an older person till it is quite big to keep away the scavenging dogs and pigs. It is cleaned, and taught to clean itself with sticks and leaves."[52]

India – the Sikhs

Sikh mothers generally begin toilet training in infancy. They quickly learn to sense when their babies need to go through observation of, or advice from, more experienced women. They use timing, intuition and cues from baby. A mother will either squat and hold her baby in position in her arms or else sit on the floor or ground and use her feet to form a toilet seat for the baby.

Infants are conditioned to have a bowel movement first thing in the morning. If smaller infants defecate more than once a day for some months, this pattern is taken into account. Urination frequency is gauged and anticipated in relation to feeding and sleeping times. No force or punishment is used.

In traditional Sikh society, babies do not wear diapers. From birth, they are taught modesty and wear special Sikh underwear. Extended families are still commonplace in villages, so a mother has plenty of help from other women and girls in the household. Wealthier families with individual households have live-in housekeepers who also serve as nannies. A housekeeper may have children of her own who also help around the home. Babies spend most of their time in-arms, either sitting on their mother's lap or being carried by her or one of the other women in the home.

The whole family sleeps in one room. Sturdy cots the size of a single bed are the norm. The baby usually sleeps on the mother's chest or right next to her, without diapers. A mother is so attuned to her baby that she automatically wakes up during the night when it is time for her baby to go.

Most claim their babies are toilet trained around the age of 6 to 9 months. This takes into account the fact that a child still needs some help getting to the bathroom, undressed and into position.

Bathrooms are small and plain, typically consisting of a faucet, a bucket and a drain. Many villagers depend on someone to remove the excrement from their bathroom floor. The plumbing, if any, in most villages consists of open gutters. Once children walk, they can easily find a place to squat and go in an open gutter outdoors. Some middle class families have Turkish (squat-style) toilets. The wealthiest can afford Western-style toilets.

Infant toilet training is the standard method used throughout the country (by Hindus, Muslims, etc., as well as Sikhs). In addition, this same method is used throughout heavily populated neighboring countries such as Pakistan, Bangladesh and Sri Lanka.

Indonesia – the Alorese

Alor is a small and obscure island in Indonesia, about 50 miles long and 30 miles wide, north of Timor. Cora Du Bois reached Alor in 1938 and published *The People of Alor* in 1944. Her tome contains detailed information on the child-raising practices of the Alorese. "After completing birth, the mother picks up the child, wraps it in the softest piece of woven or bark cloth available, and joins the group of friends and visitors in the living room. People present suggest various names; those of maternal and paternal grandparents are preferred. If a child begins to urinate or to nurse after a name is suggested, that is the one adopted. . . .

"No effort is made during infancy to teach the child to talk. . . . Toilet training, too, is completely disregarded during the prewalking period. Adults exhibit no anger or disgust when a child soils the carrying shawl or the body of the person caring for it. The caretaker cleans up after the child with the most casual matter-of-factness, wiping off its buttocks with a bit of leaf, a corn husk, or a bamboo sliver.

"Toilet training is taught gradually and easily. When the child can walk and 'when it is old enough to understand,' the mother makes a point of taking it with her morning and evening when she defecates either in the privy or outside at the edge of the village. Also, the child is watched and told to withdraw whenever it needs to eliminate. Mothers report that children learn within a few months to use the proper places and to clean themselves with leaves. Children are sometimes careless in cleaning themselves and as a result may suffer a certain amount of anal irritation.

"A child who is slow in establishing toilet habits may irritate the mother; then she may shout at him or rap him on the head with her knuckles. However, since sphincter control is instituted relatively late it seems to be a source of

Martha Mikkelson

little annoyance. Children certainly by the age of three, or five at the latest, are thoroughly trained.

"Bladder control, or at least modesty about urination, seems to come slightly later than sphincter control. I judge this to be the case since it is not unusual to see children of between three and five years standing at the edge of a group and casually urinating without anyone's paying much attention to it. A comparable lack of sphincter control was observed only twice and both times it brought angry scolding from adults."[53]

Indonesia – the Balinese

Margaret Mead and Frances Macgregor explain in their 1951 photographic study of Balinese childhood that the normal place for a child under 15–18 months is in human arms or otherwise physically close to its caregiver, by means of a sling. An infant's first experience of clothing is the sling which is used to bind baby and mother together. The sling also serves as a diaper, a shawl for warmth, a pillow, a towel and a wrapper and carrier for the baby.

"Elimination is treated very lightly. No fuss at all is made over urination by an infant. . . . Little babies experience only the shout for the dog that is to clean them up, or the attention of the dog when they are placed on the ground. As they learn to walk steadily, they toddle a little away from a group and squat, and the distance gets greater as they get older. . . . Children slowly learn to regard defecation as mildly shameful. . . . A child's chief learning from the culturally imposed elimination habits is to watch where it is and to move away from inappropriate spots. It never has to go far, so that the emphasis on foresight and self-control, which American children learn and generalize to other areas of life, is missing."[54]

Japan

The village of Taira in Okinawa, Japan, is the focus of one of the studies in the 1963 book *Six Cultures*. Thomas and Hatsumi Maretzki explain that although babies are diapered and swaddled until they are about a year old, mothers begin a form of toilet training during this time. "When the infant is anywhere from 22 days to 10 months old, the mothers start trying to anticipate urination before the baby wets his diapers. Each mother trains herself to the child's particular cues, squirming, peculiar facial expressions, and so on, or keeps a kind of mental time check. Holding the infant in a semi-sitting position out over the edge of the porch, and supporting him under his knees with her hands and at his back with her chest, she coaxes gently, repeating 'shi-shi' until he urinates onto the ground outside. If the mother is successful in her efforts, she hugs, kisses, and praises the infant. On the other hand, if she does not reach him in time and he is already wet, she will hold the child over the wet diaper and say 'shi-shi.' This is to ensure that he has fully eliminated, or if the interval between diaper checks has been long, to make certain that he does not need to urinate again before putting on a fresh change. In these instances she does not praise unless the infant does urinate or eliminate at her coaxing, but she does not punish him for urinating in his diapers."

Mothers appeared to believe that children are incapable of toilet learning at this early age. Their main concern seemed to be the number of diapers they had to wash or buy. More serious toilet training begins after the child learns to walk, with completion reported at 2 and 3 years of age. Overall, toilet training is a relatively casual affair. [55]

Kurdistan

In 1951, doctoral candidate William Murray studied the Kurds living in the town of Rowanduz, Iraq. His thesis on Kurdish life in Rowanduz provides a general description of the local method of infant toilet training. "Toilet training begins early, at five or six months, by the repetition of a nonsense word which signifies evacuation and is accompanied by the initial use of a pot. Gradually utilization of the latrine and its ewer of water is learned. After two or three years the mother and others of the family begin to punish a child who soils himself."[56]

Micronesia – the Ifaluk

Ifaluk is an atoll in the Caroline Islands, part of the Trust Territory of the Pacific Islands. Information was gleaned during a 6-month study on the island in 1947–48. Ifaluk, population 250 at the time, was chosen for study because it had had a minimum of outside influence. "The [newborn] baby itself is wrapped in cloth, as a kind of diaper, and is then covered completely with another cloth. . . . When the baby soils itself, the diaper is replaced with a clean one, and excrements are carried to the ocean, and the soiled diaper is washed.

"The infant wears swaddling clothes until it has learned to crawl. When an adult holds an infant on his lap, he usually holds the cloth under the infant so that he should not be soiled should the infant choose to defecate or urinate. This precaution is necessary because sphincter control is not taught the child until it can walk and talk; that is, not until he can understand the demand, and has mastered the motor behavior to carry it out. The infant's faeces [sic] are disposed of in the lagoon, whereas its urine is merely wiped up. Not only is there no attempt made to toilet-train the infant, but the adults do not convey to the infant by means of facial expressions or gestures any exaggerated abhorrence for excrement. Adults themselves, however, are ashamed of excretory processes . . . And this attitude, of course, is reflected in their reaction to the excretory behavior of their infants. For example, while I was sitting in a house with a young man and his infant daughter, the daughter defecated on the bare thigh of her father. He gave no overt indications of disgust or anger, but laughingly called to his wife to remove the faeces from his thigh.

"Once the child learns to walk and to talk, however, he is not only trained in sphincter control, but he learns that his parents are concerned about his bowel movements. He is taught to defecate in the lagoon, not in the house or on land. If he does not readily learn to use the lagoon he is reprimanded and shamed, though not beaten. Any person, parents and stranger alike, will rebuke a child for polluting the ground or the house. The parents often invoke the authority of the chiefs in chastising the child, warning the child that when a chief visits, he will be angry at the mess. My observations indicated that few, if any, children rebel against this training, and I observed none who did not observe the practice of repairing to the lagoon, after they had been so taught.

"The attitude towards urine is much more lax. Children who do not as yet wear clothes may urinate on the ground, but not in the house, with impunity. "The theory behind this indulgence is that the baby is completely innocent, and is not responsible for its behavior. This theory is consistent with the lack of punishment of the child."

Puritanism and a sense of shame play significant roles among the Ifaluk. These "puritanical attitudes are displayed with reference to excretory behavior. All people excrete in the lagoon, and though their faces are in public view their behavior is concealed. But if a person, even of their own sex, sees them urinating or defecating on land, with genitalia exposed, they are terribly ashamed. If a man must urinate, and other men are present, he bends down on his haunches, so that his penis is concealed. If a person is in a group and must defecate or urinate, he will not tell where he is going when he leaves. He says, 'I am going over there.'" A "verbal taboo applies to excretory references as well. No mention may be made of them in mixed company" including spouses.[57]

Micronesia – Truk Islands

Ann Fischer studied child-rearing practices on Romonum Island, Chuuk State, in Micronesia from 1946–49. Her 1950 report details the role of the Trukese mother and its effect on child training. The topic of toilet training is included in her publication.

Mothers are very sensitive to their children's elimination schedule. "Time and again the mother will put the child off the mat just before it urinates. One mother stated that she knew her child would urinate right after it awakened, and after it ate. The mother, seated on the floor, stretches her legs out in front of her and places the child with its head on her knees and its body lying along her legs toward the ankles. The child urinates in this position. After it is placed in this manner, the mother makes a sound with lips moving which sounds like 'pspspsps.' There is a special Trukese word for this sound, and it is always used when the child urinates at the direction of its mother. Supposedly it represents the sound of flowing urine, and should give the child the idea that it is now time to urinate. This direction is not always obeyed by the child, and accidents do occur on the mat. In this case, the mother wipes up the urine with a towel or rag and does not express concern over it. . . .

"Most Trukese children begin to go outside the house to eliminate when they are between two and three years old. Between three and four years of age they begin to take the more difficult step to the *penco*, the outdoor privy built over the sea for sanitation. . . . All in all, the toilet training of the child is not extremely severe nor extremely lenient. After he is one year old the child may begin to show some concern over pleasing his elders in this respect, and it is during this time that he is told what is desired of him although never in severe terms."[58]

In another study of the people of Romonum on the island of Truk, authors Thomas Gladwin and Seymour Sarason state, "Because there is no early emphasis on the control of elimination and [a child] is asked to observe the social norms at a time when he is able to do so readily, toilet training never becomes a problem either for parents or for children.

"Babies are not diapered and in fact seldom clothed, but practically no attempt is made to train them not to urinate or defecate in the house. Mothers will take small babies out of the house when they awake or at other times when they may be expected to urinate, and will carry them out also if they begin to defecate, if this is convenient; but if it is not, the feces are simply cleaned up off the mat or the mother's legs or wherever they may be with no apparent concern. The child's buttocks are usually cleaned with the mother's finger and rinsed with water. Later, when the child can walk, he will be gently directed outside when he eliminates, but a lapse is not punished."[59]

New Guinea – the Arapesh and the Manus

Margaret Mead studied "primitive peoples" in the South Seas between 1925 and 1933. In *Growing up in New Guinea*, she states that the Manus conception of social discipline is lax and based on "a proper observance of the canons of shame. Children must learn privacy in excretion almost by the time they can walk; must get by heart the conventional attitudes of shame and embarrassment."[60]

In *Sex and Temperament in Three Primitive Societies*, Mead wrote, "[W]hen an [Arapesh] infant urinates or defecates, the person holding it will jerk it quickly to one side to prevent soiling his or her own person. This jerk interrupts the normal course of excretion and angers the child. In later life, the Arapesh have notably low sphincter-control, and regard its loss as the normal concomitant of any highly charged situation."[61]

In *New Lives for Old*, she wrote, "Children are expected almost as soon as they can walk alone to get up and walk away from their sleeping mats and to lift a slat in the floor if they have to urinate or defecate at night. They are expected to walk a little distance if there is a light in the house, but only to get off the edge of the mat or blanket if there is no light. They are expected to point out next morning just where they have defecated so that the parent can carry away the feces."[62]

New Guinea – the Kwoma

The Kwoma live in the Peilungua Mountains of New Guinea. Anthropologist John Whiting spent 7 months among the Kwoma in 1936. In his book, he provides fairly detailed information on the Kwoma method of toilet training.

"Bladder and colon tensions give an infant little trouble. He simply evacuates when the pressure becomes strong enough. The mother makes no attempt at toilet training while the child is still an infant; she simply learns to anticipate his bowel and bladder movements, quickly lifting him from her lap and holding him over the earth floor. The feces are then wiped up with a leaf. Sometimes the mother does not lift the child quickly enough and he urinates on her leg. In such cases the leaf is again used, and the child is not held accountable for the mistake.

"Cleanliness training begins at approximately the same age as weaning. The mother is comparatively gentle in teaching her child toilet habits. She tells him that adults go outside near the garbage heap to urinate and that he is big enough to do likewise. Similarly, she points out that adults do not defecate in the house but in the household latrine. She takes the child with her to the latrine and holds him while he relieves himself until he has learned to do this without assistance. When I asked an informant whether a mother punishes her child if he persistently defecates in the house, he answered: 'No, of course not. He is her own child, isn't he? Why should she punish him? It is her duty to clean up after him if he defecates in the house.' Although this may express the theoretical position of the Kwoma native, in actual practice the infant is more recalcitrant, and the mother less patient, than the statement would indicate.

"Cleanliness habits are usually already established by the time a boy or girl reaches childhood. Informants stated that if a slip occurs it is the child's own business except that he is forced to clean up after himself."[63]

Oman

In *Behind the Veil in Arabia* (1982), Unni Wikan portrays the lives of the Soharis of Oman, including their method of toilet training. "Swaddling is common in the winter. The baby is wrapped in a large piece of cloth that covers all of his body, except for the head and buttocks. Training the infant to control his bowel movements begins as early as between four and six months of age (bladder control is considered of less importance) and thus the buttocks must be left uncovered.

"When the child begins to talk, around the age of two or three, he is expected to ask to be taken to the toilet, and he is scolded if he fails to do so. Until then, failures have been sanctioned with no more than discontent glances from the mother. After repeated mishaps, he may be threatened with spanking or the red-hot iron (*wasum*), or (since the inception of the hospital) injections."[64]

Philippines – the Tarongans

William and Corinne Nydegger describe life in Tarong, an Ilocos barrio in the Philippines, in one of the studies of *Six Cultures*. Infants are never left to cry. Clothing consists of a short shirt or dress. No diapers or underwear are worn. "The infant is covered loosely, if at all, below the waist. When he urinates, the puddle is wiped up or the cloth is changed; if the mother's clothing is wet, it is ignored. While interviewing or chatting with mothers of infants, we noticed that in almost all instances of the child's wetting the mother, her response was to merely shift the child to a dry part of the lap and shift the wet portion of the skirt so that it would dry. There was no verbal or facial recognition of the incident. . . . Precautions are taken, however, against the mother's clothes being soiled by feces. A folded cloth is kept under the buttocks of infants, and after defecation, the cloth is replaced. . . . At 6 months or so, training is begun by moving the child to a corner of the kitchen porch over the waste-puddle for both urination and defecation.

"Toilet training is intensified some time before weaning, usually at about 1½ years when the child is able to understand simple verbal instruction and express his need to urinate or defecate . . . bowel, like bladder control, is attained with no apparent resistance." By age 2, children use the outhouse to defecate. Bladder control is accomplished at the very latest by age 3.[65]

Taiwan

In her 1969 book, Norma Diamond explains how toilet training is done in the Taiwanese village of K'un Shen. "Carrying the child on her back, the mother soon becomes sensitized to motions or cries indicating that the child is about to urinate or defecate and she removes it from her back and holds it over the ground or a ditch to relieve itself. Toilet training thus begins at a very early age, for when the child urinates the mother makes a whistling sound. Soon, she begins holding the child and making the whistling sound to encourage it to urinate."

More serious toilet training begins around the end of the first year. Once children can walk, they have no problem continuing on their own, in part because they wear open pants. All they have to do to stay clean and dry is squat. Most children finish toilet training by the time they are 2. As soon as they are old enough to understand, they are encouraged to squat over the nearest ditch or on the dirt floor. Use of the outhouse is not encouraged until they are about 4 or 5 years old.[66]

Bernard Gallin and his wife conducted research in Hsin Hsing village, Taiwan, for 16 months in 1957–58. Their study of sociocultural change in this Taiwanese peasant village covered the time frame 1900–1959. Babies rarely cry for very long since they are never left alone and receive a lot of attention and affection. They are often cared for by older siblings.

"Toilet training, like weaning, is not considered a problem by the villagers. It is not emphasized until the child is considered ready for this new stage— that is, until he is physically capable of controlling the sphincter and bladder and able to understand what is expected of him. By the time the child is six-or-seven-months-old, his diaper is replaced by training pants—pants slit open at the crotch. However, toilet training does not begin until the child is almost two-years-old, walking, and beginning to talk and understand what he is told. At this time he is taught to ask to be taken to an inconspicuous spot to perform. Eventually, he will go there by himself. If the child has a lapse, he is slapped on the hand. Village mothers note that toilet training is usually accomplished in about a week after it is begun and that the child usually offers little resistance."[67]

Margery Wolf observed and studied rural Taiwanese women in 1959–1961. Taiwanese mothers consider it dangerous to carry an infant very much before the age of at least 6 weeks. Infants spend most of their time on the family bed or in a bamboo crib on wheels, which is rolled around the house. After about 6 weeks, a baby is tied on her mother's back with a long strip of cloth that swaddles the baby and binds her to the mother.

"Toilet training is not something that arouses much concern or interest among Taiwanese mothers. The intimate contact between mother and child during the first few months allows the mother to 'know' her baby very well. Mothers claim to be able to identify the restless movements the child makes before she urinates and to use this signal to spread the child's legs and hold her away from their own body. The mother accompanies this act with a whistling noise so that in time the child associates the sound with the activity and empties her bladder on command. Diapers are used only at night, and many mothers claim even these can be dispensed with after six weeks. Mothers say they can keep a dry bed by holding the baby over the edge several times each night (the advantage of earth or concrete floors) and whistling. Bowel control is equally undramatic. When a child can walk she is encouraged to go to a garbage heap or drainage ditch. Accidents are not punished, unless one counts the looks of disgust by an older sister who has to clean it up. Undoubtedly the great number of acceptable toilet areas takes the emotional pressure off both mother and child."[68]

Tibet

In their 1997 book *The Tibetan Art of Parenting* Anne Maiden and Edie Farwell include a general description of Tibetan toilet training. "Toilet training often begins with association by sound. The mother makes a specific sound and then the child slowly identifies that sound with the need to use the toilet pot. Soon the child learns to make these sounds, and in response the mother points to a place for the child to go, or bring the pot herself. By one-and-a-half or two years old, the child does this independently."[69]

Turkey

A 1970 report from secluded villages of Eastern Anatolia does not give an age for beginning toilet training. Diapers are not used, "the child being put to sleep in his cradle bundled up with a type of soil that soaks up the urine." The wet soil is dried in the sun and used again in the same way. "Occasionally a kind of wooden apparatus is fitted to the child's genital area, the urine passing through a pipe to a receiving cup on the floor." Children wear dresses without underwear so as to make it easy to eliminate. Defecation is a private function which is performed out of sight while urination is performed casually in public. As soon as they can walk, toddlers are taken by older children to specified defecation locations. "Appropriate toilet behavior is regulated by shaming, and the children seem to learn quickly and sensitively about what is required of them. Here too, as observed by anthropologists, bodily possessions carry the bodily identity which it is superstitiously believed can be used for evil purposes by their enemies."[70]

chapter 4

arctic regions & the americas

Arctic Regions

Anthropologist Joëlle Robert-Lamblin has visited the Arctic (Greenland, Siberia, Aleutians) many times since 1967. In an overview of IPT in the Far North, she stated that it is the mother who "makes sounds and gives encouragement to prompt her baby to eliminate. She never scolds or punishes her baby in this regard. Toilet training is gentle and carried out by joyful and affectionate enticement."[71]

David Damas spent a year (1962–63) with the Copper Eskimos of the Northwest Territories in Canada and wrote, "Toilet training is patiently but persistently pursued. The child is removed several times during the day and stimulated to urinate. The child is never reprimanded for defecating or urinating inside the mother's coat when he is carried."[72]

Observations in *Babies Celebrated* note that the Inuit use a deep and warm hood as a baby bag. When the mother "feels that her baby has to urinate, she takes the child out of the hood, often with the help of another woman." On long trips, "she slips lichen or rabbit skin into her anorak to serve as a diaper. There is not one specific material that is always used—mothers take what they find, according to the season. In spite of the restrictions of the region, each woman is inventive enough to improvise solutions, which are then repeated if they work well. However, the baby is not always put into the mother's hood—in some areas in the East Asian Arctic, when the weather is nice and the women sit outside to sew or just talk, they slip their babies into their large waders. With only his or her head sticking out of these seven-league boots, the little one begins to discover the world."[73]

In 1963, Jean Briggs went to the Canadian Northwest Territories to make a 17-month anthropological field study of the Utkuhikhalingmiut or "Utku." The 20–35 Utkuhikhalingmiut Eskimos were the sole inhabitants of an area of 35,000 square miles. "The toilet training that is considered such a critical experience in the life of a *kapluna* [Caucasian] child does not appear to be a crisis for the Utku child, who from the time he is born is held over a can at appropriate moments: when he wakes, after (and sometimes while) he eats, before he goes to sleep, and in general whenever he shows signs of discharging. I did not observe the transition from this stage to the next, in which the child learns to call attention to his need for the can. Allaq told me that children learn a verbal signal by themselves, by imitating slightly older children."[74]

In Skolt Lapp society, Finland, "the general attitude toward toilet training is a relaxed one. Parents do not teach the child any marked feelings of revulsion towards feces and urine" and rarely punish for accidents. They wait until a child "begins to understand the situation" (18–24 months) before starting.[75] Among the Saami in Norwegian Lapland, babies urinate and defecate freely on the floor. "The child is not ordinarily toilet trained until he decides to become continent at two or three years of age."[76]

Bolivia – the Siriono

Anthropologist Allan Holmberg spent about 12 months with small groups of Siriono Indians (population 2,000) in Bolivia in 1940–1942. They lived as semi-nomadic aborigines and inhabited the tropical rainforest area of northern and eastern Bolivia. "An infant receives no punishment if he urinates or defecates on his parents. Almost no effort is made by the mother to train an infant in the habits of cleanliness, until he can walk, and then they are instilled very gradually. Of course, if a mother hears her infant fart or feels that he is about to defecate on her, she holds him away from her body so as not to be soiled, but about the only punishment that an infant is subjected to by defecating on her is that of being set aside for a while until she cleans up the mess. Children who are able to walk, however, soon learn by imitation, and with the assistance of their parents, not to defecate near the hammock. When they are old enough to indicate their needs, the mother gradually leads them further and further away from the hammock to urinate and defecate, so that by the time they have reached the age of three they have learned not to pollute the house. Until the age of four or five, however, children are still wiped by the mother, who also cleans up the excreta and throws them away. Not until a child has reached the age of six does he take care of his defecation needs alone. Little training is given a child in the matter of urination. Contact with urine is not regarded as harmful, and I frequently observed mothers who did not even move when babies on their laps urinated. Since no clothes are worn by either the mother or the child, the urine soon dries or can readily be washed off."[77]

Bolivia & Brazil – the Chácobos and the Matis

Philippe Erikson has worked extensively with the Matis in Brazil and the Chácobos in Bolivia and reported, "The information I'm providing on infant toilet training applies mainly to the Matis in Brazil and somewhat to the Chácobos in Bolivia. My impression is that the Amerindian method of toilet training is very casual, mainly a matter of handling the situation until a child can walk and take care of business on his own. Mothers are relaxed about elimination. "If a baby 'goes' inside the house, the mother simply cleans up after the child. As far as I know, women are the only ones who clean up after children. I have never seen fathers help in this regard. I do not recall seeing a mother get angry at a baby about elimination. Also consider that in the tropics, people tend to get diarrhea, so even adults often have little choice as to where they will go. Diarrhea is so prevalent that the Matis sing magic chants to prevent children from getting it. They chant special verses while slapping a child's buttocks with a grub. A typical chant invokes the child in question by name followed by, 'Show me your back so I can beat your rear end so you won't have diarrhea.'

"Outdoors, with the climate, bugs, etc., waste material all disappears in a matter of hours so there is no outdoor mess to worry about. Dogs also help clean up excrement. This is reminiscent of Haudricourt's theory that dogs were domesticated because of their usefulness as scavengers and house-cleaners.

"Children are visually exposed to excretion at an early age in forest-dwelling societies. One point to consider is that toddlers have more opportunities of seeing their mothers in action than in societies such as ours where people lock themselves in the bathroom and don't take their babies along. Of course, women will sometimes hand their baby to someone in order to have privacy, but this is not always possible.

"The Amazonian peoples I have lived with are very casual when it comes to mentioning excretion. No euphemisms are used such as *petit coin* in French. They just say something like, 'Wait a second, I'm going to shit.' If you meet someone on a trail and (s)he asks where are you going, you can answer, 'I'm going for a shit.'

"The Matis live in long-houses while the Chácobo live in individual ones. The floors are either dirt or palm wood (which is full of holes). It does not matter at all if a baby eliminates in a dwelling. The Matis, like most (if not all)

Amazonian peoples, bathe several times a day, perhaps another reason for not being uptight about elimination.

"Supernatural beliefs play a role in toilet behavior. The most striking aspect of Amazonian toilet behavior has to do with the contrast between the extreme caution when it comes to adults and the very relaxed attitude in the case of babies. Grownups are very careful not to leave their feces lying around because it could be used against them by witches. (Some people such as the Machiguenga in Peru go as far as burying their feces). They are also very careful not to urinate on trails (even trails which are rarely ever used or miles from any house) because someone else might step on it and be harmed (their feet might itch). These considerations are important regarding adult defecation but barely come into play in the case of children.

"Another ethnographic detail of interest is that during major rituals, i.e., tattooing ceremonies, the initiates are separated by gender, boys on one side and girls on the other, but each group must stick together as a unit for a while and only go out at night. One of the things they do collectively is going out for their daily defecation.

"The Cashinahua, living along the border of Brazil and Peru (mainly in Peru), consider urine and feces as two of the five spirits of an individual. The other three are the eye spirit, body spirit and dream spirit. The urine and feces spirits are volatile, meaning they don't last long and certainly disappear after death."[78]

Brazil – the Tenetehara

Fieldwork was conducted by Charles Wagley and his team of assistants in the Brazilian rainforest during the period 1941–42 and later in 1945. At that time, the Tenetehara Indians were merging into Brazilian rural life. "During the first year, parents pay little attention to sphincter and bladder control of the child. Several times each day the mother places the infant on the ground to urinate or to defecate. She then simply calls an older child to sweep up the feces on a banana leaf and to throw it into the nearby underbrush. At night the mother, without even leaving her hammock, holds a child out over the floor to urinate or even to defecate. After the child is able to walk, however, she sometimes shames it when it soils the hammock or the house floor. Older siblings or cousins usually take a two or three-year-old child just outside the house for such necessities. These older children laugh at the child who does not ask to be taken outside, and both adults and older children shame the child who urinates or defecates in the house in front of the family. Although several people told us that it was customary to 'spank the child lightly' (on the buttocks) when it continued to lack sphincter and bladder control after it was walking, we did not observe one instance of such punishment for these reasons. Instead we often saw children three or four years old defecate on the floor of a Tenetehara house without being punished at all. Children are soon, however, made to feel ashamed of these body functions and by the time they are adult, they are not only ashamed to urinate or defecate in view of a person of the opposite sex but also in the company of people of the same sex. Men on hunting trips move a distance away from their companions to urinate and go to infinite trouble for privacy for excretory functions. The same is true for women with other women. The attitudes of personal shame in regard to sphincter and bladder functions are passed on to children during the first three or four years of their life—not by corporal punishment but by ridicule and shame."[79]

Canada – the Kwakiutl

The Kwakiutl of Vancouver Island are described in Clellan Ford's 1941 book. "When it was old enough to talk, the mother or father would take the child out of the house and down to the beach to defecate. Somewhat earlier, it was taught to urinate in the chamber vessel, and this is said to have been readily accomplished without punishment. The child was taught the verb 'to urinate' and learned first to tell his mother his want and then to go by himself. Children were not punished for wetting the bed; this, it was thought, would have had no effect since children do not know what they are doing in their sleep. They were, however, repeatedly asked to wake up in the night if they wanted to use the chamber vessel."[80]

Colombia – the Kogi

Among the Kogi, the attitude toward infant elimination is one of indifference. "Defecation, urination and breaking wind rather cause hilarity among the adults and older children, not with the object of ridiculing the baby, but rather because these acts are regarded as improprieties, which, in the case of a baby who 'does not yet know,' are not of great importance. If the baby is outside the pouch and naked, frequently the mother gently massages his genital region. It is very common for babies to defecate or urinate while nursing. In this case, the mother nearly always gets up quickly and holds the baby at some distance in the air so that his secretions will not dirty her clothing. Also on such occasions she looks for an old rag, either to wipe herself off or to put on her thighs to seat the baby on. In any case, the act of elimination at these moments is almost always followed by hasty movements by the mother, the breast being taken away, and frequently the definitive interruption of the nursing. The babies react with shrieks, but at the age of 3 or 4 months these accidents no longer occur, and they evidently begin to retain the secretions." The mother teaches with words and gestures that it is bad to go in the house or in the presence of others. Punishment (exclamations of displeasure, slaps with the pouch or aggressive gestures) is used for accidents after 6 months. Full control is gained around 18–20 months.[81]

Mexico – the Maya

In the village of Pustunich, Yucatán Peninsula, toilet training is gradual and permissive. The field date of this report was 1964. When a baby eliminates, it is held out at arm's length. "An attempt is made to get the child outside first, though floors are usually dirt. Its pants or huipil are then changed." There is no punishment used during approximately the first 18 months. "Little concern is given to soiling the hammock, as it is string mesh, dries fast, and is easily wash-able." As a child learns to walk, he is taken outdoors to eliminate whenever other family members themselves "feel the need." As the child's understanding increases, family members talk with him, admonish him to leave the house when he needs to urinate or defecate, and encourage him to communicate his elimination needs to them. Once he indicates that he understands what is desired of him, he will be punished (slapped) for soiling the floor, hammock or clothing. Toddlers wear only the huipil (traditional Mayan blouse), without any pants, which allows accidents with minimal soiling of clothing. Parents expect accidents and "try to avert them by learning the child's moods."[82]

Paraguay – the Ache

Anthropologist Kim Hill of the University of New Mexico has lived part-time with and observed the Ache Indians for 20 years. When I asked him in December 1999 about infant elimination training among the Ache, Hill explained, "Babies simply urinate or defecate whenever they want and often all over the person holding them. This does not bother the Ache much at all. Only when they are quite a bit older (maybe 18 months) does training start to encourage them to move a few steps away from others when they want to eliminate."[83]

United States – the Apache

The lifestyle and cultural patterns of the Apache of Arizona are described in detail by Grenville Goodwin in his 1942 book *The Social Organization of the Western Apache*. The author began his fieldwork in 1929 and was in close touch with the Apache for over 10 years. "On the few occasions observed, when babies and small children soiled, the Apache took it as a matter of course, and no remarks of disgust or anger were made. When one old woman, sitting on her own bed, placed her hand by mistake in a mess which her two-year-old great-granddaughter had made on her blanket, she merely cleaned it off, remarking that when children were about such things happen. On another occasion, a man stepping in some human feces quite close to the door of a wickiup, attributed it to a small child, saying, 'You have to watch out for this in a camp where there are small children.' A little girl two years and nine months old, visiting in my house for several days, with her mother and father and two older sisters, more than once wet or soiled the floor, but when she did this she usually went behind a barrel in one corner of the room where she was partially out of sight. Her mother cleaned up after her good-naturedly and without remark, but, if she happened to see what the little girl was up to, she hurriedly carried her outside the house and let her relieve herself there unconcealed.[84]

United States – the Hopi

The Hopi Indians are descendants of prehistoric cliff dwellers and inhabit mesas in northern Arizona. Wayne Dennis observed and studied the Hopi in 1937 and 1938. His book *The Hopi Child*, published in 1940, includes information about toilet training. Dealing with the function of elimination starts with wrapping the infant and placing him in the cradleboard. "He is placed on a blanket. A piece of cotton cloth is placed over his chest and passed between the chest and the arms so that the arms will not be brought against bare flesh. Rags are placed under the buttocks and between the legs. Nowadays diapers are sometimes used in place of the rags. Then one side of the blanket is brought over one arm of the infant and passed between the chest and the arm of the opposite side and tucked under the infant's body. The other side of the blanket is passed over both arms, which are extended along the body of the infant, and it too is tucked under the infant. Thus wrapped, the infant is placed upon the cradleboard. "The baby is bound to the cradle during the first day. The purpose of this binding is to ensure that the child will be straight and of good carriage. The child is taken off the cradle only for changing the soiled cloths and for bathing. He is put to the breast and nursed while on the board.

"Formerly the rags which were the primitive antecedent of diapers were dried in the sun and rubbed clean with fresh dry sand, although periodically they were washed. At present soap and water are used as the cleaning agents, and, as was noted earlier, modern diapers are used by some mothers. However, no other element of American baby clothes has yet come into use. Aside from rags or a diaper, the child within the blankets is naked. No toilet training is attempted until the child is able to walk, and to understand some words.

He is then told to go outside when he needs to defecate and urinate. To the beginner, this means literally just outside the door, although older children go to a corner of the plaza, and adults go outside of the village. If the child fails to go out of doors at the proper time, he is spanked. At a slightly later age he is supposed to tell his mother when he needs to eliminate during the night, but he is not expected to avoid all bedwetting until he is two years of age."[85]

United States – the Navaho

Dr. Clyde Kluckhohn of Cambridge University observed, interviewed and studied the Navaho in the late 1930s and early 1940s. Navaho babies were kept tightly wrapped up to the neck in a number of cloths (usually old flour or sugar sacks) and on a cradleboard. Use of the cradleboard started anywhere from as soon as the navel healed, after the umbilical cord fell off, to 1 month of age. The cradleboard contained one or more small holes in the lower part to allow urine to drain. The hours spent on the cradleboard steadily decreased as the child grew older. Some parents freed the child at the onset of crawling or scooting while others waited until the child could walk independently.

Navaho diapers were originally made from cliff-rose bark which was rubbed together to make straw. This material is very absorbent. After drying it in the sun, it is nearly odorless and can be used again and again. Later, cloth replaced the straw. Wet cloths were dried (not washed) and reused. Soiled cloths had the fecal matter scraped off, then were dried and reused in the cradle. Babies were changed at bath time (every day or every other day) plus a few other times a day, depending on individual family circumstances. "Navaho clothing for children is such that 'accidents' seldom render the garments completely unfit for further wear without washing. Neither sex ordinarily wears underwear." Little boys wear open pants, and little girls wear skirts.

Training in most areas of life, including elimination, was gradual, gentle and delayed during the first 2–3 years of life. There was basically no sphincter discipline used for a year or more and only very gentle discipline thereafter. "Babies under six months often urinate or defecate while nursing, and this not infrequently occurs with older children as well. These occurrences are accepted as a matter of course until the child talks or at least responds to words. At most the mother will interrupt the nursing briefly in order to clean her clothes or protect herself with additional dry cloths.

"Not until he can talk and understand is pressure put on a child to learn Navaho conventions of excretion. If a child who can walk and talk (or at least respond to speech) starts to urinate inside the hut, he is told to go outside to do this, and an older child will gently lead him out. At first elimination is permitted just outside the door; later the child is expected to go away into the bushes or behind a rock ledge. For a long time he is not punished for lapses or accidents but encouraged to act like his elders. Before going to sleep at night, he is taken out and is also advised not to eat or drink much for some time before going to bed. No special 'baby words' are used with children in referring to urine or feces.

"It is important to realize that bowel control is not expected of the Navaho child until he is old enough to direct his own movements and merely accompany an elder at night and in the morning. The mother or an older sister takes the child out in the morning when she herself goes to defecate and tells the little one to imitate her position and her actions. . . . After a time, the youngster who continues to wet or soil himself is teased or scolded by his relatives. In some families the buttocks of older children are slapped, though ordinarily Navaho children are switched on the legs, not on the buttocks. Even babies of under two who urinate or defecate within the hogan will be observed to have a slightly guilty look. Some children who are about to perform give an advance signal (such as a hand on the buttocks) which is recognized by the family, and they are hurriedly taken outside.

"Little feeling of disgust for urine or feces is inculcated. There is no exaggerated emphasis upon the unpleasantness of odors or consistency of excreta. A little girl of four will scrape out the diapers of her young brother in a perfectly matter-of-fact manner. Indeed, once a diaper is dry, she may use it for a head covering. Feces within the hogan are usually covered with sand or dirt and carried out in a shovel, but they may also be scraped into the firepit or under a stove. Adults do avoid stepping in urine or excreta, but their behavior conveys the notion that these materials are merely mildly unpleasant—not disgusting and certainly not shameful. When a baby urinates or defecates in someone's lap (which frequently occurs) the event is taken very calmly. In short, the two evacuation activities of the child are uniquely free from parental interference for a long time. Whatever may be the sensations associated with evacuation or retention of urine and feces, the processes are subject for some time to the impulses of the child, unmixed with parental punishment."[86]

United States – the Papago

In 1949, Jane Chesky wrote about life on the Papago Indian Reservation in southern Arizona. The Papago call themselves "the Desert People" and believe that "a little child should be happy and therefore he should be humored as often as possible. Corporal punishment of any sort is seldom used on children under five." Toilet training starts when a child can walk and understand instructions. The exact age is hard to determine since parents don't know their children's birthdays. Babies use diapers when in public but are usually bare-bottomed at home. There is no negative reaction when a baby urinates on the dirt floor or in the yard. When he can walk, his mother begins taking him to the bushes away from the dwelling and tells him to urinate there. His brothers and sisters take him there whenever they go to the bushes, and he learns mainly by imitation. "He soon becomes aware of the extreme modesty of his relatives during elimination, and by the time he is three and a half or four years old he knows that he is supposed to go to the bushes with members of his own sex." If he soils himself after this time, his mother makes a face and shows disapproval by saying "dirty" or "nasty" or else warns him that wild animals or ghosts will get him. "It is significant that, in using threats of the supernatural or the enemy, the mother sidesteps responsibility for the denial; it is not she who refuses the baby but an outside agency potentially harmful to them both."[87]

Venezuela

The Warao Indian culture and way of life focus on canoes. The name of the tribe means "boat people." Boys and young men receive extensive training in both the craft and spiritual aspects of canoes. "Behavior offensive to the canoe, or rather to the spirit of the canoe, called Masisikiri, can occur as early as during a child's infancy. . . . The child first learns to refrain from urinating or (worse still) defecating in or near the canoes." Toilet training is gentle, and no one gets upset if a child has accidents in the house. "But both mother and father will not tolerate similar defilement of a large canoe and the child is scolded severely. Usually they are told to stay away from it altogether."[88]

Jean Liedloff provides a brief but colorful glimpse into the toilet training attitudes of the Yequana in her 1977 book *The Continuum Concept*. Yequana do not wear diapers. Elimination by a baby is almost a nonevent, except for the gleeful laughter that follows an occasional soaking. "When he wets or defecates, [his mother] may laugh, and as she is seldom alone, so do her companions, and she holds the infant away from her as quickly as she can until he finishes. It is a sort of game to see how fast she can hold him away, but the laughter is louder when she gets the worst of it. Water sinks into the dirt floor in moments and excrement is cleared away immediately with leaves. Later, when house training takes place, the toddler is chased outside if he sullies the hut floor."[89]

NOTES

PART 1 - THE CONCEPT & THE METHOD

Chapter 2 – Philosophy
1. Brazelton & Cramer, 1990.
2. Brazelton & Cramer, 1990.
3. Brazelton, 1962.
4. Montessori, 1966.
5. Messmer, 1997.

Chapter 3 – The In-Arms Phase
6. Sears, 2001.

Chapter 4 – The Potty Phase
7. Lorentzen, e-mail to the author, 1999.
8. Michel, 1999.
9. Wilde, e-mail to the author, 2002.
10. Wang, e-mail to the author, 2002.
11. Fietser, from internet bulletin board, 2001.
12. Bradfisch, 2002.
13. Kayser, 2007 & 2010.

Chapter 5 – Baby Signals
14. Sears & Sears, 1993.
15. Tronick, 1989.
16. Ainsworth & Bell, 1969. In Small, 1998.
17. Dunstan, 2006.
18. Small, 1998.
19. Volterra & Erting, 1990.
20. Petitto & Marentette, 1991.
21. Volterra & Erting, 1990.

Chapter 6 – Nighttime
22. Baas, e-mail to the author, 2002.
23. Sonna, 2003.

Chapter 8 – Part-Time Pottying
24. Lorentzen, 2007.

Chapter 10 – Doctors & Other Experts
25. Susskind, 2006.
26. Dunham & Crane, 1938.

27. Ball, 1971.
28. Gersch, 1978.
29. Ravindranathan, 1978.
30. Smeets et al., 1985.
31. Fischer, 1990.
32. Schaefer & DiGeronimo, 1997.
33. Bakker & Wyndaele, 2001.
34. Bakker et al., 2002.
35. Sun & Rugolotto, 2004.
36. Rugolotto, Ball, Boucke, Sun & deVries, 2007.
37. Ball & Boucke, 2007.
38. Rugolotto, Sun, Boucke, Calò, Ma & Tatò, 2008.
39. Duong, Jansson & Hellström, 2012.
40. Boucke, Sun, Rugolotto & Ball, 2013.
41. Lamb, 1993.
42. Gablehouse, 2000.
43. Gablehouse. In Sonna, 2005.
44. Rugolotto, e-mail to the author, 2002 & 2007.
45. Davis, e-mail to the author, 2007.
46. Sonna, 2005.
47. Sonna, e-mail to the author, 2002.
48. Sonna, 2005.
49. Ball, e-mail to the author, 2007 & 2013.
50. Isbit, 2007.
51. Hyman, 2004.
52. Hull, 2007.
53. Hull, 2007.
54. Sonna, 2005.
55. Klassen et al., 2006.
56. Sonna, 2003.
57. Touchette et al., 2005.

Chapter 11 – Diapers

58. Sonna, 2005.
59. Labor, 2007.
60. Brecevic, 1998.
61. Milder, 1997.
62. Greene, 1999.

Chapter 12 – Environmental Issues

63. MacEachern, 1990.
64. Lamb, 1990.
65. Vallely, 1990.
66. MacEachern, 1990.
67. Richer, 1999.

68.   Brecevic, 1998.
69.   Wikipedia, 2013.
70.   Stortenbeek, letter to the author, 1991.
71.   Vallely, 1990.
72.   Vallely, 1990.

Chapter 13 – Dispelling the Myths
73.   Brazelton & Sparrow, 2005.
74.   Mothering, 1998.

Chapter 14 – History & Theories
75.   Bagellardo, 1472. In Beekman, 1977.
76.   Stone, 1979.
77.   Fontanel & D'Harcourt, 1997.
78.   Fontanel & D'Harcourt, 1997.
79.   Holt, 1894. In Beekman, 1977.
80.   Tweddell, 1913.
81.   West, 1914.
82.   West, 1921.
83.   Hull & Hull, 1919. In Brackbill & Thompson, 1967.
84.   Pouliot, 1921. In Fontanel & D'Harcourt, 1997.
85.   Litchfield & Dembo, 1930.
86.   Faegre & Anderson, 1930.
87.   Messmer, 1997.
88.   Sears & Sears, 1993.
89.   Montagu, 1971.
90.   Blurton-Jones, 1972.

PART 3 - TESTIMONIALS – AROUND THE WORLD

Chapter 7 – Short Reports

1.   Dedace, letter to the author, 2002.
2.   In many countries, cow and buffalo dung is shaped into patties and
      baked in the sun. The dung has a variety of uses in third world
      countries. For example, it is often used as fuel to cook food
      and heat homes. Once it has been treated, it is not considered
      unhygienic.
3.   Olson, e-mail to the author, 2002.
4.   Wang, e-mail to the author, 2002.
5.   Strawn, e-mail to the author, 2002.
6.   Rowat, e-mail to the author, 2004 & 2007.

PART 4 - CROSS-CULTURAL STUDIES
Chapter 1 - Cross-Cultural Comparisons
1. Tronick et al., 1987.
2. Whiting & Edwards, 1988.
3. LeVine, 1977. In Leiderman et al., 1977.
4. LeVine, 1970. In Paden & Soja, 1970.
5. LeVine, 1980. In Fantini & Cárdenas, 1980.
6. Goldberg, 1972.
7. Briffault, 1931.
8. Warren, 1972.
9. Super, 1981. In Triandis & Heron, 1981.
10. Kilbride, 1980.
11. deVries & deVries, 1977.
12. Landers, 1989. In Nugent et al., 1989.
13. Keefer et al., 1989. In Nugent et al., 1989.
14. Keefer et al., 1989. In Nugent et al., 1989.
15. Ainsworth, 1967.
16. Kilbride et al., 1970.
17. Ainsworth, 1967.
18. Konner, 1977. In Leiderman et al., 1977.
19. Super, 1973. In Kilbride, 1980.
20. Kilbride, 1980.
21. Kilbride, 1980.
22. deVries, 1999.
23. Goldsmith, 1984.
Chapter 2 - Africa
24. Konner, 1977. In Leiderman et al., 1977.
25. Konner, 1972. In Blurton-Jones, 1972.
26. Pearce, 1977.
27. Konner, e-mail to the author, 1999.
28. Marshall, 1965. In Gibbs, 1965.
29. deVries & deVries, 1977.
30. LeVine, 1963. In Whiting, 1963.
31. Sangree, 1965. In Gibbs, 1965.
32. Linton, 1933.
33. Linton, 1939.
34. Wanono, e-mail to the author, 1999.
35. Herskovits, 1938.
36. Cohen, 1967.
37. Cohen, 1960. In HRAF, 2007.
38. Epelboin, e-mail to author, 2000 & 2007.
39. Thomas et al., 2006.

40. Epelboin, e-mail to author, 2000.
41. Rabain, e-mail to the author, 1999.
42. Cederblad, 1970.
43. Raum, 1940.
44. Fontanel & D'Harcourt, 1998.
45. Ainsworth, 1967.
46. Kilbride & Kilbride, 1990.
47. Geber, 1998.
48. Pearce, 1977.
49. Stork, 1999.

Chapter 3 – Asia

50. Linton, 1939.
51. Martini & Kirkpatrick, 1981.
52. Gorer, 1938.
53. Du Bois, 1944.
54. Mead & Macgregor, 1951.
55. Maretzki, 1963. In Whiting, 1963.
56. Murray, 1953. In HRAF, 1999.
57. Burrows & Spiro, 1954.
58. Fischer, 1950. In HRAF, 1999.
59. Gladwin & Sarason, 1953. In HRAF, 1999.
60. Mead, 1930.
61. Mead, 1935.
62. Mead, 1956. In HRAF, 2007.
63. Whiting, 1941.
64. Wikan, 1982.
65. Nydegger, 1963. In Whiting, 1963.
66. Diamond, 1969.
67. Gallin, 1966. In HRAF, 1999.
68. Wolf, 1972. In HRAF, 1999.
69. Maiden & Farwell, 1997.
70. Sümer, 1970.

Chapter 4 – Arctic Regions & the Americas

71. Robert-Lamblin, e-mail to author, 1999.
72. Damas, 1972.
73. Fontanel & D'Harcourt, 1998.
74. Briggs, 1970.
75. Pelto, 1962. In HRAF, 2007.
76. Anderson, 1978. In HRAF, 2007.
79. Holmberg, 1985.
78. Erikson, e-mail to author, 1999.
79. Wagley, 1949.
80. Ford, 1941.

81.   Reichel-Dolmatoff, 1951. In HRAF, 2007.
82.   Press, 1975. In HRAF, 2002.
83.   Hill, e-mail to author, 1999.
84.   Goodwin, 1942.
85.   Dennis, 1940.
86.   Kluckhohn, 1947. In Roheim, 1947.
87.   Chesky, 1949.
88.   Wilbert, 1976. In HRAF, 2002.
89.   Liedloff, 1977.

RESOURCES

Books

Infant Potty Basics, Laurie Boucke, White-Boucke Publishing, 2003.
Diaper Free! Ingrid Bauer, Plume, 2006.
The Diaper-Free Baby, Christine Gross Loh, Harper Collins, 2007.
Diaper-Free Before 3, Jill Lekovic, Three Rivers Press, 2006.
Early-Start Potty Training, Linda Sonna, McGraw-Hill, 2005.

Foreign editions:

Je baby op het potje, Laurie Boucke, Thoeris, 2006.
Senza Pannolino, Laurie Boucke, Terra Nuova, 2006.
TopfFit!, Laurie Boucke, Tologo / Anahita, 2004.
Un orinal para mi bebé, Laurie Boucke, Vida Kinesiologia, 2013.
親子で楽しむ！おむつなし育児 (Japanese), Kawade Shobo Shinsha, 2009.

DVD

Potty Whispering, White-Boucke Publishing, 2006.

Websites with IPT articles and much more

www.pottywhisperer.com
www.godiaperfree.com
www.tribalbaby.org
www.diaperfreebaby.org
www.freewebs.com/freetoec
www.white-boucke.com
www.en.wikipedia.org/wiki/Infant_Potty_Training_(book)
www.123-Windelfrei.de (in German/auf Deutsch)
www.babysohnewindeln.de (in German/auf Deutsch)

Assisted Infant Toilet Training Board

aitt.evassist.it

Playgroups and Meetings

www.diaperfreebaby.org

Clothing and Gear

www.theECstore.com

www.babybunz.com

www.babylegs.com

www.thepottyshop.com.au (Australia)

www.nooneewilga.com (Australia)

www.mamaroo.com

www.tadpoles.ca (Canada)

www.nordicwoollens.com (Canada)

www.mokoshop.eu (Czech, Austria, Italy)

www.ohne-windeln.de (in German/auf Deutsch)

www.abhala.de (in German/auf Deutsch)

www.mummysmilk.com (Singapore)

www.edenbaby.se (in Swedish)

Online Support Groups

- In yahoogroups http://groups.yahoo.com, visit the "Elimination Communication" and "IPT LateStarters" groups.
- On Mothering magazine's site www.mothering.com/discussions, visit the "elimination communication" subforum.
- On Facebook, visit the diaperfreebaby page and many others including local and international Facebook pages.

IPT COUNTRIES

Africa

Algeria, Botswana, Cameroon, Central African Republic, Egypt, Ethiopia, Ghana, Ivory Coast, Kenya, Madagascar, Mali, Nigeria, Senegal, South Africa, Sudan, Swaziland, Tanzania, Togo, Uganda, West Africa, Zaire, Zambia

Asia and Oceania

Afghanistan, Azerbaijan, Bangladesh, Cambodia, China, Georgia, India, Indonesia, Iran, Iraq, Japan, Kazakhstan, Korea, Kurdistan, Kyrgyzstan, Laos, Lebanon, Malaysia, Micronesia, Mongolia, Myanmar (Burma), Nepal, New Guinea, Oman, Pakistan, Philippines, Polynesia, Sikkim, Singapore, Sri Lanka, Syria, Taiwan, Thailand, Tibet, Turkey, Turkmenistan, Uzbekistan, Vietnam

Central & South America and Caribbean

Argentina, Belize, Bolivia, Brazil, Costa Rica, Dominican Republic, El Salvador, Guatemala, Honduras, Jamaica, Mexico, Nicaragua, Panama, Paraguay, Peru, Venezuela, West Indies

Europe

Bulgaria, Czech Republic, Poland, Romania, Russia, Serbia, Slovakia, Turkey

Polar Regions

Alaska (Inupiat, Eskimos), Aleutians, Canada (Inuit, Kwakiutl, Netsilik and Utkuhikhalingmiut), Greenland, Siberia

REFERENCES

Ainsworth, Mary D. Salter. *Infancy in Uganda*, Johns Hopkins Press, pp. 77–78, 83–84, 1967.

Ainsworth, Mary D. Salter, and Steven M. Bell. "Some Contemporary Patterns of Mother-Infant Interactions in the Feeding Situation," 1969. In Meredith F. Small, *Our Babies, Ourselves*, Doubleday, 1998.

Anderson, Myrdene. *Saami ethnoecology: resource management in Norwegian Lapland*, University of Michigan, 1978.

Baas, Lois. E-mail to the author re: infant potty training, Mar.–Apr. 2002.

Bagellardo, Paolo. *Book on Infant Diseases*, 1472. In Daniel Beekman, *The Mechanical Baby,* Lawrence Hill, 1977.

Bakker, E. and J. J. Wyndaele. "Changes in the Toilet Training of Children during the Last 60 Years: The Cause of an Increase in Lower Urinary Tract Dysfunction?" *British Journal of Urology International* 86:248–252, 2000.

Bakker, E. and J.D. van Gool, M. Van Sprundel, J.C. Van Der Auwera and J. J. Wyndaele. "Results of a questionnaire evaluating the effects of different methods of toilet training on achieving bladder control," *British Journal of Urology International* 90(4):456-461, 2002.

_____. "Risk factors for recurrent urinary tract infection in 4,332 Belgian schoolchildren aged between 10 and 14 years," *European Journal of Pediatrics* 163(4-5):234-238, 2004.

Ball, Thomas S. "Toilet Training an Infant Mongoloid at the Breast," *California Mental Health Digest* 9:80–85, 1971.

_____. E-mail to the author re: infant potty training, Aug. 2007.

Ball, Thomas S. and Laurie Boucke. "Toilet Training Initiated Before Age One and Stool Toileting Refusal: A Survey of Successfully Trained Children," unpublished data, 2007.

Beekman, Daniel. *The Mechanical Baby,* Lawrence Hill, 1977.

Blurton-Jones, N. G., ed. *Ethological Studies of Child Behaviour*, Cambridge University Press, 1972.

Boucke, Laurie. *Trickle Treat: Diaperless Infant Toilet Training Method*, White-Boucke Publishing, 1991.

Boucke, Laurie, Min Sun, Simone Rugolotto & Thomas S. Ball, 2010-2013 "Prospective Studies on Assisted Infant Toilet Training," unpublished data, 2013.

Brackbill, Yvonne, and George G. Thompson, eds. *Behavior in Infancy and Early Childhood*, The Free Press, 1967.

Bradfisch, Friederike. E-mail to the author re: infant potty training, Feb.– Mar. 2002 & Sep. 2007.

Brazelton, TB. "A child-oriented approach to toilet training," *Pediatrics* 29:121-128, 1962.

Brazelton, T. Berry, and Bertrand G. Cramer. *The Earliest Relationship: Parents, Infants, and the Drama of Early Attachment*, Adison-Wesley, 1990.

Brazelton, T. Berry and Joshua Sparrow. "'Elimination Communication' isn't just baby talk," *New York Times* syndicated online article, Nov 7, 2005.

Brecevic, Candace. "The Diaper Debate," www.diaperingdecisions.com, 1998.

Briffault, Robert. *The Mothers: The Matriarchal Theory of Social Origins*, Macmillan, 1931.

Briggs, Jean L. *Never in Anger: Portrait of an Eskimo Family*, Harvard University Press, 1970.

Burrows, Edwin G., and Melford E. Spiro. *An Atoll Culture: Ethnography of Ifaluk in the Central Carolines*, Human Relations Area Files, 1954.

Cederblad, Marianne. "A Child Psychiatric Study of Sudanese Arab Children." In E. James Anthony and Cyrille Koupernik, eds., *The Child in His Family*, Wiley-Interscience, 1970.

Chesky, Jane. "Growing up on the Desert." In Alice Joseph, Rosamond B. Spicer and Jane Chesky, *The Desert People: A Study of the Papago Indians,* University of Chicago Press, 1949.

Cohen, Ronald. *The Kanuri of Bornu*, Holt, Rinehart and Winston, 1967.

_____. *The structure of Kanuri society.* Dissertation, Ann Arbor: UMI, 1960.

Damas, David. *The Copper Eskimo*, Holt, Rinehart and Winston, 1972.

Davis, Natalya. E-mail to the author re: infant potty training, Sep. 2007.

Dedace, Eric. Correspondence to the author re: IPT in the Philippines, 2002.

Dennis, Wayne. *The Hopi Child*, Appleton-Century, 1940.

deVries, Marten W. "Babies, Brains and Culture: Optimizing Neuro-development on the Savanna," *Acta Pædiatrica Suppl* 429:43–8, 1999.

deVries, Marten W., and Rachel M. deVries. "Cultural Relativity of Toilet Training Readiness: A Perspective from East Africa," *Pediatrics* 60:170–177, 1977.

Diamond, Norma. *K'un Shen: A Taiwan Village*, Holt, Rinehart and Winston, 1969.

Douglas, J. W. B., and J. M. Blomfield. *Children under Five*, George Allen & Unwin, 1958.

Duong, Thi Hoa, Ulla-Britt Jansson and Anna-Lena Hellström. "Vietnamese mothers' experiences with potty training procedure for children from birth to 2 years of age," *Journal of Pediatric Urology*, 2012 Nov 23. pii: S1477-5131(12)00262-8. doi:10.1016/j.jpurol.2012.10.023 (in press).

Du Bois, Cora. *The People of Alor: A Social-Psychological Study of an East Indian Island*, University of Minnesota Press, 1944.

Dunstan Baby Language–Learn the meaning of your baby's cries. Priscilla Dunstan, DVD, 2006.

Epelboin, Alain. E-mail to the author re: Senegal and Central African Republic, Dec. 1999–Sep. 2007.

Erikson, Philippe. E-mail to the author re: Amerindians and Matis of Brazil, Dec. 1999–Jan. 2000.

Faegre, Marion L., and John E. Anderson. *Child Care and Training*, University of Minnesota Press, 1930.

Fantini, Mario D., and René Cárdenas, eds. *Parenting in a Multicultural Society*, Longman, 1980.

Field, Tiffany M., Anita M. Sostek, Peter Vietze and P. Herbert Leiderman, eds. *Culture and Early Interactions*, Lawrence Erlbaum, 1981.

Fischer, Ann M. *The Role of the Trukese Mother and Its Effect on Child Training*, Pacific Science Board, 1950.

Fischer, Paul. Letters to the Editor, "Early Toilet Training," *The Journal of Family Practice* 30:262, 1990.

Fontanel, Béatrice, and Claire D'Harcourt. *Babies Celebrated*, Trans. Jack Hawkes, Harry N. Abrams, 1998.

_____. *Babies: History, Art, and Folklore*, Trans. Lory Frankel, Harry N. Abrams, 1997.

Ford, Clellan S. *Smoke from Their Fires: The Life of a Kwakiutl Chief*, Yale University Press, 1941.

Gablehouse, Barbara. In Linda Sonna, *Early-Start Potty Training*, McGraw-Hill, 2005.

Gallin, Bernard. *Hsin Hsing, Taiwan: A Chinese Village in Change*, University of California Press, 1966.

Geber, Marcelle. *L'enfant africain dans un monde en changement, Étude ethno-psychologique dans huit pays sud-africains*, Presses Universitaires de France, 1998.

_____. "The Psycho-motor Development of African Children in the First Year, and the Influence of Maternal Behavior," *Journal of Social Psychology* 47:185–195, 1958.

Gersch, Marvin J. Letter to the Editor, "Early Toilet Training," *Pediatrics* 61:674, 1978.

Gibbs, James L. Jr., ed. *Peoples of Africa*, Holt, Rinehart and Winston, 1965.

Gladwin, Thomas, and Seymour B. Sarason. *Truk: Man in Paradise*, (Viking Fund Publications in Anthropology, No. 20, 1953), by permission of the Wenner-Gren Foundation for Anthropological Research, New York, 1953.

Goldberg, Susan. "Infant Care and Growth in Urban Zambia," *Human Development* 15:77–89, 1972.

Goldsmith, Judith. *Childbirth Wisdom*, Congdon & Weed, Inc., 1984.

Goodwin, Grenville. *The Social Organization of the Western Apache*, University of Chicago Press, 1942.

Gorer, Geoffrey. *Himalayan Village: An Account of the Lepchas of Sikkim*, Michael Joseph, 1938.

Greene, Alan. Re: diaper rash. In Carlos E. Richer, "I have been told that cloth diapers are better for the skin of my baby . . .?". www.giga.com/~cricher/FAQ.htm, 1999.

Herskovits, Melville J. *Dahomey: An Ancient West African Kingdom*, vol. 1, J. J. Augustin, 1938.

Holmberg, Allan R. *Nomads of the Long Bow: The Siriono of Eastern Bolivia*, Waveland Press, 1985.

Holt, Luther Emmett. *The Care and Feeding of Children*, 1894 & 1903. In Daniel Beekman, *The Mechanical Baby*, Lawrence Hill, 1977.

Hull, Clark L., and Bertha Iutzi Hull. "Conflict between Overlapping Learning Functions." In Yvonne Brackbill and George G. Thompson, eds., *Behavior in Infancy and Early Childhood*, The Free Press, 1967.

Hull, Jeffery W. Parents' Common Sense Encyclopedia *"Dyschezia, Straining with Stools"* and *"Constipation, Infant,"* www.drhull.com, 2007.

Human Relations Area Files (HRAF). Toilet training, Yale University, sourced via the Internet, Nov. & Dec. 1999, April 2002 and Sep. 2007.

Hyman, Paul. "Infant Dyschezia: Looking out for Number Two," www.aboutkidsgi.org, 2004.

Isbit, Jonathan. *Nature Knows Best*, InstantPublisher.com, 2007.

Kardiner, Abram. *The Individual and His Society: The Psychodynamics of Primitive Social Organization*, Columbia University Press, 1939.

Kayser, Gigi. E-mail to the author re: infant potty training, Oct. 2007 & online forum message, Apr. 2010.

Keefer, Constance H., Suzanne Dixon, Edward Z. Tronick and T. Berry Brazelton. "Cultural Mediation between Newborn Behavior and Later Development: Implications for Methodology in Cross-Cultural Research." In J. Kevin Nugent, Barry M. Lester and T. Berry Brazelton, eds., *The Cultural Context of Infancy: Biology, Culture, and Infant Development*, vol. 2, Ablex, 1989.

Kilbride, Philip Leroy. "Sensorimotor Behavior of Baganda and Samia Infants: A Controlled Comparison," *Journal of Cross-Cultural Psychology* 11:131–152, 1980.

Kilbride, Philip Leroy, and Janet Capriotti Kilbride. *Changing Family Life in East Africa*, Pennsylvania State University Press, 1990.

Kilbride, Philip Leroy, Janet E. Kilbride and M. C. Robbins. "The Comparative Motor Development of Baganda, American White, and American Black Infants," *American Anthropologist* 72:1422–1428, 1970.

Klassen, Terry, Darcie Kiddoo, Mia Lang, Carol Friesen, Kelly Russell, Carol Spooner and Ben Vandermeer. "The Effectiveness of Different Methods of Toilet Training for Bowel and Bladder Control," *Agency for Healthcare Research and Quality* (AHRQ) Publication No. 07-E003, Dec 2006.

Kluckhohn, Clyde. "Some Aspects of Navaho Infancy and Early Childhood," 1947. In Geza Roheim, ed., *Psychoanalysis and the Social Sciences*, vol. 1, International Universities Press, 1947.

Konner, Melvin J. "Aspects of the Developmental Ethology of a Foraging People." In N. G. Blurton-Jones, ed., *Ethological Studies of Child Behaviour*, Cambridge University Press, 1972.

_____. "Infancy among the Kalahari Desert San." In P. Herbert Leiderman, Steven R. Tulkin and Anne Rosenfeld, eds., *Culture and Infancy: Variations in the Human Experience*, Academic Press, 1977.

_____. "Maternal Care, Infant Behavior and Development among the !Kung." In Richard B. Lee and Irven DeVore, eds., *Kalahari Hunter-Gatherers*, Harvard University Press, 1976.

_____. E-mail to the author re: !Kung in Botswana, Dec. 1999.

Labor of Love, The. "Cloth Diapers Versus Disposable Diapers–Pros and Cons, www.thelaboroflove.com, 2007.

La Leche League International. "FAQ on Normal Bowel Movements of Breastfed Babies," www.lalecheleague.org, 1999.

Lamb, Jan Leah. Interview with the author, June 1993 and e-mail to the author re: infant potty training, Nov.–Dec. 1999 & Sep. 2007.

Lamb, Marjorie. *Two Minutes a Day for Greener Planet: Quick and Simple Things You Can Do to Save Our Earth,* Harper Paperbacks, 1990.

Landers, Cassie. "A Psychobiological Study of Infant Development in South India." In J. Kevin Nugent, Barry M. Lester and T. Berry Brazelton, eds., *The Cultural Context of Infancy: Biology, Culture, and Infant Development*, vol. 1, Ablex, 1989.

Leiderman, P. Herbert, Steven R. Tulkin and Anne Rosenfeld, eds. *Culture and Infancy: Variations in the Human Experience*, Academic Press, 1977.

LeVine, Robert A. "A Cross-Cultural Perspective on Parenting." In Mario D. Fantini and René Cárdenas, eds., *Parenting in a Multicultural Society*, Longman, 1980.

_____. "Child Rearing as Cultural Adaptation." In P. Herbert Leiderman, Steven R. Tulkin and Anne Rosenfeld, eds., *Culture and Infancy: Variations in the Human Experience*, Academic Press, 1977.

_____. "The Relative Absence of Separation Anxiety and Related Affects." In John N. Paden and Edward W. Soja, eds., *The African Experience*, Northwestern University Press, 1970.

LeVine, Robert A., and Barbara B. LeVine. "Nyansongo: A Gusii Community in Kenya." In Beatrice Blyth Whiting, ed., *Six Cultures: Studies of Child Rearing*, John Wiley, 1963.

Liedloff, Jean. *The Continuum Concept*, Knopf, 1977.

Linton, Ralph. "Marquesan Culture." In Abram Kardiner, *The Individual and His Society*, Columbia University Press, 1939.

_____. *The Tanala: A Hill Tribe of Madagascar*, vol. XXII, Field Museum of Natural History, 1933.

_____. "The Tanala of Madagascar." In Abram Kardiner, *The Individual and His Society*, Columbia University Press, 1939.

Litchfield, Harry R., and Leon H. Dembo. *Care of the Infant and Child: A Book for Mothers and Nurses*, Waverly Press, 1930.

Lorentzen, Vanessa. E-mail to the author re: infant potty training, Aug.– Dec. 1999, Jan.–Apr. 2000 & Oct. 2007.

MacEachern, Diane. *Save Our Planet: 750 Everyday Ways You Can Help Clean up the Earth*, Dell Trade Paperback, 1990.

Maiden, Anne Hubbell, and Edie Farwell. *The Tibetan Art of Parenting*, Wisdom Publications, 1997.

Maretzki, Thomas W., and Hatsumi Maretzki. "Taira: An Okinawan Village." In Beatrice Blyth Whiting, ed., *Six Cultures: Studies of Child Rearing*, John Wiley, 1963.

Marshall, Lorna. "The !Kung Bushmen of the Kalahari Desert." In James L. Gibbs Jr., ed., *Peoples of Africa*, Holt, Rinehart and Winston, 1965.

Martini, Mary, and John Kirkpatrick. "Early Interactions in the Marquesas Islands." In Tiffany M. Field, Anita M. Sostek, Peter Vietze and P. Herbert Leiderman, eds., *Culture and Early Interactions*, Lawrence Erlbaum, 1981.

Mayo Clinic. "Choosing diapers." www.mayohealth.org, 1996.

Mead, Margaret. *Growing up in New Guinea: A Comparative Study of Primitive Education*, Blue Ribbon Books, 1930.

_____. *Sex and Temperament in Three Primitive Societies*, W. Morrow, 1935.

_____. *New Lives for Old: Cultural Transformation–Manus, 1928-1953*, Morrow, 1956.

Mead, Margaret, and Frances Cooke Macgregor. *Growth and Culture: A Photographic Study of Balinese Childhood*, G. P. Putnam's Sons, 1951.

Michel, Robert S. "Toilet Training," *Pediatrics in Review* 20:240–245, 1999.

Milder, John. "Choosing Diapers," National Association of Diaper Services, www.diapernet.com/choose.htm, 1997.

Montagu, Ashley. *Touching: The Human Significance of the Skin*, Columbia University Press, 1971.

Montessori, Maria. *The Secret of Childhood*, Fides, 1966.

Mont-Reynaud, Randy. E-mail to the author re: mother training and Vietnam, July–Dec. 1999.

Mothering. "Your Letters," Nov.–Dec. 1998.

Murray, William M. *Rowanduz: A Kurdish Administrative and Mercantile Center,* Ph.D. Dissertation, University of Michigan, 1953.

Nugent, J. Kevin, Barry M. Lester and T. Berry Brazelton, eds. *The Cultural Context of Infancy: Biology, Culture, and Infant Development*, Ablex, 1989.

Nydegger, Corinne. "Tarong: An Ilocos Barrio in the Philippines." In Beatrice Blyth Whiting, ed., *Six Cultures: Studies of Child Rearing*, John Wiley, 1963.

Olson, Katambra. E-mail to the author re: infant potty training, Mar. 2002.

Paden, John N., and Edward W. Soja, eds. *The African Experience*, Northwestern University Press, 1970.

Pearce, Joseph Chilton. *Magical Child: Rediscovering Nature's Plan for Our Children,* Dutton, 1977.

Pelto, Pertti J. *Individualism in Skolt Lapp society*, Suomen Muinaismuistoyhdistys (Finnish Antiquities Society), 1962.

Petitto, Laura Ann, and Paula F. Marentette. "Babbling in the Manual Mode: Evidence for the Ontogeny of Language," *Science* 251:1483–1496, 1991.

Potty Project for Babies, The. Barbara Gablehouse, DVD, Five Star Parenting, 2000.

Potty Whispering: The Gentle Art of Infant Potty Training. Dir. Colin White & Laurie Boucke, DVD, White-Boucke Publishing, 2006.

Pouliot, L. *Hygiène de maman et de bébé*, 1922. In Béatrice Fontanel and Claire D'Harcourt. *Babies Celebrated*, Trans. Jack Hawkes, Harry N. Abrams, 1998.

Press, Irwin. "Tradition and Adaptation: Life in a Modern Yucatan Maya Village," Greenwood Press, 1975.

Rabain-Jamin, Jacqueline. E-mail to the author re: the Wolof of Senegal, Dec. 1999.

Raum, Otto Friedrich. *Chaga Childhood: A Description of Indigenous Education in an East African Tribe*, Oxford University Press, 1940.

Ravindranathan, S. Letter to the Editor, "Early Toilet Training," *Pediatrics* 61:674, 1978.

Reichel-Dolmatoff, Gerardo. *The Kogi: a tribe of the Sierra Nevada de Santa Marta, Colombia*, Editorial Iqueima, 1951.

Richer, Carlos E. www.giga.com/~cricher/FAQ.htm, 1999.

Robert-Lamblin, Joëlle. E-mail to the author re: the Arctic (Aleutians, Greenland and Siberia), Dec. 1999.

Roheim, Geza, ed. *Psychoanalysis and the Social Sciences*, vol. 1, International Universities Press, 1947.

Rowat, Kira. E-mail to the author re: infant potty training, Sep. 2007.

Rugolotto, Simone, Thomas S. Ball, Laurie Boucke, Min Sun and Marten deVries. "A surging new interest on toilet training started during the first months of age in Western countries," *Techniques in Coloproctology* 11(2):162-3, 2007.

Rugolotto, Simone, Min Sun, Laurie Boucke, Daniela G. Calò, Aqin Ma, and Luciano Tatò. "Toilet Training Started During the First Year of Life: A Report on Completion Age, Presence of Elimination Signals, and Stool Toileting Refusal," *Minerva Pediatrica* 60(1):27-35, Feb 2008.

Rugolotto, Simone. E-mail to the author re: infant potty training, Apr. 2002 & Oct. 2007.

Sangree, Walter H. "The Bantu Tiriki of Western Kenya." In James L. Gibbs Jr., ed., *Peoples of Africa*, Holt, Rinehart and Winston, 1965.

Schaefer, Charles E. *Childhood Encopresis and Enuresis,* Jason Aronson, 1993.

Schaefer, Charles E., and Theresa Foy DiGeronimo. *Toilet Training without Tears*, Signet, 1997.

Sears, William. "Toilet-Training: Tips to Tell Potty Times," www. AskDrSears.com, 2001.

Sears, William, and Martha Sears. *The Baby Book,* Little, Brown and Company, 1993.

Small, Meredith F. *Our Babies, Ourselves*, Doubleday, 1998.

Smeets, Paul M., Giulio E. Lancioni, Thomas S. Ball and Dorette S. Oliva. "Shaping Self-initiated Toileting in Infants," *Journal of Applied Behavior Analysis* 18:303–308, 1985.

Sonna, Linda. *Early-Start Potty Training*, McGraw-Hill, 2005.

_____. *The Everything Potty Training Book*, Adams Media, 2003.

_____. E-mail to the author re: infant potty training, Feb.–Apr. 2002.

Stone, Lawrence. *The Family, Sex and Marriage in England 1500–1800*, Harper & Row, 1979.

Stork, Hélène E. *Introduction à la psychologie anthropologique*, Armand-Colin, 1999.

Stortenbeek, Willem. Correspondence with the author re: diseases spread via diaper waste in landfills, Nov. 1991 and e-mail to the author, Mar. 2000.

Strawn, Katie. E-mail to the author re: infant potty training, Mar. 2002.

Sümer, Emel A. "Changing Dynamic Aspects of the Turkish Culture and Its Significance for Child Training." In E. James Anthony and Cyrille Koupernik, eds., *The Child in His Family*, Wiley-Interscience, 1970.

Sun, Min. E-mail to the author re: infant potty training, Apr. 2002 & Sep. 2007.

Sun, Min and Simone Rugolotto. "Assisted Infant Toilet Training in a Western Family Setting," *Journal of Developmental and Behavioral Pediatrics* 25(2):99-101, 2004.

Super, Charles M. "Cross-Cultural Research on Infancy." In Harry C. Triandis and Alastair Heron, eds., *Handbook of Cross-Cultural Psychology: Developmental Psychology*, Allyn and Bacon, 1981.

_____. "Patterns of Infant Care and Motor Development in Kenya," *Kenya Education Review* 1:64–69, 1973.

Susskind, Karin. In *Potty Whispering: The Gentle Art of Infant Potty Training*, Dir. Colin White & Laurie Boucke. DVD, White-Boucke Publishing, 2006.

Thomas, Jacqueline M.C., Serge Bahuchet, Alain Epelboin and Susanne Fürniss. *Encyclopédie des Pygmées Aka Techniques, langage et société des chasseurs-cueilleurs de la forêt centrafricaine (Sud-Centrafrique et Nord-Congo)*, Vol 11(3), Editions Selaf Peeters, 1981-2007.

Touchette, Évelyne, et al. "Bed-wetting and Its Association With Developmental Milestones in Early Childhood," *Archives of Pediatrics & Adolescent Medicine* 159:1129–1134, 2005.

Triandis, Harry C., and Alastair Heron, eds. *Handbook of Cross-Cultural Psychology: Developmental Psychology*, vol. 4, Allyn and Bacon, 1981.

Tronick, Edward Z., and Jeffery F. Cohn. "Infant-Mother Face-to-Face Interaction: Age and Gender Differences in Coordination and the Occurrence of Miscoordination," *Child Development* 60:85–92, 1989.

Tronick, Edward Z., Gilda A. Morelli and Steve Winn. "Multiple Caretaking of Efe (Pygmy) Infants, *American Anthropologist* 89:96–106, 1987.

Tweddell, Francis. *How to Take Care of the Baby: A Mother's Guide and Manual for Nurses*, Bobbs-Merrill, 1913.

Vallely, Bernadette. *1001 Ways to Save the Planet,* Ivy Books, 1990.

Volterra, V., and C. J. Erting, eds. *From Gesture to Language in Hearing and Deaf Children*, Springer-Verlag, 1990.

Wagley, Charles, and Eduardo Galvao. *The Tenetehara Indians of Brazil: A Culture in Transition*, Columbia University Press, 1949.

Wang, Angie. E-mail to the author re: "no" phase, Feb.–Mar. 2002.

Wanono, Nadine. E-mail to the author re: the Dogon of Mali, Nov. 1999–Jan. 2000.

Warren, Neil. "African Infant Precocity," *Psychological Bulletin* 78:353–367, 1972.

West, Mrs. Max. *Infant Care*, U.S. Dept. of Labor, Children's Bureau, GPO, 1914; 1921.

Whiting, Beatrice Blyth, ed. *Six Cultures: Studies of Child Rearing*, John Wiley, 1963.

Whiting, Beatrice Blyth, and Carolyn Pope Edwards. *Children of Different Worlds: The Formation of Social Behavior*, Harvard University Press, 1988.

Whiting, John W. M. *Becoming a Kwoma: Teaching and Learning in a New Guinea Tribe*, Yale University Press, 1941.

Whiting, John W. M., and Irvin L. Child, eds. *Child Training and Personality: A Cross-Cultural Study*, Yale University Press, 1953.

Wikan, Unni. *Behind the Veil in Arabia: Women in Oman*, Johns Hopkins University Press, pp. 76 & 78, 1982.

Wikipedia. *Diaper,* www.en.wikipedia.org/wiki/Diaper, September 2013.

Wilbert, Johannes. "To Become a Maker of Canoes: An Essay in Warao Enculturation," UCLA Latin American Center Publications, University of California, 1976.

Wilde, Rosie (pseudonym). "Upright Baby Kinesiology," www.howtoparent.net/media/ecsite, 2001.

Wolf, Margery. *Women and the Family in Rural Taiwan*, HRAF, Stanford University Press, 1972.

INDEX